ALSO BY DANIEL GORDIS

God Was Not in the Fire: The Search for a Spiritual Judaism

Does the World Need the Jews?

RETHINKING CHOSENNESS AND
AMERICAN JEWISH IDENTITY

Daniel Gordis

SCRIBNER

SCRIBNER
1230 Avenue of the Americas
New York, NY 10020

Designed by Brooke Zimmer
Set in Dante
Manufactured in the United States of America

3   5   7   9   10   8   6   4   2

Library of Congress Cataloging-in-Publication Data
Gordis, Daniel.
Does the world need the Jews? : rethinking chosenness and
American Jewish identity / Daniel Gordis.
p.   cm.
Includes bibliographical references and index.
1. Judaism—United States. 2. Jews—United States—Identity.
3. Jews—Election, Doctrine of. I. Title.
BM205.G67   1997
296'.0973—dc21   97-13246
CIP

ISBN 0-684-80389-5

For My Parents

שמע בני מוסר אביך
ואל תטש תורת אמך

PROVERBS I:8

All the nations of the earth
shall bless themselves
by your descendants.

Genesis 22:18

As I see them from the mountaintops,
Gaze on them from the heights,
There is a people that dwells apart,
Not reckoned among the nations.

Numbers 23:9

Contents

PART THREE: BRINGING THE MESSAGE TO LIFE

Acknowledgments

THE EXPERIENCE OF writing this book afforded me constant reminders of how fortunate I am to have teachers, colleagues, students and friends from whom I have learned much and upon whom I continue to rely. It gives me great pleasure to be able to formally thank them, however inadequately.

I have been at the University of Judaism for virtually all of my professional career. The university has been an extraordinary supportive and nurturing environment in which to grow and to learn. I am particularly grateful to the university's president, Dr. Robert Wexler, for his treasured friendship, support and encouragement over the past years. Ever since we met, Bob has taken an avid interest in my work and has always sought to make my roles at the university as challenging and satisfying as they could possibly be. I have learned a great deal by watching him implement his vision for the university, and look forward to many years of continued partnership. I would also like to express my appreciation to the chairman of our board of directors, Mr. Francis S. Maas, for his enthusiastic interest in this and my other projects. He has brought great vision to the university, and my family and I are honored to count the Maas family among our friends.

I am also indebted to my colleagues on the faculty of the University of Judaism for their ideas, the challenging intellectual environment they create and their friendship. Several members of the staff of the University of Judaism provided critical assistance along the way. To Rick Burke and the entire library staff of the university, my thanks. Dr. Louis Shub, director of the university's Documentation Center, has spent decades collecting thousands of documents that I am certain I would never have found without him. My thanks as well to Betty Brasky for help in enhancing the argument about text in Jewish life, and to Dr. Aryeh Cohen for multiple assists along the way.

Special thanks are due to my students, rabbinical students in the university's Ziegler School of Rabbinic Studies, from whom I have learned much more than I have taught, and whose sensitivities and insights are woven throughout this text. In particular, I benefited from the hard work of several students who generously gave of their time and assisted with various stages of the work on this book. Jeff Pivo did preliminary literature searches as the idea for this book first took form. Elliot Cosgrove's superb research assistance aided me immeasurably during the summer of 1995 as this project got underway. To Sharon Brous and Jeremy Wiederhorn, who read the manuscript with care and did much of the work on the Glossary, my deepest thanks. Jeni Friedman, a student in the UJ's College of Arts and Sciences, served as my research assistant in the fall of 1996 as the manuscript was completed. I am grateful for her assistance as well.

Beyond the University of Judaism community, I am fortunate to have friends who have shared their ideas and insights and who, over the years, have profoundly shaped my thinking. For all that they have taught me in the past, and for their assistance with this particular project, the following brief thanks are wholly insufficient.

Many of the initial thoughts that ultimately led to this book emerged during conversations with Rabbi Levi Lauer when we were both teaching at the Brandeis Collegiate Institute in the early 1990s. A treasured friend, Levi has also shaped my thinking through the profundity of his thought, the breadth of his reading and the passion of his convictions. I am grateful to Robert Bleiweiss for affording me continued association with the *Jewish Spectator*, and for his publication of two brief early drafts of sections of this book in that journal. The feedback I received on those pieces has been extremely helpful.

A number of teachers, friends and colleagues assisted with specific dimensions of this project, pushing an idea further, helping me find a reference or steering me away from error. To Jacki Cooper, Rosemary Cullen, Lauren Eichler, Rabbi Yosef Kanefsky, Dalia Levine, Rabbi Jay Miller, Professor Aviezer Ravitsky, Professor Jack Schuster, Rami Wernick and Rabbi David Wolpe, my thanks.

Other people and institutions contributed to the ideas in this book and to the way they are expressed. I am grateful to the students in my fall 1994 San Diego Wexner Heritage Foundation class and my classes at the 1996 Wexner Heritage Aspen Summer Institute and Basic Judaism Institute for extraordinarily enriching conversations about this material. To the president of the Wexner Heritage Foundation, Rabbi Nathan Laufer, my mentor, teacher and friend, many thanks for inviting me to teach those courses and for experiences that have been profound far beyond what I had dared expect.

I'm particularly grateful to Shawn and Tom Fields-Meyer, ever-present friends, critics and editors. Despite their many other responsibilities, they each read major portions of the manuscript several times. Their insightful comments and suggestions improved the text immeasurably. How they found the time to read the manuscript as carefully as they did is beyond me, but my gratitude for their time and my appreciation for their friendship is enormous.

Jane Rosenman, executive editor at Scribner, is the consummate professional and a superb editor. I am grateful not only for her talent but for her friendship as well. Virtually every page of this book bears the mark of her skill, insight and sensitivity. To Jill Feldman and Caroline Kim, Jane's editorial assistants, my thanks for critical insights about the argument for "text" and for their attention to the many details involved in the production of this book. I am also grateful to my colleagues at Touchstone Books, and in particular wish to thank Sydny Miner for her insightful thoughts about the Jewish condition in contemporary America.

Few authors are fortunate enough to work with literary agents as fine as Richard Pine. But I am convinced that even fewer can point to pivotal ideas that came from conversations with their literary agents and that ultimately shaped the course of a book. Richard is a deeply thoughtful person who has had a profound impact on my thinking about many of the ideas found in these pages, and I remain more than grateful that we have worked together. I hope we continue to do so for many years to come.

No one has shaped the ideas in this book more than my wife, Beth. Beth not only read the manuscript with care, making critical suggestions about argument, organization and style, but has consistently challenged me to rethink many of the ideas found in these pages as well as many that I decided to discard after her critique. We still don't agree completely about all the ideas that follow, but every single page of this book has been enriched by her insight, her keen intelligence and her passion for Jewish life. As always, she is proof that your toughest critic can also be your best friend.

Our children, Talia, Aviel and Micha, provide inspiration to think about these questions on a daily basis. While Beth and I want many things for them, passionate and meaning-filled Jewish lives top the list. Watching them learn to love being part of the Jewish people gives both of us cause to view the future with great optimism and hope.

I have dedicated this book to my parents, Leon and Hadassah Gordis, but I fear that this gesture is wholly inadequate to the challenge of expressing my love for them and the gratitude they merit. My parents are truly extraordinary people. My brothers and I grew up in a home lined with books, in which passions for thinking and for Jewish life were woven into the fabric of our everyday lives. It was from my parents that I first intuited that a devotion to Jewish life needed to share space with an appreciation for the dignity of other traditions. My parents taught us from early on that a deep commitment to Jewish life did not have to come at the expense of involvement in the world around us. Through their care for other human beings and their ability to see the good in every person, they have taught me the most important lessons I've learned.

My parents have also been models of devotion and loyalty to their children, and more recently, to their grandchildren as well. They have trusted us, believed in us, guided us and helped us at critical junctures in our lives in ways that are too numerous to name. It is no exaggeration to say that Beth and I have the friendship and family that we do in no small part due to my parents' support. If Beth and I can love and nurture our own children as wholeheartedly as my parents have loved us, our own children will be deeply blessed.

December 1996
Hanukkah 5757

Andersen Versus Disney—
Modern Jews and Their Crisis of Identity

What would happen if the world woke up one day and there were simply no Jews left? No genocide, no persecution. Just a gradual fading away. Would the world be worse off?

As strange as that scenario sounds, some people are beginning to argue that it is not all that preposterous. For Judaism in America is in crisis. While not everyone agrees on the exact nature of the crisis, its causes or its solution, most observers of the contemporary Jewish scene have implicitly agreed on its name. We have, they say, a "continuity" crisis in Jewish America. Throughout the Jewish community, in all walks of Jewish life, leaders have sprung to action, trying to stem the tide of rapid and wholehearted assimilation, trying to ensure the continuity of Jewish life in the freest society Jews have ever known.

Yet this crisis is not a problem only for the community's leaders. Grandparents wonder if their grandchildren will be Jewish. Parents don't know how to transmit a sense of Judaism's importance to their children. Members of the thirty-something generation often have no idea why they should make Judaism part of their lives. Occasionally, though, they feel pangs of guilt about that uncertainty. We have a problem—in virtually all segments of the Jewish community.

But people who panic rarely think clearly. We, too, have panicked, and are more prone to look for a "fix" than to think deeply about the true nature of the problem. For what does it really mean to have a "continuity crisis"? Continuity, after all, is something that we measure in behavior. We assess the likelihood of our continuity by looking at synagogue affiliation, levels of Jewish education, patterns of giving to Jewish charitable causes. Our challenge, we therefore believe, is to change these patterns of behavior. If we could only change the numbers, we try to convince ourselves, we would solve the problem.

Solutions are premature. We have to ask ourselves *why* we have a crisis, and what kind of crisis we have. Do we really have a continuity crisis? I think not. We do have a crisis, but it is not a crisis of continuity. It is a crisis of identity. Our problem is not that Jews are not affiliating with their community, but that they have no idea why they should want to affiliate. Before we can take steps to ensure Jewish continuity, we need to begin to bolster Jewish identity. The challenge is not to figure out how to get Jews to "join"; rather, it is first to figure what being Jewish in our era ought to mean. That is what demands our immediate attention, and that is why the question, what is Jewish identity?—what does it mean to be a Jew?—lies at the heart of this book.

The contemporary crisis in Jewish identity is an ironic one for Jews. For much of our history, we have been wondering how to survive poverty, oppression, resentment and hatred. Now, "confronted" by relative security, unprecedented accomplishment and almost boundless acceptance by the society around us, many Jews wonder not how we ought to survive, but why.

We ask, why be Jewish? not because Judaism seems bad or objectionable, but simply because we're no longer certain why it matters. Our grandparents, perhaps, believed that Judaism was unique, important—a real contribution to the world. We're no longer certain.

To understand the disposition of American Jewry on the eve of the twenty-first century, it helps to start with a story. Not a Jewish story, but a universal one. In Hans Christian Andersen's fairy tale "The Little Mermaid," a young mermaid makes her first trip to the surface of the sea and falls in love with a world that is completely unlike her own. It sparkles and is wondrous beyond anything she has known. Her own sea world now seems drab in comparison. She dreams of joining the human world, of gaining a soul, of marrying the Prince. Suddenly, her fish tail, which had always seemed natural to her, is an impediment, and she wants nothing more than to trade it for human legs.

So the mermaid goes to the wicked sea witch, who offers to create a brew that will dissolve the mermaid's tail and replace it with legs—but at a devastating cost. Though her legs will be beautiful, they will be painful, and every step the former mermaid takes will feel as though she is stepping on sharp knives. The mermaid will also have to risk her life. If the Prince won't marry her, she won't get a soul, and she will dissolve into the foam on the sea.

Finally, the witch reveals an even higher price. In exchange for the magic brew, she demands the mermaid's voice, renowned throughout the mermaid kingdom for its sweetness and beauty. The mermaid can become human, but only at tremendous and horrifying sacrifice. She must leave her family forever. She'll lose the near immortality that mermaids have, will no longer be able to speak, and will be in perpetual pain.

Yet her love for the Prince and her enchantment with his world is so deep that the mermaid decides to accept the offer. She drinks the brew, loses her tail and finds in its stead the beautiful legs the witch had promised her. Unable to return to the ocean's depths, she leaves her former world. She is cut off from her family and all that is familiar to her, from everything she had always loved. But, we quickly learn, the human world can never be hers, for she cannot speak. She is beautiful, but an oddity. The Prince loves her, but because they can't converse, it never even occurs to him to marry her. Ultimately, he marries a Princess from another kingdom, and as the witch had warned, the mermaid does not get the soul she so desires. She senses her death approaching. Soon, she turns into the foam upon the sea and disappears forever.

*   *   *

THERE IS A harrowing wisdom to Andersen's fairy tale. Andersen (1805–1875) created a story about the dangers of trying to become something we are not, of forgetting who we are. The mermaid failed to appreciate the beauty of the world from which she came. Ultimately, she destroyed herself by trying to be something else.

Such dire consequences do not fit into modern Americans' view of the world. We have been taught, and have come to believe, that we can be anything we want to be. With enough effort or money, we think, we can become virtually anything we wish.

That is why in the 1990s version of *The Little Mermaid* produced by Disney studios, things had to work out differently. Ariel (the mermaid's name in the movie version) gets human legs, but suffers no pain. She loses her voice, but gets it back when the Prince kills the sea witch. It is the sea witch, not Ariel the mermaid, who dies in this version. Because the mermaid-turned-human *can* ultimately speak, the Prince does marry her. Her mer-family is present at her wedding, delighted at her newfound happiness. She and the Prince sail into the horizon and presumably "live happily ever after."

ANDERSEN OR DISNEY?
THE MODERN JEWISH DILEMMA

On the eve of the twenty-first century, American Jews are a community that has tried to believe the Disney version, but that now wonders if there was more truth in Andersen's. Like the mermaid, the early masses of Jews who came to this country arrived in a new place and fell in love with a culture different from anything they had seen before. It was a culture that seemed open to new ideas, in which it appeared that Jews could be participants rather than outsiders, in which talent and hard work were rewarded. It appeared there was no limit to what we could accomplish. Jews were attracted to this brave new culture with a passion. The allure was much too powerful to resist.

So American Jews set out to become as much a part of this new world as they could. But they had their own version of the mermaid's fish tail. They had come predominantly from Europe, laden with accents, ethnic behaviors and religious rites that seemed to make them stick out. They didn't need a witch to tell them that the way into American life was to discard those old-fashioned ways and traditions; that was obvious. So they quickly moved to create a version of Judaism that could still tie them to their roots, but that would not make them different. They acquired American clothes and accents. They attended the finest American universities. They created synagogues and Hebrew schools that didn't make them feel different, but rather, let them feel Jewish and wholly American at the same time. They imagined that to join this new world, they needed synagogues to which they felt comfortable inviting non-Jewish friends for celebrations of births, Bar and Bat Mitzvah celebrations and weddings. American Jews stopped learning Hebrew in any meaningful way. They moved away from traditions that seemed like superstitions, from anything that did not seem proper, rational, universal. They would keep Judaism, they decided, but it had to be a fully American form of Jewish life.

For a while, it seemed that Disney had it right. It appeared that we *could* become anything we wanted, and it seemed that we had. Anti-Semitism, a scourge that seemed to follow the Jews wherever they went, did not disappear entirely, but it was no longer a daily threat for most American Jews. In American definitions, we seemed to have found success. Seymour Martin Lipset and Earl Raab, two sociologists of the modern American Jewish community, offer staggering statistics documenting the success story of Jews in America. According to them, Jews represent only 3 to 5 percent of American society (some put the figure as low as

1.8 percent). But what has that tiny minority achieved? According to Lipset and Raab:

> During the last three decades Jews have made up 50 percent of the top two hundred intellectuals, 40 percent of American Nobel Prize winners in science and economics, 20 percent of professors at the leading universities, 21 percent of high level civil servants, 40 percent of partners in the leading law firms in New York and Washington, 26 percent of the reporters, editors, and executives of the major print and broadcast media, 59 percent of the directors, writers, and producers of the fifty top-grossing motion pictures from 1965 to 1982, and 58 percent of directors, writers, and producers in two or more prime-time television series.

But just when it seemed that we, like Disney's Ariel, would "live happily ever after," our community began to notice warning signals that something is amiss. Particularly in the aftermath of the Council of Jewish Federations' landmark demographic study in 1990, Jews who care about Jewish life in this country have begun to fret. Unprecedented numbers of Jews are leaving the Jewish community. In some major cities, only two Jews in ten affiliate with the community by joining a synagogue or by having some other formal relationship with a Jewish institution. Intermarriage rates have gone beyond the 50 percent mark in many places. Of the children of intermarried couples, more than three quarters (78 percent, to be precise) don't even call themselves Jewish.

Among Jews who are still identified as part of the community, there is little about their lives on a daily basis that reflects their Jewish connection. Jewish life is no longer the animating core of our identity. Even for many affiliated Jews, being Jewish is part of who we are, but it is not usually the essence of who we are. It sometimes seems that Judaism, like the mermaid of Andersen's tale, is fading away like the foam on the sea.

Those who downplay this identity crisis among American Jews are quick to point out that ours is not the first generation of Jews who could leave their community. They note that Jews have always had that option, and they are right. But they are wrong to suggest that nothing is new. They are wrong because of the sheer numbers of people making this choice. But more importantly, they are wrong because ours is a generation in which people leave Judaism not by making a conscious decision to leave, but just by drifting away. Ours is the first generation in which huge numbers of Jews left the world of Jewish life without even giving it much thought, lured away by the currents of a culture that makes Judaism seem of little consequence.

Like the mermaid of the fairy tale, we have lost our voice. It is not, of course, that we're unable to speak; we simply have no idea what to say. We have no clear conception of what might be special or important about our culture, our religion or our way of life. We have no clue as to why we matter. Free at last, we have no vision of what to make of our freedom.

REJECTING OUR VOICE—
JEWISH STUDENTS IN AMERICA

Were it only the case that we had lost our voice, that we no longer knew what to say, our problem would be serious enough. But it goes deeper. At times, it even seems that we don't want our voice back, that even when it is obvious that we might have something to say, we want to blend in so badly that we consciously choose silence. Two relatively recent incidents on American college campuses illustrate this tendency.

Our first example comes from America's premier Jewish institution of general higher education, Brandeis University. Founded in 1948, Brandeis was originally established to offer Jewish faculty—who were excluded from the faculties of other universities—a place to teach and to build their careers. When many of the nation's most prestigious universities dropped their quotas and opened their doors to Jews, Brandeis recast itself as an American Jewish university that would represent the very best of the academic world.

But as outstanding an institution as it is, Brandeis has not found it easy to be both thoroughly American and purposefully Jewish. For the first four decades of its existence, Brandeis had two kinds of kitchens: a kosher kitchen and two non-kosher dining halls. In deference to Jewish aesthetics, even the two non-kosher dining halls did not serve pork or shellfish. The university also had the Hebrew word *emet*—"truth"—at the center of its logo, and the university calendar was closed for some (though not all) major Jewish holidays.

In the late 1980s, however, the university apparently could no longer manage this delicate balance of being a university in the American model, and consciously Jewish as well. Its distinctively Jewish aura was becoming uncomfortable for some elements of the university's leadership. Eventually, in moves that were immediately controversial (and in several cases, ultimately reversed), the university decided to allow pork and shellfish in its non-kosher cafeterias. It deleted the Hebrew word *emet* from the university seal (even though other schools, such as Columbia and Yale, still had Hebrew in their seals) and eliminated all references to the Jewish holidays in its official calendar, inserting the strange (and rather obfuscating) phrase "No University Exercises."

But, one might ask, wasn't all this change and the strident objection to much of it "much ado about nothing"? Does it really make any difference, one might ask, whether Brandeis has a Hebrew word in its university seal? And if committed Jewish students already know when those holidays fall, is it ultimately significant whether Brandeis mentions them in its official publications? Brandeis administrators thought not. Several years later, however, Brandeis students gave the Jewish community reason to wonder.

In the early 1990s, a Californian named Bradley Smith began

placing advertisements in college newspapers across the country that essentially denied the Shoah.* Under the name of CODOH, the Committee for Open Debate on the Holocaust, Smith claimed that if universities were genuinely committed to free and open inquiry, then they had no reason not to publish his ads, most of which had titles such as "You Have the Right to Know the Truth! A Revisionist's View of the U.S. Holocaust Memorial Museum," or "The Holocaust Story: How Much Is False? The Case for Open Debate."

In December 1993, Smith submitted an ad to the Brandeis daily, *The Justice*. Astonishingly, the newspaper decided to run the ad, and it did so in the December 7 issue without even indicating that the piece was a paid-for advertisement. Though many fine colleges had previously accepted Smith's ads, there was already a tradition among many others of refusing them. Prior to Brandeis's decision, Smith had been turned down by such universities as Brown, the University of California at Berkeley, Santa Barbara and Los Angeles, the University of Chicago, Dartmouth, Emory, Georgetown, Harvard, the University of Pennsylvania and Yale, among many others. What did his ad say? Some excerpts:

> But were the prisoners killed or did they die of typhus or some other disease during the last terrible weeks of the war? Autopsies made by Allied medical personnel found that inmates died of disease. Not one was found to have been "gassed." . . . *We don't even know that the dead pictured in the photo are Jews!* [italics in original]

---

*Shoah, the word that many Jews today use to refer to the Holocaust, is a biblical Hebrew word that means "calamity" or "utter destruction." "Holocaust" is an English word that means "burnt offering" or "sacrifice to God." The Jews of Europe in the 1930s and 1940s were not sacrificed—they were murdered. There is a tremendous difference; this book uses the word "Shoah" in order to take that difference seriously.

That the gassed prisoners were also cremated is obviously omitted from Smith's diatribe. But he went further. At the bottom of the ad, he inserted the following paragraph:

> Contact CODOH to inquire about speakers or more background on the scandal of the gas-chamber stories. Demonstrate to the fuhrers of conformity on your campus that you want intellectual liberty, not "leaders."

The irony that less than fifty years after the gas chambers had ceased burning, Jewish students at a Jewish-sponsored university would be willing to publish an ad such as this was not lost on members of the Jewish community. Reaction was swift, and it was voluminous. Indeed, *The Justice* subsequently devoted virtually an entire (and expanded) issue to the publication of numerous letters to the editor that had been received on the subject. The debate on that issue was fierce. Some students decried the ad's appearance, while others suggested that its publication served as a valuable reminder that anti-Semitism persists, that all sides of an issue need to be explored.

What was striking about the debate at Brandeis, however, was that no one seemed to reflect on a possible connection between the diminution of Jewish symbols on campus a few years earlier and this new strain of Jewish indifference. Obviously, this was not a case of direct cause and effect. But what had happened at Brandeis several years earlier was at least symptomatic of a growing discomfort with the university's Jewishness. The decision to publish the ad reflected that same discomfort. Just decades earlier, it would have been unthinkable that any committed Jew would publish such an ad. The need for the preservation of Jewish memory, revulsion at this blatant anti-Semitism, and a feeling of horror that anyone would deny what was so patently obvious would have "trumped" all else.

But the desire to be thoroughly American has erased some of those visceral Jewish loyalties. Brandeis's students' desire to join the larger and alluring culture into which America welcomed them, ultimately led them to give up the unique and authentic voice that was rightfully theirs. They didn't even realize that CODOH was an attack on them.

But Brandeis's Jewish students are hardly the only example of this phenomenon. On October 12, 1995, the Columbia *Spectator,* once regarded as one of the finest campus dailies in the country, published a column by an African-American Columbia College student named Sharod Baker. In his piece, a weekly column called "Blackdafide," Baker had the following to say:

> . . . I single out Jews because their oppression of blacks cannot go unnoticed while they disguise their evilness under the skins and costumes of the Rabbi. Lift up the yarmulke and what you will find is the blood of billions of Africans weighing on their heads. . . . How dare any Jewish person ask me why I am obsessed with Jews. I speak of Jews because of those from their race who are always on our backs like leeches sucking the blood from the black community then pretending to be our friends. If you look at the resources leaving Africa you will find them in the bellies of Jewish merchants.

When the *Spectator* was assailed for publishing Baker's virulently anti-Semitic piece, Peter Freeman, editor-in-chief of the paper and a Jew, defended the decision to publish. He asserted, "this was a column we thought we should have a discussion about," and added, "I'm Jewish . . . but that didn't factor into our decision to publish."

Why not? Consider: would an African-American editor have published similar comments about the black community so nonchalantly? Obviously not. American Jews have produced an environment in which even our finest and most sophisticated students are rarely able to (or even want to) think in consciously Jewish terms.

CAN WE LEARN TO SING AGAIN?

Yet many contemporary Jews are not willing to give up on the possibility of a fulfilling and meaningful Jewish life in America. They believe that if contemporary Jews could come to feel the power and majesty of Jewish life, more would decide to stay. So the American Jewish community has begun to produce a veritable flood of books and essays, many suggesting reasons for American Jews to remain Jewish.

In many cases, authors have argued for Jewish life by pointing to its profound spiritual richness. In my earlier book, *God Was Not in the Fire: The Search for a Spiritual Judaism,* I took exactly this approach. I sought to show how Jewish tradition is not only ancient and venerated, but, perhaps more importantly for contemporary Jews, that it helps us express our profound questions and dreams; it affords us a powerful way of living our humanity.

But that response—the idea that Judaism is a deeply spiritual tradition—is important but often not enough. Many Jews do not think in spiritual terms, are not interested in that intimate, deeply personal side of Jewish life. Other Jews know that Judaism is not the only tradition that provides spiritual fulfillment. Christianity, they note, is also a spiritually compelling tradition. Others are attracted to Eastern traditions, or other contemporary varieties of spiritual expression. What does Judaism say that is unique?

It is not enough for Judaism to be spiritual, though that is important. Judaism must also have its own distinct voice. This book makes a simple claim: we *can* still go home, we *do* have something unique to say, and we *can* recapture the voice with which to say it.

WHY SHOULD JEWS SURVIVE?

This is certainly not the only book to ask, why should Jews survive? But this book answers the question in a way that is different from most; it does not insist that we have to know what we believe about God, revelation, suffering or other classic religious questions in order to see the importance of Jewish survival. This book argues that even without certainty about those issues, we *can* make a compelling case for Judaism's significance.

That is very different from other approaches to this question. One recent volume, for example, answers the question of why Jews should survive by assuring us that Jewish survival is not a question—it is guaranteed. Its author, Rabbi Michael Goldberg, explains that

> contemporary Jews who obsess about "Jewish survival" may . . . stew about how many Jews will survive, but that Jews will survive they need never doubt—unless they doubt that there is a God who makes and keeps his promises. But should they doubt that, then why care about Jewish survival at all?

But many contemporary Jews *do* doubt that there is a God who keeps promises. Some doubt God, and especially in the aftermath of the Shoah, they doubt that God keeps promises. Goldberg's system of faith in God's promise may work for those already committed to traditional theologies, but it will not satisfy a generation of Jews unsure about God's existence or omnipotence.

This is certainly not to suggest that Goldberg is wrong. His book is fascinating, and he may well be right; but for many Jews, his vocabulary is simply foreign. The vast majority of Jews wondering why they should choose Judaism want answers that do not depend upon theology, upon absolute belief in God, upon acceptance of precepts they find questionable at best.

Our goal is to find compelling reasons for Jews to remain Jewish that do not necessarily require God as the foundation of the argument. The point, of course, is not to deny the reality of God. It is simply to recognize that so many Jews are unsure about God that arguments for Jewish life in which God is a precondition will too often fall on deaf ears.

For many people, the suggestion that God need not be at the center of our arguments for Jewish survival may seem strange, even heretical. But this book does not deny either God's being or God's centrality in Jewish life. It only seeks to provide rationales for choosing Judaism that can speak even to Jews who are not yet sure what they believe about God.

None of this is meant to suggest that God is unimportant in Jewish life. Quite the contrary—I think one can make a compelling case that a version of Judaism that leaves no room for faith divorces itself from the tradition of the Bible, from the spiritual power of the prayer book, from the emotional nurturing that Judaism affords through its claim that the world was fashioned by a benevolent and caring Creator who knows the value of each and every human being. None of this is unimportant.

The issue for us is not "God" versus "no-God." It is a matter of gates, of points of entry. Our interest is in affording Jews who still have problems with the "God issue" a way into Jewish tradition. I would like to offer them a take on Jewish life that will address their sense that for Judaism to matter, it has to enrich the world in some distinctive and profound way. There are people who are potentially interested in Jewish life, yet who want to know not what Judaism will do for them, but what it might do for the world. These people, too, deserve answers.

The question is: How can we make it possible for Jews to find their way home, to locate in Jewish life a system of meaning that will attract their attention and merit their commitment? This book argues that Judaism does bring something unique and profound to the world. It is a book about what that something is, and what we need to do to rediscover it. It is a book about who we have been, who we are, and about—if we are courageous enough—who we can still become.

Part One

DOES THE WORLD NEED THE JEWS?

CHAPTER ONE

The Promise and the Reassurance— "You Shall Be a Blessing"

*T*here is perhaps no better analyst of the American Jewish psyche than Philip Roth. Thus, it should not surprise us that Roth's reflections on his own Jewish upbringing and the creation of his own Jewish identity cut to the heart of our challenge:

> . . . what one received, I think, was a psychology, not a culture and not a history in its totality. The simple point here is, I think, that what one received of culture, history, learning, law, one received in strands, in little bits and pieces. What one received *whole*, however, what one feels whole, is a kind of psychology; and the psychology can be translated into three words—"Jews are better." . . .
>
> So one had to, then, I think, as one grew up in America, begin to create a moral character for oneself. That is, one had to invent a Jew. . . . There was a sense of specialness and from then on it was up to you to invent your specialness; to invent, as it were, your betterness.

But most Jews in America have not wanted to invent a Judaism with "betterness" at its core. They wanted something less objectionable, more populist and American. As long as they sensed that substantive Jewish identity had to have betterness at its core, they were not interested. So many have simply drifted away. Is that, perhaps, what happened to the Jewish students at Brandeis and Columbia?

If Philip Roth intuited that building a Jewish identity was a matter of "inventing our betterness," there are critical questions that we need to ask: Is "betterness" necessarily part of the picture? Does the Jewish tradition offer other images of our relationship with the rest of the world?

It has to. Transcending the ambivalence that is at the heart of the American Jewish experience will require that we seek the richness of the Jewish tradition at its best. Recovering a modern Jewish identity that will inspire and motivate contemporary Jews requires more than the "little bits and pieces" of culture, history, learning and law that Roth inherited. It requires a confrontation with the majesty and power of the tradition, with its sophistication, with its most ennobling qualities.

HOW DO WE SEARCH FOR RICHNESS?
"TEXT" AS THE ROADMAP FOR THE JOURNEY

But before we can begin the task of recovering Jewish identity, we need to learn *how* to recover it. How will we know if the images of Jewish identity we discover are genuinely *Jewish* images? Quite simply, our search for a meaningful Jewish future has to be rooted in the meaning of the Jewish past.

As this book works through the tension between being part of the larger world and retaining Jewish uniqueness and authenticity, between "blending in" and "standing out," it will look carefully at classic Jewish texts. As we ask why Judaism should survive, we need to look at the stories Jews have been telling, not just for centuries, but for millennia. To uncover these stories, we will look at biblical sources, liturgical compositions, folklore and even poetry. We will base our quest for a future in the words of our past. Why? Because in doing so we will gain roots. Jews have typically looked to our sacred texts not out of an antiquated sense of obedience, but out of love and loyalty—a conviction that in figuring out who we want to become, we also need to know where we have come from.

In that sense, Torah is collective memory. Though the Torah and the many later works that make up the Jewish tradition contain much more than stories, we should not overlook the importance of those stories, even when we become adults. For these are the stories of our family; these are the stories that make up what some people call the Jewish "master story."

In many ways, the stories that the Torah tells function like a family photo album. Why do families treasure their albums so deeply? Why do even people who pride themselves on not being overly sentimental cherish grandparents' wedding pictures, their parents' baby pictures, faded portraits of ancestors whose names they struggle to recall?

There's nothing rational about all this. Our reasons for cherishing the past are far more complex. We prize these portraits because they tell us who we are and where we have come from. In the faces of our great-grandparents, we find our children's eyes. In the smile of a distant relative, we recognize our own.

As we hear stories of our ancestors or learn details about them, something intangible suddenly seems to make more sense. We understand not only the roots from which we've come, but the future to which we're headed as well. Uncovering our past is more than the recovery of history. It is self-discovery, coming to terms with our own narrative, perhaps even our own destiny.

Why do adopted children often feel an overwhelming need to find their birth parents? Do they have any doubt that their adoptive parents are the ones who have given them love, warmth and nurturing? Of course not. And surely, they understand that parents who gave them up long ago may have no desire to see them or to establish an ongoing relationship. So why the need to find people who gave them up so long ago?

There is something about our past that beckons to us. We are a society that photographs and videotapes virtually everything. We videotape visits to grandparents or to the zoo that we know we will probably never watch again. But we record these events because of a deep-seated need to bequeath a past to our children.

If we, as Jews, wish to embark on a search to find out who and what we must be, we must turn to the past. It is no accident that for literally thousands of years, the *words* of the Jewish tradition have beckoned to Jews no less powerfully than Homer's Sirens lured Odysseus. Text has been critical to Jews in a variety of ways. Because books, unlike temples or towns, are portable, Jews were able to take sacred words with them wherever they went. Even occupation by foreign powers and forced migrations could not separate Jews from their tradition's words. Amazingly, some Jews even managed to smuggle a page or two of some sacred text into the Nazis' death camps. Why? Because these words were their links to a world that honored people, in which sanctity still prevailed and in which life had meaning. For Jews, words are links to worlds of the past, to idealized worlds, to worlds that might still come to be.

But there is more. The words of the tradition linked Jews across the globe in ways that no other tradition or belief could. Jews in different places have different rituals and customs, speak different languages and believe very different things. But the words of Torah link them. The phrase *Shema Yisrael,* "Hear O Israel," is something that virtually every Jew would recognize. Hearing another person utter those words creates a bond, a sense of trust, a perception of shared destiny that would be virtually indescribable to an outsider.

But perhaps most importantly, texts have always been critical to Jewish life because Jews never saw the laws of the Torah as simple law handed down to be mechanically obeyed. Of course, law was and is an important element of Jewish tradition. But for centuries, Jews have found in their texts not just law and not just fairy tales. We have seen these words as part of an ongoing conversation, a dialogue about life's most critical questions: Who are we? What ultimately really matters? Where shall we find meaning for the too few years we have yet to live?

For centuries, Jews have been wedded to each other in part by their conversations and their books. What has tied Jews to each other has been a sense that with other Jews, they could begin these lifelong conversations with sacred Jewish texts as their guide. Perhaps no one has put it better than Allan Bloom (1930–1992). A professor of political philosophy at the University of Chicago who was deeply influenced by his Jewish upbringing, Bloom explains his love of books:

> The friend is the man with whom Socrates can talk about their shared interests in the good. Good horses and dogs are not companions on this hunt; only human beings are. Shared taste and interest are a real common ground for them. And here we come to the core of what is of concern to us: awareness of shared interest and nourishment for it come from books of the wise men of old. Lovers of the good become friends because they think about it with the help of wise old books. . . . Friends spend their lives together reading and talking about the life they would like to lead while they are leading it.

Modern Jews need such conversations; we need conversations between ourselves and "wise old books." We turn to ancient Jewish texts because in their company we can have a conversation about who we ought to be, a conversation that is directly and noticeably linked to the past from which we herald.

The stories we tell about our past will help us determine if our dreams for the future are Jewish dreams. If we have no conception of the Jewishness of our past, how can we assess the Jewishness of our visions for the future? There would be questions about our hopes we could never answer: Does anything that Jews happen to decide to stand for become "Judaism," or is there some other standard? How shall we know whether a serious encounter with Judaism's mission demands that we shun the rest of the world or encounter it as deeply as possible? We answer these questions, and many others, by turning to the words of a tradition that for centuries has defined our sense of who we are.

JEWS AND THE WORLD AROUND US:
MODELS FROM OUR TRADITION

We are alone. At first blush, the story our tradition tells about us describes us as existentially alone, often in a cruel and uncaring world. Recall the story that our "collective autobiography"—the Torah—tells about our origins. The vast majority of the Torah's narrative takes place while the Jews are in the midst of their forty-year expedition through the desert. The Torah makes a point of reminding us that in the desert we were without friends. We were vulnerable. We were the "Other."

But aloneness is not always a problem. It can also be a wellspring of vitality. Jews and non-Jews alike have recognized in the Jew's aloneness a deep reservoir of purpose and of meaning. Thus, our aloneness is sometimes portrayed as a compliment, even by the non-Jewish nations. Indeed, one of the most poignant blessings bestowed upon the Jews in the Bible describes their aloneness as a cornerstone of what is wondrous about them. When Balak, King of Moab, saw the Israelites traversing the desert, he grew fearful of them, and decided to protect himself and his people by hiring a seer to curse them. He sent a message to Balaam, asking him to curse the Israelites whom he feared so deeply. The Torah describes Balaam as deeply spiritually sensitive, filled with misgivings about his assigned role. Eventually, Balaam made his way to a mountaintop from which he could glimpse part of the people. He then returned to Balak, the Moabite king, and recited the following:

> [7]From Aram has Balak brought me,
> Moab's king from the hills of the East:
> Come, curse me Jacob,
> Come, tell Israel's doom!

8How can I damn whom God has not damned,
How doom when the LORD *has not doomed?*
9As I see them from the mountaintops,
Gaze on them from the heights,
There is a people that dwells apart,
Not reckoned among the nations,
10Who can count the dust of Jacob,
Number the dust-cloud of Israel?
May I die the death of the upright,
May my fate be like theirs!

(NUMBERS 23:7–10)

Balaam's famous phrase, *hen-am levadad yishkon*—"there is a people who dwells apart"—is among the most famous phrases of the Torah. While this passage describes the Jews as dwelling alone, that characterization is not an indictment, but rather, a compliment! Balaam ends his soliloquy saying, "May I die the death of the upright, may my fate be like theirs!" Over the centuries, Jews have often understood this verse to suggest that Judaism's spiritual richness comes, in part, from its being differentiated from the rest of the world.

But contrary to what many contemporary Jews might like to believe, the "differentness" implied by the Torah does not mean that we ought not care about the rest of the world. True, the Torah seems to see us as distinct from the rest of the world. It also believes, however, that this distinctiveness ought to be used in the service of the world. Ironically, our tradition claims, we are different so we can make a difference; we cannot blend in because the rest of the world needs us.

To many of us, however, this rhetoric sounds disconcertingly similar to the tired, worn-out and boring rhetoric of 1960s liberal Jews, whose Judaism essentially consisted of liberal, Democratic values and actions in a Jewish package. Don't we know better by now, we cynically wonder? Isn't it obvious that those Jewish communities that seem most authentic, most "religious," are those with virtually no connection to the outside world? How, then, can we even suggest that the Torah's vision for Jews is a separateness devoted to the rest of the world?

"AND YOU SHALL BE A BLESSING"

Admittedly, the image of the Jews as different so as to serve the rest of the world does seem to have been rejected by today's most religiously observant Jews. In our minds, Hasidim have nothing to do with the world around them; they represent virtually absolute insularity. The political agenda of the Haredi (ultra-Orthodox) Jews in Israel revolves around funding for their schools and their religious establishments, and to a lesser extent, their desire to impose the rule of Jewish law on all citizens of Israel, religious or not. But they have less interest in Israel's foreign policy, and apparently no concerns whatsoever for issues such as civil liberties or the status of Israel's non-Jewish citizens. As far as they seem to be concerned, those people might as well live on a different planet.

But no matter. The Torah insists unabashedly that this perspective is simply wrong. The Torah argues that to retreat from the world is to betray who we are.

To understand what the Torah is saying, we need to recall that although it is primarily a book about the Jews (whom it calls Israelites), the Torah is not *only* about Jews. In fact, it begins in very universal terms. Genesis, the first of the Torah's five books, opens with a description of the creation of the world, the first murder (when Cain kills his brother, Abel), the flood of Noah and the sinfulness of all humankind, and a number of other stories that address humanity at large, not just the Jewish people. By avoiding all discussion of Jews in its opening chapters, our tradition makes clear that it has a larger picture in mind.

Eventually, of course, the Torah gets to the story of Abraham (or Abram, as he is originally called) in Genesis 12. At that point, the Torah's universal perspective gives way to a more specific interest in the Jewish people. Yet even there, it is clear that Abram's life and story matter not only to him, his family and his people, but to the entire world. God's first words to Abraham are a command to leave his native land and his father's house, in order to journey to a new land. Then God continues with a promise that has since shaped the Jews' conception of themselves, and in many ways, still does:

> *I will make of you a great nation,*
> *And I will bless you;*
> *I will make your name great,*
> *And you shall be a blessing.*
>
> (GENESIS 12:2)

What does the Torah mean when it says that Abraham must "be a blessing"? At this point, we cannot be sure. But we *can* imagine what Abraham must have been experiencing.

Before God promises Abraham that he will become a great nation, God commands Abraham: "Go forth from your native land and from your father's house to the land that I will show you" (Genesis 12:1). For us, obeying such a command is unimaginable. Not only might we not be inclined to heed such a call, the world in which we live makes Abraham's dislocation impossible for us. For God was asking Abraham to do more than relocate. God demanded that Abraham permanently leave behind everything he knew. Never again would he see the people he left behind. Never would he get news about their children, their destinies, their fates.

Our world, made ever smaller by air travel now so commonplace, a world in which the Internet gives any computer user access to virtually anyplace on the globe and transmits pictures, information and even voices almost instantaneously, is a world in which we cannot experience what Abraham was being asked. No matter where we go, we do not need to leave our past behind. Our friends can remain in instantaneous touch; their pictures and voices often remain with us. Indeed, even when we *want* to leave parts of our past behind, we learn that we can't.

No matter what else Abraham may have felt, his reaction had to have been at least partly one of terror. A past forever severed; a future wholly unknown. The terror of such dislocation is scarcely describable. In reaction to that unspoken but palpable terror, God assures Abraham that he has a destiny of importance, that his terror is in service of an ultimate good. "And you shall be a blessing."

But to whom? At this point in its narrative, the Torah is unclear. The picture is filled out as the Torah repeats the phrase "and you shall be a blessing" three times. God utters this phrase first to Abraham (again), then to his son Isaac, and finally, to his grandson Jacob. Each time, interestingly, God's promise comes in response to terror, to the ultimate existential fear that the Patriarch's life is of no meaning.

Our next destination is the "Binding of Isaac" narrative. Here, too, Abraham faces terror, but terror of a different sort. Here, he risks losing not only his past, but his future as well. After all, when God commands him to sacrifice his son, he confronts not only the potential loss of his child, but with that child, any hopes of fathering a great nation.

To Abraham, God must have seemed almost capricious at this point. When God had commanded him to leave Mesopotamia, Abraham obeyed immediately. He asked for no "proof" of God's existence, no fail-safe indication that God's promise would come to pass. He simply obeyed; his was a pure and seemingly absolute faith.

But in the ensuing years, God gave Abraham plenty of reason to begin to doubt. Abraham and Sarah grew old, but had no children. After Sarah's handmaid, Hagar, finally gave birth to a son, hatred and jealousy eventually split the family so that Abraham had to send his son, Ishmael, into the desert, presumably to die. Ultimately, Sarah does give birth to Isaac, but now God commands Abraham to sacrifice his son, his only hope for a future, the only remaining reason to believe that his life of service to God has had any meaning at all.

Imagine Abraham's devastation! Why, he might have wondered, did I leave my father's homeland? To die childless in a strange land? How can I possibly be the beginning of a great nation if God will not even permit me a single son? Has my whole life been lived for naught? Though the Torah never tells us what Abraham was thinking, as the Binding of Isaac passage concludes, we *do* learn more about the destiny God has in store for him. At the last moment, an angel of God commands Abraham *not* to kill his son, and then

> [15]The angel of the LORD called to Abraham a second time from heaven, [16]and said, "By Myself I swear, the LORD declares: Because you have done this and have not withheld your son, your favored one, [17]I will bestow My blessing upon you and make your descendants as numerous as the stars of heaven and the sands on the seashore; and your descendants shall seize the gates of their foes. [18]All the nations of the earth shall bless themselves by your descendants, because you have obeyed My command."
>
> (GENESIS 22:15–18)

Just as it was not clear what the Torah meant by "and you shall be a blessing," it is far from clear what God means by the words "all the nations of the earth shall bless themselves by your descendants." Who blesses whom? And what is the substance of that blessing?

At this point, we do not know. Yet one message does begin to emerge clearly. In the face of terror, in the face of the possibility that our existence might be utterly devoid of meaning, the Torah says: Your life is *not* without meaning. You are needed. And your importance is not just internal, but external as well. Your mission is to bring something to the world. In that mission, the Torah suggests, Jews will find their voice.

Abraham's terror, of course, is not unlike our own. Faced with the new question, why be Jewish? wondering whether we really do make a difference, whether there was any enduring value to the struggles of our past, many of us as individuals respond with confusion, or even apathy. But on a communal level, these questions strike terror into the heart of American Jewry. We are terrified of the possibility that our own collective future is disintegrating in front of our very eyes. Images abound: Jewish college students who are blind to anti-Semitism. Grand-children of survivors who have no connection to Jewish life. Jews who are afraid of being "too Jewish." A Jewish community that too often sees Zen, rather than Judaism, as the natural starting point for spiritual searching.

All these force us to ask the questions that Abraham asked: Was the whole journey meaningless? Is this the last stop? And if this Jewish odyssey in a free, democratic world is going to be so difficult, who needs it? The Torah's answer: the world needs it.

So far, however, God has made this assurance only to Abraham. Had the Torah's discussion of the promise ended here, we might have assumed that this was a private "arrangement" between God and Abraham, and that it has little to do with contemporary Jews searching for meaning. Thus, to indicate that God's assurance was not simply a promise to Abraham as an individual, but rather, to the entire people descended from him, the Torah quickly repeats the promise, this time to Abraham's son Isaac.

Again, the pledge comes in response to terror. Here, the terror is not that of leaving an entire lifetime behind, nor is it the terror that accompanies the command to kill a son. If anything, *this* fear is even more primal; it is fear in the face of death. Famine has struck Canaan. Isaac contemplates leaving Canaan for Egypt in the hope of finding food. But will leaving the land mean the end of God's promise? After all, the promise that God made to Abraham began with Abraham's willingness to go to "the land that I will show you," the Promised Land. Isaac seems caught between impossible alternatives. If he stays, he risks death. If he leaves, he risks losing his destiny.

And as before, we moderns must struggle to understand Isaac's terror. Famine is a foreign concept for us. We read about a citrus crop that has failed, and assume that the price of orange juice will rise a few cents. But real hunger is no longer part of our vocabulary. The possibility of famine does not move us. Even the evening news sound bites only show us famine once somebody is doing something about it. We don't know—and therefore can't appreciate—the terror of dying slowly and alone for lack of food. But if we are to appreciate how critical this message of "being a blessing" is to *us*, we need to appreciate better the terror Isaac felt at the moment he heard it.

Perhaps, if we are to experience Isaac's dread, we should substitute the word "cancer" for "famine." Cancer, after all, does evoke that sort of fear for us. The terror, the uncertainty, the image of a future about to be stolen from us. The fear of being alone, of being forgotten, of having planned for a future that will never come to be. *That* is Isaac's terror.

But God does not want Isaac to leave the Promised Land. The Torah recounts the "conversation" that then ensues:

> ²The LORD had appeared to him and said, "Do not go down to Egypt; stay in the land which I point out to you. ³Reside in this land, and I will be with you and bless you; I will assign all these lands to you and to your heirs, fulfilling the oath that I swore to your father Abraham. ⁴I will make your heirs as numerous as the stars of heaven, and assign to your heirs all these lands, so that all the nations of the earth shall bless themselves by your heirs—⁵inasmuch as Abraham obeyed Me and kept My charge: My commandments, My laws, and My teachings."
>
> (GENESIS 26:2–5)

Before moving on to God's similar promise to Jacob, we should note a brilliant literary detail in the Torah. Immediately prior to this story, the Torah foreshadows its theme. It does this with the tale of Rebekah (Isaac's wife) becoming pregnant with twins. As the twins, who will later be known as Jacob and Esau, struggle in her womb and cause her great discomfort, she asks rhetorically, "Why do I exist?" (Genesis 25:22). "Why do I exist?" is not only Rebekah's question. It is Isaac's implicit question in this passage, and it is ours. It is the question American Jews must answer before they can reclaim an authentic voice, before Jews will know why they should choose Judaism.

Finally, God's blessing is repeated to Abraham's grandson Jacob. In the midst of a journey, Jacob stops to sleep for the night, and dreams a strange dream:

> [12]. . . a stairway was set on the ground and its top reached to the sky, and angels of God were going up and down on it. [13]And the LORD was standing beside him and He said, "I am the LORD, the God of your father Abraham and the God of Isaac: the ground on which you are lying I will assign to you and to your offspring. [14]Your descendants shall be as the dust of the earth; you shall spread out to the west and to the east, to the north and to the south. All the families of the earth shall bless themselves by you and your descendants."
>
> (GENESIS 28:12–14)

But what sounds like an idyllic pastoral setting was nothing of the sort! What was Jacob doing sleeping alone in the field? As we search for the origins of this story in Genesis 27 and Genesis 28, we are reminded that Jacob is fleeing his brother, Esau, the very one with whom he had struggled in his mother's womb. Years earlier, Esau had "sold" his birthright for a bowl of soup, but now that Jacob has "collected the debt" by tricking his near blind father into blessing *him* rather than his older brother Esau, Esau is enraged. As the more powerful of the two brothers, he can clearly kill Jacob. So Rebekah, Jacob's mother, urges Jacob to flee and to save his own life.

Jacob, therefore, is also facing terror. It is the terror of violent death. And here, too, the Torah's answer to terror is "meaning," purpose. It is assurance not only of survival, but of meaningful survival. The substance of that meaning, we clearly see, has something to do with Jews and their engagement with the families of the earth.

Carefully, almost painstakingly, the Torah makes clear to us that the "promise" that "all the families of the earth shall bless themselves by you and your descendants" is not simply a promise to one of the Patriarchs. "Being a blessing" is not a rhetorical flourish here; it is part of the fundamental reason that the very lives of these people and their families make a difference. The blessings all come at a moment when life seems devoid of meaning; the blessings suggest that through their descendants, Abraham, Isaac and Jacob have the opportunity to find purpose, to make their lives matter, to live with the sense that they are part of an important, possibly world-changing, process.

The Torah, of course, is speaking to us. Just when *we* wonder whether to go on, whether being Jewish matters, our tradition cries out and says that it does. It says that to be a Jew cannot, ultimately, mean being just like everyone else. Nor can being Jewish be about disengaging from the world. Jews need to survive not (as some would insist) in order to rob Hitler of his posthumous victory, but because the world needs us. *We* are the ones who need to recover our conviction that we matter, that we are here for a purpose, and that the world desperately needs what we have to offer.

JEWS TODAY: THE SPIRITUAL DESCENDANTS OF ABRAHAM, ISAAC AND JACOB

If we are to be true to our history, then, we cannot simply disengage from the world, hoping to be ignored. The long-standing

American Jewish goal of becoming so Americanized that we blend in completely is fundamentally at odds with the Torah's description of who we must be. Even at this early stage, our tradition—the story we tell about ourselves—suggests that we need to stand out. That, of course, is not always comfortable for us. Indeed, it might even be a burden.

For that reason, Jewish history is filled with examples of Jews trying to turn attention *away* from our distinctiveness. More than one hundred years ago, in 1885, the leaders of Reform Judaism in America adopted a document known as the "Pittsburgh Platform" as a general statement of their principles. Many of these Reform Jews were from families of German-Jewish descent who had come to the United States decades earlier. These West European Jews, comfortable, thoroughly American and largely assimilated, were horrified and humiliated by the masses of East European Jewish immigrants flowing onto American shores. They saw these impoverished, "uncultured" new Jewish arrivals as far too obviously foreign. Perhaps that is why these Reform leaders—some of the most significant figures of American Jewry—wrote:

> We recognize, in the modern era of universal culture of heart and intellect, the approaching of the realization of Israel's great messianic hope for the establishment of the kingdom of truth, justice, and peace among all men. We consider ourselves no longer a nation, but a religious community. . . .
>
> We recognize in Judaism a progressive religion, ever striving to be in accord with the postulates of reason. We are convinced of the utmost necessity of preserving the historical identity with our great past. Christianity and Islam being the daughter religions of Judaism . . . we extend the hand of fellowship to all who operate with us in the establishment of the reign of truth and righteousness among men.

For these thinkers, Judaism was now a universal faith. Calling themselves "no longer a nation" and "extending the hand of fellowship" to Christianity and Islam were subtle but critical phrases: they were those rabbis' way of saying that it was time to lessen the differences between Judaism and the outside world, time to see the fulfillment of Judaism's ideal as the establishment of a universal, human family. And it was time, finally, to integrate Jewish life into the world around it.

The Pittsburgh Platform was hardly sui generis. Indeed, much of American Jewish life has been committed to the ideal of giving up our distinctive voice. As late as 1939, when it was already becoming clear that European Jewry was in grave danger, American Jewish leaders were still trying to ignore the need for a distinctively Jewish perspective on the world. Samuel Goldenson, rabbi of New York's famed Temple Emanu-El, wrote in that year:

> If we insist, as I believe we should, upon the moral basis and universal validity of democracy, we should at the same time emphasize less and less the particularisms in our Jewish heritage, those particularisms that separate us from others, and stress the universal concepts and outlooks more and more.

Rabbi Goldenson, a leading Reform rabbi of his generation, understood the tension between American universalism (or at least the myth of that universalism) and Jewish distinctiveness. Perhaps he suspected that most American Jews would not make the commitment that real distinctiveness demanded. We cannot be certain. But what *is* clear is that almost three quarters of a century ago, he realized that American Jews would have to choose. He, like many of us, decided that in order for us to "make it" in America, Judaism's particularisms would have to go.

Although Goldenson's choice was honest, for those of us today wondering why we should choose Jewish life at all, it rings hollow. How does a universalist conception of Jewish life help us answer our question about a world in which no Jews are left? If Judaism is simply "the moral basis and universal validity of democracy," how is it different (in that regard) from Christianity? Or from a host of nonreligious options, such as ethical humanism or Democratic liberalism, which also value democracy and ethical living?

Though more than a century has passed since the Pittsburgh Platform, some American Jewish leaders are still wedded to this universalist conception of Jewish life and purpose. In 1995, when the $65 million multimedia Skirball Cultural Center opened in Los Angeles, visitors were greeted by an open Torah scroll and, on the wall, a translation of the displayed passage. That passage, Genesis 12:1–3, is translated exactly as follows: "Go forth . . . and be a blessing to the world." That, of course, is a highly condensed form of the original, which actually says:

> [1]*The* LORD *said to Abram, "Go forth from your native land and from your father's house to the land that I will show you.*
> [2]*I will make of you a great nation,*
> *And I will bless you;*
> *I will make your name great,*
> *And you shall be a blessing.*
> [3]*I will bless those who bless you*
> *And curse him that curses you;*
> *And all the families of the earth*
> *Shall bless themselves by you."*

Asked about the omissions in the translation, the center's program and core exhibition director explained, "We put an ellipsis in our translation because we did not want to emphasize unduly the middle lines, which promise a particular land and future to Abraham's offspring. We wanted instead to bring out the universal aspect of the command." Rabbi Uri Herscher, the center's founder, went further. He added that this approach was designed to bring unaffiliated Jews back to the fold. "We have a marketing plan for reaching Jewish people who are not members of synagogues. We're going to make it clear to all of them that we're not . . . dogmatic."

But why is distinctiveness equated with being dogmatic? Perhaps because it is simply not comfortable. Some Jews want to resolve the tension between the Torah's vision and our own contemporary preferences by using an ellipsis. For these Jews, our ambivalence about Jewish distinctiveness is not a serious problem. Indeed, universalism is for them the key to the solution.

But is universalism a fair reflection of the tradition and what it has to say? Of course, there is a universalist streak in much of Jewish classical tradition. When Genesis 1:27 states that human beings were created in God's image, it refers to all people, not just Jews. The Book of Job, the Bible's gripping discussion of why innocent people suffer, is about a non-Jew. Similarly, the *Aleinu* prayer, which concludes many Jewish worship services, ends with a vision of all the earth's peoples recognizing one God. And other examples abound.

But this universalist strain is not the only voice in our tradition. Even while insisting on the universal, Judaism argues for Jewish particularism as well. In religious language, the tension in the Jewish tradition is one of a universal God forging a contract with one distinctive people.

Maintaining that healthy tension has been difficult for American Jews. When we hear that the goal of a major Jewish cultural center (which interestingly does not have the word "Jewish" in its name) is to "bring out the universal aspect of the command" in Genesis 12, we need to ask, "What is that universal aspect?" Where is it in the words of the Torah? Isn't the passage's basic point that the Jews have special work to do, a unique mission to carry out?

ARE MODERN JEWS UP TO THE CHALLENGE?

It is one thing to know our history, and another to be burdened by it. Why should modern Jews give any consideration to what the Bible might say about people who lived long ago?

No one can force modern Jews to take the Torah's claims about Abraham, Isaac and Jacob seriously. Each of us has the right to see the Patriarchs as mere historical curiosities. However, our tradition would claim that inheriting this special sense of destiny is akin to being the oldest child in a family. There is no logical reason that the oldest child in a family often feels a sense of obligation for her siblings once they've reached adulthood, or that parents often look to the oldest of their adult children for care as they grow older. No one can force an eldest child to play this role; but the role somehow comes with the territory. When firstborn children decide not to play that role, they often sense that they are walking away from a part of themselves, denying a piece of who they really are.

Responsibility is like a shadow. We can run from it, but we can never really escape it. As we hold ourselves up to the light in different ways and in different angles, we can make the shadow loom larger, or we can diminish the area it reaches. But it is always with us.

The same is true with contemporary Jews and the responsibilities our tradition ascribes to us. No matter how far some Jews stray from Jewish life, there is a call from the depths of our consciousness that seems to forbid us to forget where we've come from. Our ears perk up at what we think might be disparaging remarks. We are immediately ashamed when Jews in public office fail in their responsibilities; when Jews murder their own leaders, we feel shame, personally wounded. But we also feel deeply connected. Our connections to Jewish life die hard, not because we've been convinced of anything, but because they transcend reason.

If we're serious about recovering Jewish identity on the eve of the twenty-first century, we must stop pretending that identity is simple or that the search will be easy and undemanding. Rather, we will have to ask hard and pointed questions: Can contemporary Jews find a thoughtful way of being what Isaiah called a "light unto the nations" (Isaiah 42:6, 49:6, 51:4), the bearers of a message that the world needs to hear? And why is it that so many Jews today never find it? These are all crucial questions, issues that we will address throughout the coming chapters.

But as we move closer to answering them, we need to pause; for there is another side to the Bible's "promise" that we will make a difference. If we look carefully, we will see that Jewish tradition has never believed that Jews will make a difference simply by virtue of existing. Contrary to what some of us may have heard or may wish to believe, the simple presence of Jews in the world guarantees nothing. Jews will make a difference only if they live in certain ways, do certain things. There is a subtle, conditional quality to the promise that God made us. Being a blessing is not automatic; it demands something from us.

How do we know that? And what are those behaviors upon which our making a difference depends? We need to return once again to the words of the tradition, and explore the other side of the "challenge" that our ancestors accepted so long ago.

CHAPTER TWO

To Be the Chosen People—
"That Cunningest of Races" or
"A Treasured People and Holy Nation"

*T*he Chosen People." It would be hard to imagine any other combination of three simple words that could arouse such passion, devotion, ire and embarrassment among Jews. Mentioned in one group, the phrase elicits nods of approval, occasionally even knowing glances of native superiority. In such a group, when pressed about why Jews should survive, people will often answer obliquely, "Because we're the chosen people; God *wants* us to survive." What that argument actually means is often unclear. What these people mean by chosenness is usually left unsaid—and often, is not well thought through. But the superficial folk-notion that Jews are somehow God's "favorites" is so reassuring to many Jews that they are content simply to accept the idea at face value.

But in other groups, the very same phrase evokes the opposite reaction. These are Jews who are uncomfortable with or even ashamed of the "chosen people" concept, who say that it is that idea alone that moved them away from Judaism. Some among them insist (quite incorrectly, I believe), that the mere words "chosen people" have been responsible for generations and centuries of anti-Semitism. "If only we had not rubbed the faces of the non-Jewish world in this haughty, arrogant concept," the argument goes, "they would have had much less reason to hate us."

For still others, the concept is too painful even to contemplate in light of the horrific events of Europe in the 1930s and 1940s. "If we're God's chosen people," they ask with understandable cynicism and bitterness, "where was God when Jews were marched to their deaths in Auschwitz?" Some add to their bitter complaint, "If that's what God has in mind for the chosen people, let God choose somebody else." For those of us who did not personally live through the Shoah, what can we say to those who did?

But more common than any of these groups are another sort who dismiss the chosen people concept entirely. These are Jews—often representing the liberal side of the political and social spectrum, often those with more exposure to the secular world of America—who find the phrase not ironic or painful, but rather, patently offensive and virtually unmentionable. It seems to them to demean other peoples and traditions. Just as there are certain offensive racial epithets that these Jews would never use about another group, "the chosen people" is one they avoid when describing themselves.

Nor is this an entirely new phenomenon. The following, written just after the Shoah, almost half a century ago, could have been written today. It is part of a letter to the editor of *Judaism* magazine, attacking an article by Will Herberg, one of this century's most important Jewish philosophers. Herberg had argued for the importance of "chosenness," and the reader wrote back:

> [this] doctrine suffers from an ethnocentric arrogance which denies the validity of the moral experiences of other peoples. It teaches that God selected one people to be the moral teachers of mankind. Therefore, the rest of mankind is morally benighted. The claim of moral superiority of a people, forever, and with the stamp of God, is unacceptable no matter how cloaked in piety. . . .
>
> I am afraid of people who believe they are God's direct agents in spreading the Truth. You cannot argue with those people. There is no listening to reason with them. There is no voting with them. There are no minority rights with them, except those that they graciously grant for reasons suf-

ficient to their own interests. . . . This doctrine has been a destructive and divisive factor in the attempt to build democratic Jewish communities in America. Mr. Herberg's idea of the "covenant" is parallel to racist thinking. . . .

It's all here: the fear of appearing superior, the absolute dedication to building a "democratic" community in *America,* the concern about pluralism, and the list goes on. Even in the 1950s, American Jews found the notion unacceptable. Their resistance to it has only grown in the interim.

All of this leads us to an important question: How critical is the chosen people concept in Jewish life? Consider once again the Torah, the document that tells our communal story.

"CHOSEN PEOPLE"— TRADITIONAL CONCEPT OR RECENT DEVELOPMENT?

Jews who dislike (or detest) the phrase "the chosen people" might take comfort in the fact that the Torah never mentions it. The phrase is so common in certain Jewish circles, and so frequently uttered *about* the Jews, that many of us assume that it simply must have been mentioned somewhere in those early narratives about Abraham, Isaac and Jacob, in which the relationship between God and Israel is first established. But it is not. Nowhere in the Torah does God use the term "chosen" to speak about the Israelites either.

But the issue is more complex than it initially seems. For although it is true that the word "chosen" does not appear in the Torah this way, God's various promises to Abraham, Isaac and Jacob certainly do seem to argue for a unique relationship between their descendants and God.

Moreover, later works in Jewish life use the term "chosen" freely. When we include *these* compositions in our survey, we find something very different; the phrase "chosen people" is not only present, but is rather common.

Let's look first at some brief examples from the Bible itself. In the Hebrew Bible, the book that most commonly speaks of chosenness is the Book of Isaiah. Isaiah, a prophet who lived in the eighth century B.C.E., seems entirely unabashed by the idea that God had selected the Jews for some special role in the world. In Isaiah 41, God says

> *⁸But you, Israel, My servant,*
> *Jacob, whom I have chosen,*
> *Seed of Abraham My friend—*
> *⁹You whom I drew from the ends of the earth*
> *And called from its far corners,*
> *To whom I said: You are My servant;*
> *I chose you, I have not rejected you—*
> *¹⁰Fear not, for I am with you. . . .*
>
> (ISAIAH 41:8–10)

In the next chapter, the image of "chosenness" is distinctly tied to the idea that the Jews are to be a blessing:

> *This is My servant, whom I uphold,*
> *My chosen one, in whom I delight.*
> *I have put My spirit upon him,*
> *He shall teach the true way to the nations.*
>
> (ISAIAH 42:1)

And there are numerous other examples. Soon thereafter, we find: "For I provide water in the wilderness, rivers in the desert, to give drink to My chosen people" (Isaiah 43:20) and "For the sake of My servant Jacob, Israel My chosen one" (Isaiah 45:4).

But if Isaiah introduces the "chosen people" to our vocabulary, the liturgy of the prayer book makes the phrase ubiquitous. Consider, for the moment, just two examples. Immediately prior to the morning recitation of the *Shema*, those famous words that read "Hear O Israel, the Lord our God, the Lord is one"

(Deuteronomy 6:4), the liturgy inserts a paragraph called *Ahavah Rabbah*, "Abundant Love." That passage concludes with a phrase that is critical for our discussion. *Ahavah Rabbah* is a long blessing, on the theme of love, but the concluding words say something particular about the nature of God's love for Israel: "Blessed are You, Lord, Who chooses His people Israel with love."

And *Ahavah Rabbah* is not the only place that we find this theme of "chosenness" in the *siddur*. The *siddur* (the Hebrew term for the prayer book) says that when a person is called to the Torah for an *aliyah* at a service, they should recite the following blessing: "Praised are You, Lord our God, Ruler of the Universe, who has chosen us from among all the nations and who has given us His Torah." Other examples abound.

The Torah itself may not mention chosenness. And many modern Jews may struggle with it, even to the point of rejecting it. But the tradition is equally clear. Isaiah speaks proudly about his belief that God chose the Jews for a significant "mission." In critical places, the liturgy makes exactly the same point. And even in the opening chapters of our history, as God establishes relationships with Abraham, Isaac and Jacob, chosenness of some sort is implicit. What else can "All the nations of the world will be blessed by your descendants" really mean? Whether we are comfortable with it or not, our "photo album" is clear. The story we have long told about ourselves is a story that ascribes to us a critical role. No matter how uncomfortable we may be with this idea now, we cannot avoid the conclusion that at pivotal and formative junctures in Jewish intellectual history, "being a blessing" or "chosenness" have been central ideas for us.

How, then, shall we proceed? Can we simply ignore chosenness, relegating it to the garbage heap of ideas that no longer appeal to us? Not if our goal is to reclaim our authentic voice. Not if we want our emerging conception of the Jews and their purpose to speak with the legitimacy that comes with thousands of years of history. Not if we want to be intellectually and spiritually honest.

Uncomfortable though chosenness may make us, if we are to be sincere about asking why the Jews exist, we're going to have to confront it. We shall have to ask tough questions about it, and of ourselves.

MISGUIDED SEARCHES FOR JEWISH UNIQUENESS

Before we can begin to figure out what to make of chosenness, we need to be honest about one of the sadder sides of the issue: Jewish racism. Often, what turns contemporary Jews off to Jewish life is the elitism that they sense in Jews' attitudes to the rest of the world. Many modern Jews sense that when other Jews—traditional or even largely secular—use Yiddish terms such as *schwartze* (which means "black" but has a very derogatory implication), or *shiksah* (a term for a non-Jewish woman that comes from a biblical Hebrew root that means "abomination"), or *goy* (a term that literally means "nation" but that also has ugly overtones), they are denying the humanity of the non-Jewish world. Some contemporary Jews also suspect— quite possibly correctly—that these offensive attitudes come from the notion of chosenness.

Is chosenness inherently racist? Certainly not. But honest searchers need to acknowledge that the opponents of chosenness, who believe that it often reveals an ugly side of Jewish communal life, are often right. All too often, Jews conflate "chosenness" with "betterness." Too many Jews assume that the Bible's conception of chosenness— of being a "blessing"—means that God somehow likes Jews better.

"That Cunningest of Races"?

In our desperation to believe that we still make a difference, we tend to rely on definitions of who we *are*, rather than what we do. There remain, for example, numerous Jews who believe, or at least claim to believe, that Jews are somehow naturally more intelligent than non-Jews. Generations of immigrant Jews, most of whom spoke or even still speak Yiddish, used a phrase that reflected this attitude. They spoke of a *yiddishe kop*, or a "Jewish head." "She has a *yiddishe kop*" was their way of saying "she's bright." The implication about Jews was clear. So, too, unfortunately, was what it suggested about non-Jews.

While most Jews today do not openly hold these beliefs about Jews and non-Jews, the notion of Jewish superiority still lurks not far below the surface of Jewish identity. It needs to be confronted, especially if we have any hope of making the search for a modern Jewish identity not only meaningful, but moral as well.

Dismissing inherent Jewish superiority does not have to mean denying our legitimate accomplishments. No one can deny that Jews have amassed an impressive record of accomplishment in this society. Recall the figures provided to us by Seymour Martin Lipset and Earl Raab, cited in the Introduction. Jews are represented far beyond their numbers in the best universities, among Nobel Prize winners, and the list goes on.

Those figures are impressive. But what do they really mean? There are still some Jews, and even a few non-Jews, who hold on to the notion that there is a magical quality to Jewish accomplishment; but most Jews respond, probably correctly, that Jews inherited a tradition of serious study. That tradition, they claim, is how we ought to explain Jews' success. Perhaps. Jews were also born to parents and grandparents who desperately wanted to succeed in this society, and who therefore consistently pushed them to climb the social, economic and academic ladders that America had suddenly made accessible.

Today, other more recent immigrant groups evince the same qualities. Asian-Americans, another group with a powerful drive to succeed, are now radically overrepresented in top American universities relative to their numbers in society. Some Jews may be bright, and some may be driven and hardworking. But deep in our hearts, most of us do not believe that we are intrinsically smarter than anyone else.

We may be proud of our accomplishments, but we don't consider them sufficient reason for choosing Judaism, for making this tradition part of our lives. Ultimately, we'll need something far more compelling as an explanation of what we contribute to society. Indeed, even though some Jews like to speak of native Jewish intelligence, almost nobody—even in the Jewish community—believes it.

How do we know this? All it takes is a quick look at Jewish public policy and our open-arms approach to conversion and to "Jews by Choice." If we really believed in some form of native Jewish intellectual superiority—if we thought that Jews were somehow naturally "smarter" than everyone else—the logical thing to do would be to put an immediate stop to conversion. Each year, thousands of non-Jews convert to Judaism. But the American Jewish community has not even tried to stop conversion; indeed, we encourage it. Our leadership recognizes that precisely because we *are* so much like our neighbors, some Jews will inevitably fall in love with non-Jews, and will often marry them.

Of course, many people convert to Judaism for other reasons as well. Nonetheless, a radical shift has taken place. Sociologists playfully suggest that the non-Jewish world by and large no longer wants to murder Jews, but many want to marry Jews. In the eyes of many Jewish leaders, therefore, conversion of these future spouses has been one of the great sources of hope for Jewish continuity. Many American rabbis argue that we can lessen the impact of intermarriage not by preventing these marriages (for that is often unrealistic), but by inviting the non-Jewish partner into our tradition. Almost all the major movements of Jewish life, from the most liberal to the most traditional, willingly accept serious converts. But if we really believed that we were somehow more intellectually equipped, why would we tamper with this gene pool?

The answer: we don't really believe Jews are more intelligent. We know it's not true, and we know it's offensive. Even the classic works of the Jewish tradition suggest that such views are anathema. Consider an interesting ruling found in the Mishnah, the first major work of the rabbinic tradition, codified in approximately 220 C.E. This simple rule holds that once a person converts to Judaism, we are forbidden from ever mentioning that the convert had once been non-Jewish. The Mishnah puts it this way:

> If he was a child of converts, one may not say to him, "Remember the deeds of your ancestors" [when they were gentiles], for it is said, "You shall not wrong a stranger or oppress him" (Exodus 22:20).
>
> (BAVA MEẒI'A 4:10)

Though deceivingly simple, the Mishnah's law is making an important point. After conversion to Judaism, a person's transformation is complete. Indeed, the convert may recite all of the liturgical prayers that include the phrase "Our God, and God of *our* ancestors." There are no lingering vestiges of the convert's former spiritual life. As far as the tradition is concerned, this "new" Jew is as much a part of the Jewish people as anyone who was born Jewish.

THERE IS YET another reason we ought to give up this idea that Jews are naturally more intelligent than their neighbors. It's quite simple: not only is the claim untrue, but some people believe it is also dangerous. If the world at large came to believe that Jews were natively more intelligent, they argue, the natural response would be either jealousy or deep mistrust. We have lived through too much history to dismiss the results to which that might lead.

Sounds absurd? Perhaps it's not. After all, the notion that Jews are inherently "smarter" is essentially a racial argument. It sees Jews not as a religion, as a culture or as a people, but as a biological entity—a race. Wasn't that Hitler's tactic? Haven't Jews been trying to insist ever since the Third Reich that speaking of Jews as a race has inherent, or at least potential, anti-Semitic overtones? We can't have it both ways.

At times, the argument for Jewish intelligence is seen as part of an argument against other groups. In Richard Herrnstein and Charles Murray's famous *The Bell Curve,* which has at its core an argument that African-Americans are less intelligent than whites, Jews are again singled out as a race. They note that Jews "of European origins . . . test higher than any other ethnic group," indeed, "between half and a full standard deviation above the mean." How comfortable are we with the idea of being used as the high end of a scale, when the argument against those on the bottom end of the scale is seen as so vicious? Shall we construct our identity on *that* foundation?

But there is a danger to the argument that Jews are inherently smarter. Some have argued that as a result of this native intelligence, Jews need to be watched more carefully; they suggest that the Jews' attempt to become unified ought to be curtailed. Consider the example of Mark Twain, generally regarded as a friend of the Jews. In a letter to his friend, the Reverend Joseph Twitchell, Twain once wrote that

> the difference between the brain of the average Christian and that of the average Jew—certainly in Europe—is about the difference between a tadpole's and an archbishop's. It's a marvelous race—by long odds the most marvelous race that the world has produced, I suppose.

But elsewhere in his writings, Twain's apparent awe of Jews and their intellectual abilities led him to fear them. Reacting to Theodor Herzl's plans for the creation of a Jewish national entity in Palestine, he wrote in *Harper's Magazine:*

> If that concentration of the cunningest brains in the world was going to be made in a free country . . . I think it would

be politic to stop it. It will not be well to let that race find out its strength. If the horse knew theirs, we should not ride anymore.

Some scholars have suggested that there is yet another danger: the portrayal of Jews as more intelligent is often coupled with a claim that they are also less virtuous. One recent study points to this phenomenon in popular American culture, suggesting that even in works like F. Scott Fitzgerald's *The Last Tycoon* (especially with the character Monroe Stahr) and Robert Redford's film *Quiz Show*, Jews' native intelligence is portrayed as somehow in inverse relation to their virtue. Hardly a compliment, this "intelligence."

Much more insidious examples could be brought, but the point is clear: the idea that Jews bring a unique intelligence to the world is not only unconvincing, but double-edged as well. If we believed it, it would only make sense to "circle our wagons," to declare a moratorium on conversion and to hope against all hope that we could interrupt this rich and profound interaction between Jews and their neighbors. But we simply do not believe it. And if non-Jews really believed it, Jews might well be worse off. Thus, to answer the question, What unique contribution do the Jewish people make to the world? we shall have to look elsewhere.

"If You, Too, Only Had Power . . ."
Jews and Their Belief in Moral Superiority

But not every "elsewhere" is an improvement. There are alternatives to the intelligence argument that are just as bad, if not worse. The most notorious example of that has been the notion of the Jews and their moral superiority.

For a long time, Jews have asserted—sometimes quietly but at other times more vocally—that what differentiates Jews from the rest of the world is a higher ethical standard, a more refined sense of right and wrong. All our talk of a Judeo-Christian ethic notwithstanding, Jews have often believed that Judaism made them more ethical, more honorable, more moral—even if they couldn't explain exactly how Jewish ethics were really all that different from Christian ethics.

At times, people put this argument in historical terms. Asked why the world needs the Jews, some Jews respond, "Because we gave the world the Ten Commandments," or some variation on the theme: "Jews gave the world morality." "We taught the world right from wrong."

These historical arguments are not completely incorrect. While it might be a bit much to claim that the Jews taught the world right from wrong, it is certainly the case that the Torah *did* introduce a new moral code to the world. In a world in which Hammurabi's code was the norm, the Torah was a radical document. In many respects, the Torah's moral code *was* preferable to what the world knew. Ours was a moral code that denied the popular notion that the rich could kill the poor with impunity, that slaves had no rights, that humanity ought to work, day after day, with no opportunity for respite. On that level, the historical argument is correct.

But today, the question is, so what? After all, even if the Jews were to disappear, the Ten Commandments would remain an important part of Western culture. Even if there were no Jews left in the world tomorrow, much of the advancement that the Jews brought to morality would remain. Why? Because Christianity also represents much of the goodness of the early part of the Jewish tradition. So when we ask why the world needs the Jews, of what relevance is this history?

The answer is clear. Implicit in the answer, "We gave the world the Ten Commandments," is the assertion, "And we're still the world's beacon of morality today." Buried just below the surface of the historical explanation is a claim about the present— it's a claim that the Jews are still more moral, still a shining light of ethical behavior in a world that would otherwise be wholly corrupt. That, say many Jews, is what genuinely sets us apart.

But do Jews really believe that anymore? If anything, our unprecedented successes in America have proven the "moral superiority" argument wrong. While we've got more than our share of Nobel laureates, Wall Street partners and award-winning artists, we also have our share of shame. When the prominent careers of Robert Levine, Ivan Boesky and Michael Milken (the latter two of whom were deeply involved in the Jewish community) collapsed after their Wall Street behavior was discovered, the entire Jewish world seemed to shudder from the impact. After the initial shock, we learned an important lesson: part of the price of success, of "making it" in a world that had once been closed to us, is that we will make the same mistakes and commit the same crimes as everyone else.

We learned the same thing in Israel as well. When the Palestinian intifada forced young Israeli soldiers to shoot tear gas (and sometimes bullets) at ten-year-old boys throwing stones, American Jews grimaced. Suddenly, their image of the new Israeli state, an image of a democratic stronghold in a backward and repressive region, a society committed to liberal values even in the face of persistent threats to its survival, began to give way to a more sober realization. Israel, like all other countries, would have to engage in some unpleasant work to stay alive.

The pinnacle came with the murder of Yitzhak Rabin in November 1995. When we first came to know about Yigal Amir, an observant yeshivah graduate who was also an assassin, our grief knew no bounds. We grieved not only for a man, and for a nation suddenly thrust into adulthood. We grieved for our loss of an image of ourselves, a sense of the inevitable goodness that comes with Jewish seriousness.

Modernity has taught us the painful truth that with economic, social and military power, Jews will sometimes commit the same abuses that everyone else does. At times, we seem surprised by these realizations. But Jewish philosophers of almost a thousand years ago would have wondered at our surprise; they would insist that they knew what we have just now "discovered."

A classic example is the great medieval Jewish philosophical classic, the *Kuzari*. Written by Rabbi Judah Ha-Levi (1075–1141), it is a lengthy fictitious dialogue between a rabbi and a gentile king, in which the rabbi seeks to convince the king of the "truth" of Judaism. Ha-Levi's work is a classic apologetic argument from the Middle Ages; indeed, his subtitle for the *Kuzari* is *A Composition in Argumentation and Proof in the Defense of the Despised Faith*. Throughout this enduring dialogue, the rabbi argues for Judaism's superiority; after each argument, the king responds. Usually, whenever the king raises an objection to the rabbi's argument, the rabbi deftly shows him where he has erred.

Throughout the hundreds of small arguments that make up the *Kuzari*, there are only two instances in the entire book when the rabbi hears the king's objection and says, "You're right. I have no response." One of those two is particularly important to our discussion. In that example, the rabbi points with pride to the fact that Jews have no record of committing atrocities such as those perpetrated upon them. He notes this "clean record" as a mark of Jewish ethical superiority. But the king responds that the Jews have a clean record only because they have had no power. "If you had power," the king effectively says, "you, too, would have a sullied record." Interestingly, in this instance, the rabbi does *not* point to an error in the king's logic. The rabbi admits that he has no response (*Kuzari* 1:113–14).

That is precisely what we, too, have learned. The Jewish people does have an impressive moral code and a long history of being on the receiving end of much of the world's evil. But modernity has complicated that naive and simplistic perspective. We have access to power but we also commit crimes. Now, we achieve success but we also fail. And we have an army, and it, too, faces harrowing choices. Whatever sets us apart, it is *not* an innate proclivity to avoid evil or to do good.

"A TREASURED PEOPLE AND HOLY NATION"—THE
TRADITION'S READING OF JEWISH UNIQUENESS

As we saw in Chapter One, the Jewish tradition claims that Abraham, Isaac, Jacob and their descendants—the Jews of today—need to be a people through whom the rest of the world considers itself "blessed." But how does that happen?

Somewhat surprisingly, the Torah tells that the Israelites left Egypt with no clear signal from God as to what their role would be. Though God tells them of a special relationship with their ancestors, they actually have very little idea why God is going to such trouble on their behalf. What does God want for them? From them? Only after they have left Egypt, crossed the sea and begun their journey through the desert do they begin to get an idea. Only after it is basically too late to return to Egypt does God more fully explain how "all the nations of the earth shall bless themselves by [their] descendants. . . ." We read:

> ³And Moses went up to God. The LORD called to him from the mountain, saying, "Thus shall you say to the house of Jacob and declare to the children of Israel: ⁴'You have seen what I did to the Egyptians, how I bore you on eagles' wings and brought you to Me. ⁵Now then, if you will obey Me faithfully and keep My covenant, you shall be My treasured possession among all the peoples. Indeed, all the earth is Mine, ⁶but you shall be to Me a kingdom of priests and a holy nation.' These are the words that you shall speak to the children of Israel."
>
> (EXODUS 19:3–6)

Simple though these brief sentences sound, there is something extraordinary about them. The Israelites, like contemporary Jews, might have been tempted to assume that God's interest in them was due to some innate characteristic they had.

It might well have seemed that God was devoted to them (or to use less theological language, that they mattered), simply because of who they were. But not so, says the Torah. Despite God's love for their ancestors, God is interested not in *who* they are, but in *how* they live and *what* they do. There is nothing automatic about their special role. Either they will earn it, or they will not have it.

What a dramatically different way of thinking about Jews and their role from what we have become accustomed to. Having been taught that we ought to be Jewish but not "too Jewish," American Jews have sought to minimize their outward expressions of Jewishness, claiming that the world of Jewish tradition—the covenant, in the Torah's language—was outmoded and unnecessary.

But the tradition is clear. That covenant, ancient and antiquated as it might seem, is the critical link between Jews and their special role. Without that, the Torah implies, we have no purpose for being.

Let's examine the passage a little more carefully, searching again for hints about where to start constructing a Jewish identity that would have us make a difference. Several points become immediately clear.

First: the Torah claims that no matter what God's relationship with the Israelites (later to be called Jews) may be, God is the God of all the earth. "All the earth is Mine," says the Torah; the Jews' relationship with God must not obscure the fact that God cares about all peoples, not just the Jews.

Second: the passage then retreats from this entirely universalist picture, and describes something more particularist. Despite God's role as Ruler of the entire universe, it asserts, God does have a special relationship with the Jewish people. We are to be God's "treasured possession."

Third: God's promise that we will become "a kingdom of priests and a holy nation" is preceded by the simple but crucial condition, "if you will obey Me faithfully and keep My covenant." If and only if. The covenant is binding on the Jews no matter how they behave. But the privilege of actually bringing something important to the world is conditional. The Jews do not have this status because they are somehow better than anyone else. There is nothing genetic or innate about this. Precisely the opposite is true: Jews will come to merit this special role if—and only if—we earn it. And how do we earn it? By "obeying [God] faithfully" and "keeping [the] covenant."

The Torah's point is clear. Jews *can* be unique, indeed we must, but it will not happen without effort. There is a "price of entry" to this distinct position. It is uniqueness. It is a commitment to a community that is not only national or ethnic, but that is deeply rooted in the traditions that set us apart, that give us something distinctively Jewish to bring to the world.

That is implicit, by the way, in the promises that God makes to Isaac and Jacob. If we examine the words of that promise carefully, we notice that God does not simply promise Isaac that his descendants will make a difference. Rather, God makes clear that their making a difference is tied to the covenant, to that distinct way of living. God says, "All the nations of the earth shall bless themselves by your descendants, because you have obeyed My command" (Genesis 22:18).

The same is true with Jacob. God's promise to him, too, specifically mentions the covenant, here called "commandments, law and teaching." God promises him:

> 4I will make your heirs as numerous as the stars of heaven, and assign to your heirs all these lands, so that all the nations of the earth shall bless themselves by your heirs—5inasmuch as Abraham obeyed Me and kept My charge: My commandments, My laws, and My teachings.
>
> (GENESIS 26:4–5)

Even after the Akkedah (the Binding of Isaac), we find the same thing. As soon as Abraham demonstrated his willingness to sacrifice his son, the angel of God ties Abraham's reward to his having fulfilled God's command. The angel appeared

> ¹⁶And said, "By Myself I swear, the LORD declares: Because you have done this and have not withheld your son, your favored one, ¹⁷I will bestow My blessing upon you and make your descendants as numerous as the stars of heaven and the sands on the seashore; and your descendants shall seize the gates of their foes. ¹⁸All the nations of the earth shall bless themselves by your descendants, because you have obeyed My command."
>
> (GENESIS 22:16–18)

In each case, the promise for the future is explicitly linked to certain behaviors, to obeying God's command, to sustaining the covenant.

A single conclusion begins to emerge clearly: a Judaism that is both worth preserving and yet divorced from its traditional roots is simply not possible. We cannot have Jewish significance without Jewish substance. The more we minimize the substance of Jewish life, the more we undermine our own significance.

For understandable reasons, Jews are often inclined to try to revive the old and tired notion that Judaism can survive almost no matter what we do to it or how we live it. But arguing that we have something special to contribute to the world at the same time that we insist on living just like everyone else inevitably requires falling back on notions of some sort of innate superiority. Most of us are no longer willing to take that step. Thus, we have a choice to make. We can either give up the idea that Judaism makes any difference whatsoever (and probably give up Jewish life altogether), or we can undertake a serious investigation of our tradition to see what values it reflects that might give us something to offer the world.

But that is a profound undertaking. Perhaps that is why earlier Jewish-American leaders like Rabbi Samuel Goldenson of

Temple Emanu-El moved away from this notion. But Rabbi
Goldenson's well-intentioned vision is no longer compelling.
This is not to suggest that Rabbi Goldenson and the other leaders
of his generation made terrible mistakes. Quite the contrary.
They were responding to what they believed American Jews
needed and wanted at that time. They may well have been right.

But the times have changed. Even while sociologists point to
a dramatic rate of nonaffiliation and some suggest that the very
future of Jewish life is threatened, there is a small but pronounced movement in the opposite direction. Particularly
among younger people, some Jews have begun to move back to
tradition. They are doing their spiritual searching inside Jewish
life, looking for new ways to invest their lives with meaning,
with sanctity, with spiritual substance. As they engage in this
search, these Jews are returning to a serious engagement with
sacred Jewish texts. Today, they are not interested in forcing the
texts to conform to their American sensibilities. Rather, we
struggle to hear the authentic impulse of the tradition. Many of
us want to conform our lives and priorities to the values that
emerge from an authentic reading of our tradition. We are interested not in what American-Jewish leaders have said for a generation or two, but rather, in what our tradition has said for
thousands of years. And Genesis 22, Genesis 26 and Exodus 19 all
speak clearly: a choice needs to be made. If we want a reason to
survive as Jews, Judaism must stand for something different from
the rest of the world. And if we want to *be* different, we will have
to *live* that difference.

Again, because this conception of Jews and their place in the
world is so dramatically different from what American Jews have
been taught to think, one might be tempted to dismiss this
requirement for distinctive living as an ancient biblical concept
that makes no difference to us. But that would be a mistake, for
this link is virtually omnipresent in the Jewish tradition. It is
found not just in the Bible, but in virtually every nook and
cranny of Judaism. It *is* Judaism. To see a few more examples,

let's turn to the Jewish book with which many Jews are most familiar—the *siddur,* or prayer book.

"WHO HAS CHOSEN US FROM AMONG THE NATIONS" AND ITS LINK TO COMMANDMENTS

Earlier in this chapter, we saw that what the Torah calls "being a blessing" the *siddur* calls "being chosen." We examined two blessings that used this language: the blessing before the morning recitation of the *Shema,* and the blessing recited as a person is called up to the Torah. Let's look at them briefly again.

No words of the *siddur* are better known than the famous words of the *Shema:* "Hear O Israel, the Lord our God, the Lord is One." Traditional Jews recite the *Shema* three times each day: morning, evening and even in bed at night before they fall asleep. The *Shema* is the phrase that many Jewish martyrs have died saying. Though it first appears in the Torah (Deuteronomy 6:4), it is in many ways the quintessential Jewish prayer. Thus, whatever the tradition does to introduce the *Shema* should be particularly important.

When the *Shema* appears in the morning liturgy, it is introduced by a prayer called *Ahavah Rabbah,* or "Abundant Love." *Ahavah Rabbah* claims that God loves the people of Israel; it suggests that proof of God's love is the fact that God gave us the Torah. The prayer therefore pleads that we be enabled to live up to the demands of the Torah, and says:

> Enable our hearts to understand and to elucidate, to listen, to learn, to teach, to safeguard, to perform and to fulfill all the words of Your Torah's teaching with love. Enlighten our eyes in Your Torah, attach our hearts to Your commandments, and unify our hearts to love and to feel awe for Your name. . . . Praised are You, Lord, who chooses His people Israel with love.

Even though we have jumped from the Torah to the prayer book, a leap of many centuries, the central claim remains constant. Composed hundreds of years after the Torah, the *siddur* retains an interest in Jewish religious distinctiveness, which it calls "chosenness." And like the Torah, its point is clear: what we were chosen to do was to live up to the standards of the Torah. Distinctiveness remains part of our tradition, but so does the very conditional—almost tenuous—nature of that special role. *Ahavah Rabbah,* no less than the Torah itself, suggests that Jews must do something to remain distinct. Here is what "chosenness" might come to mean today: Jews have to choose to be chosen—there are uniquely Jewish commitments we'll have to honor if our survival is to matter.

The same point emerges in the blessing that Jews recite when they are called up to the Torah in the synagogue. People recite blessings before and after their particular selection from the Torah is read. The blessing recited before the reading—which we saw earlier—is particularly instructive:

> Praised are You, Lord our God, Ruler of the universe, who has chosen us from among all the nations, and who has given us His Torah. Praised are You, Lord, who gives the Torah.

Again, note the connection between having a special role in the world (which the liturgy again calls being "chosen") and having the Torah (a distinctive way of life). This blessing, like the one prior to the *Shema,* sees the two as intrinsically linked.

Consider one final example: the *Kiddush* recited on the evenings of major Jewish festivals. Though *Kiddush* is commonly called the "blessing over the wine," it is more accurately the blessing that declares that the day is sacred. Several times a year, as Jews usher in a major festival—Sukkot (the Festival of Tabernacles, in the fall), Passover, Shavu'ot (the Festival of Weeks, in the late spring), and with some modifications in the prayer, Rosh Ha-Shannah as well—they raise a cup of wine and recite the festival *Kiddush*. In this *Kiddush* (there are several different versions, depending on the occasion), we find the same confluence of ideas that we've seen before. The main section reads:

> Praised are You, Lord our God, Ruler of the universe, who has chosen us from among all the nations, who has exalted us above all the languages [of the earth], and who has sanctified us with His commandments. And in love You have given us, Lord our God, festivals in which to rejoice, holidays and appointed times for celebrating. . . .

All of the ideas we have seen thus far repeat themselves here. By following the "chosen" and "exalted" images with "sanctifying us through commandments," the passage links chosenness to a particular way of life. The *Kiddush* suggests that only by living in a unique way—for example, by celebrating each festival in its season—can Jews represent something unique to the world.

UNIQUENESS IN THEORY, ACCOMMODATION IN PRACTICE

Of course, contemporary American Jews have been taught something very different. We have been weaned on the idea that Jews could do whatever they wanted with Judaism, still survive, and even make a difference. We were assured that Bar and Bat Mitzvah ceremonies could be seen as graduations rather than the beginning of a lifetime of learning. But today's Jews don't know enough. When Hebrew conflicted with Little League, we assumed that Jewish study could be made up later. But when? We convinced ourselves that even if there was no sign of Jewishness in our home, the school or the *shul* could preserve our children's identity. But we've found that our kids read us well, and draw profound conclusions from what we ourselves do not do. We convinced ourselves that Jewish homes could be maintained even if one partner was not Jewish, but statistics show that is difficult to do. We were told that distinctive forms of Jewish dress could and even should be eliminated so we could seem completely American, but now we wonder: if no one knows we're Jewish, what difference do we really make? We were assured that Judaism at its "best" reflected the "most advanced" ethics and morals of American culture, but now that we have grown despondent about America and its lack of culture and ethics, we've lost the sense that Judaism might have something very different to say. We were assured that Judaism could be ful-filling without being demanding, but suddenly, the idea that a Judaism without real demands could be worth preserving has begun to sound like a hollow promise.

The evidence is in: Being just like everyone else will make it difficult to survive. The tradition goes even further; indeed, it is brutally clear. It says that if we're to be just like everyone else, survival is essentially irrelevant. Ironically, modern sociology and the ancient words of tradition agree that the very foundation of our American Jewish worldview may be misguided. Everything we've been taught about why we matter and what is at stake in our survival needs to be rethought.

Thus, a search. It is a search for the voice that made us differ-ent, the voice that set us apart. We gave up that voice because we discovered a culture that we desperately wanted to join, and rightly or wrongly, we sensed that we'd never be permitted to join that culture unless we traded our unusual voice for one that blended into the chorus.

Now we know that such a trade will not do. Virtually every Jewish-American family has some anecdotal evidence of the powerful charm of American culture. We have a vague interest in Judaism hampered by a paralyzing sense of ignorance about it. The only part of the *bris* that we understand is the medical pro-cedure; the rest of the words seem to fly by, leaving us wholly untouched. At a house of mourning, we appreciate the presence of our friends and family, but we would also like to be nurtured by ritual. Yet it feels alien. We don't know what to say or what to do. At the Passover Seder, we would like an experience that was more than social, beyond the quaint. But the *Haggadah* is complicated, and most of it seems irrelevant because making our way into America meant that we didn't have time to study it. So with time, a tradition that we no longer understand doesn't speak to us, and we begin to wonder why it is worth preserving. Our desperation to blend into America has robbed us; we are only now beginning to feel the cost of what we have lost.

The freedom of this culture—something our ancestors could only dream of—has proven itself a complicated gift. On the surface, it made Jewish life easier than it had ever been before, for in welcoming us, it removed what we thought were the key obstacles to Jewish survival and thriving.

But today, we also recognize the other side of that gift. We have come to understand that in an open and relatively accepting society it is up to *us* to remind *ourselves* that we're Jewish. The outside world has ceased pointing to our Jewishness. Secular culture and Christian society (for the most part) no longer see our heritage as our foremost defining characteristic. Now, Jews have to take on that responsibility. If we want to be able to explain to our children, to our colleagues and to our society why we matter, we need to answer that question for ourselves first. Unless we recapture a sense of why we matter and what made us different, we'll have difficulty explaining why we should go on.

RESPONDING TO THE CHALLENGE OF AN OPEN WORLD: TOWARD A NEW PARADIGM OF AMERICAN JEWISH INVOLVEMENT

There are new and radical challenges to Jewish survival in America. For the past one hundred years or even more, we have been developing models that simply cannot work in this open and tolerant society. The abject universalism of American liberalism is not the answer. It is at complete variance from our tradition. It simply doesn't keep Jews meaningfully Jewish. And it gives Jews nothing to say.

The extreme alternative, associated with the most traditional segment of our community, argues that the way to avoid rampant assimilation is to withdraw into a self-made Jewish cocoon. It suggests that Jewish concerns are just that—exclusively Jewish—and that the outside world need not figure formidably in our conception of who we are.

Yet this model will also fail. It will fail because it is highly unlikely that more than a handful of Jews will opt for it, and perhaps more importantly, because the more Jews study their tradition, the more they will realize that this cocoon is not a traditional Jewish value. Jewish tradition demands that Jews engage with the non-Jewish world.

Sometimes, it does appear that this isolation is exactly what our tradition mandates. *Kashrut,* Judaism's dietary laws, have been interpreted as a way of keeping Jews and non-Jews from socializing together. The rigors of traditional Sabbath observance strike some as designed to create insular Jewish communities. But those explanations of Jewish ritual miss the mark. Our tradition is not dedicated to Jews' ignoring the rest of humanity. The Torah makes that clear from the very outset.

The Torah's story of creation is a perfect place to start, for that is the place where we begin to encounter our tradition's universalist sensibilities. On the sixth day of creation, the Torah relates:

> [26]And God said, "Let us make man in our image, after our likeness. They shall rule the fish of the sea, the birds of the sky, the cattle, the whole earth, and all the creeping things that creep on earth." [27]And God created man in His image, in the image of God He created him; male and female He created them. [28][And] God blessed them. . . .
>
> (GENESIS 1:26–28)

It is not just the Jews whom the Bible describes as being created in God's image; it is all humanity. The creation story seems unaware of the divisions that will subsequently separate people from each other. The Garden of Eden, the Bible's version of utopia, is not inhabited by Jews; thus, it consciously undermines any vision of the Jewish future that is predicated on ignoring the rest of humanity.

Nor is the creation narrative the only part of our tradition that urges Jews to accord the non-Jewish world value and dignity. Amazingly, some Jewish sources even chastise the Jews for hating their enemies. One might imagine that no one would be viewed with more derision than the Egyptians who enslaved the Israelites, who put the male Jewish babies to death, and who, throughout the plagues, refused God's demand to "Let My people go." But the Talmud tells the following wonderful story about the song that the Israelites sang to God after the Egyptians had drowned in the sea:

> In that instant the ministering angels wished to utter songs [of praise] to the Holy One blessed be He, but He rebuked them saying, "My own Creations are drowning in the sea, and you would utter song in My presence?!"
>
> (SANHEDRIN 39B)

God won't listen to the song; nor, God seems to imply, should the Israelites even have wanted to sing it. All human beings, the Talmud insists, whether they are enemy or ally, are God's creations. Elitism and separatism as keys to Jewish self-definition have no place here either.

Lest the point of this passage be missed, the Talmud includes a similar discussion just a few pages earlier. This passage is absolutely clear in its assertion that any attempt to base Jewish pride or identity on a foundation that demeans or even ignores others is perverse:

For this reason was Adam [the first human] created alone, to teach that whosoever destroys a single soul, scripture considers him as though he had destroyed a complete world; and whosoever preserves a single soul scripture ascribes [merit] to him as though he had preserved a complete world. Furthermore, [Adam was created alone] for the sake of peace among humankind, that one should not say to his fellow, "my father was greater than yours," and that the sectarians should not say, "there are many ruling powers in heaven"; again, to proclaim the greatness of the Holy One, Blessed be He: for if a man strikes many coins from one mold, they all resemble one another, but the supreme King of Kings, the Holy One, Blessed be He, fashioned every man in the stamp of the first man, and yet not one of them resembles his fellow. Therefore every single person is obliged to say: "the world was created for my sake."

(SANHEDRIN 37A–37B)

This particular version of the passage (other manuscripts contain significant differences) makes its point clearly. Because Adam was created alone, all humanity is descended from him. Metaphorically, then, all human beings are family; and because all people are created in the image of Adam, the progenitor of all humanity, destroying any of them is tantamount in God's eye to destroying an entire world.

Thus, neither our universalist model nor its cocoon-like counterpart will work. Each is an extreme. What we need is a model of being willing to be openly Jewish and yet wholly involved in the world outside. Creating that model is the greatest challenge facing those of us who care deeply about American Jewish survival.

THE WHOLE debate about chosenness and the Jews has given rise to a well-known battle of rhymes. After W. N. Ewer penned his famous words:

> *How odd*
> *of God*
> *to choose*
> *the Jews.*

Cecil Browne replied:

> *But not so odd*
> *As those who choose*
> *A Jewish God*
> *Yet spurn the Jews.*

The "battle" that rages in these poems no longer really matters. The questions that matter are not why God chose the Jews, or even whether God chose the Jews. The question that matters is whether the Jews will choose to do something with their heritage to fulfill their tradition's commitment that they will be a blessing to the world.

In our era, chosenness is not about God peeking out from the heavens and picking one people from among many. Chosenness today is about a two-way street; it is a claim that we won't matter by default. We'll have to give up on the fundamental American Jewish assumption that we should be either invisible or completely insular. Wanting to matter requires that we be willing to be noticed. Ultimately, being that blessing—finding our purpose and recovering our voice—will require that Jews come out of hiding.

CHAPTER THREE

Blending In or Standing Out—
An Ongoing Jewish-American Dilemma

*A*s great a baseball player as he was, Sandy Koufax won a permanent place in the hearts of American Jews not for anything he did on the ballfield, but for a decision he made not to play. The Dodgers were battling the Twins in the 1965 World Series, and just when it seemed that no game could be more critical, Koufax made a stunning announcement. The game was scheduled for Yom Kippur, the holiest day of the Jewish year, and Koufax simply wouldn't play.

In American Jewish folklore, that story is a classic. For Jews, it is akin to the tales in general American culture of George Washington's honesty after he chopped down the cherry tree or Abraham Lincoln's decision to walk miles to return a penny. Koufax's famed decision made the impression it did because it suggested to us that one could be both an American and a Jewish hero at the same time. We could both publicly honor Jewish religious holidays and still be icons in the great American pastime.

That is basically what we want. We have been taught that we can have it both ways. We can be fully integrated into American life (what greater symbol of integration into American life could there be than being a world-class baseball player?) and still be committed Jews. What we don't want is what Exodus 19 seems to suggest we can't avoid—a "high-priced ticket" into Jewish continuity. We resist Genesis's suggestion and the implication of our liturgical tradition that what makes the Jews somehow special is not innate, but rather depends on our upholding some "covenant," some unique way of living.

Why are we so resistant? For a variety of reasons. To many of us, that traditional Jewish way of life is simply foreign. It's strange, and it makes us uncomfortable. For others, there is something about "religious" life in general that raises a whole litany of questions and unresolved conflicts that we would rather not address. Is there a God? How can I be certain? Can I proceed if I'm not certain? Does being uncertain make me a "bad Jew"? These are complicated questions, and for many Jews, they are insurmountable obstacles, reason enough not to want any serious engagement with Jewish tradition.

But for almost all American Jews, there is something else at stake as well—we simply don't want to be different. We would like to believe the Sandy Koufax story. We want to be different at certain key moments, but thoroughly American at virtually all others. That's the critical dilemma for many contemporary Jews: are we willing to commit to Jewish continuity and substance, even if that means giving up our camouflage?

As parents, should we keep our children out of school on Jewish holidays? If our own parents kept us out of school on Rosh Ha-Shannah, Yom Kippur or Passover, we often recall both the glee at not having to go to school and the sense of feeling different, out of place, of not completely belonging in either world.

If we make a point of eating matzoh during Passover, we've grown accustomed—but not entirely immune—to the stares we get from friends and colleagues. At Christmastime, as office lobbies and store windows fill with trees and decorations, as people wish us "Merry Christmas," we are reminded of our dilemma: do we err on the side of being more "American" and try to blend in, or does our Jewishness somehow demand that we say something like "I'm Jewish—I don't celebrate Christmas, but I wish *you* a Merry Christmas" even if that means a moment of discomfort?

In his best-selling book *Chutzpah,* Alan Dershowitz writes both amusingly and insightfully of his family's constant worry that the ways Jews acted might be a *shanda fur de goyim*—a source of embarrassment for Jews in front of the gentiles. That fear of being perceived negatively by the Christian world around them, says Dershowitz, was a major theme of his family and his youth. We chuckle at the Dershowitz family's self-consciousness, but partly because it strikes home. We know how they feel. We may pretend to be different from the Dershowitz family; we may try to believe that we live in a more accepting and self-confident time, but deep down we're not so sure. And thus, when our search for an authentic Jewish voice raises the possibility that it is time to be different, to be committed to something distinct, we bristle. To be honest, we're not certain that Judaism is worth it.

THAT IS PRECISELY why many of us have sought to create an American Judaism that would blend more into American life. Suburban synagogues began to bear a striking resemblance to churches—massive structures, stained-glass windows, immaculate interiors and an emphasis on decorum. In the early Reform movement, this included a move away from overt Jewish garb such as the *tallit* (prayer shawl) and *kippah* (or *yarmulke*) and in some cases, a decision to celebrate the Sabbath not on Saturday but on Sunday. The way to be fully Jewish in America, we convinced ourselves, was to be fully American. A new Jewish era seemed to be dawning, and as long as we were willing to adapt, Jewish life seemed filled with potential.

But fifty years later, something has changed. The unbridled optimism of the past has become but faint memory. Blending in has proven more insidious than we imagined it would be. It's not of course that anyone has attacked or maligned us, but rather, that being so thoroughly blended in has prevented us from making Judaism a central and defining characteristic of our lives. We've achieved a new identity that is American at its core; what's no longer clear is how critical *Jewishness* is to that identity.

The huge synagogues that American Jews built in the 1950s

and 1960s often search desperately for members and lack wor-shipers. National organizations like the American Jewish Com-mittee, American Jewish Congress, B'nai B'rith and Hadassah now struggle to survive. And they worry that younger genera-tions of American Jews do not join them as their parents and grandparents once did.

Have we blended in too successfully? Sociologists and demog-raphers have amassed data that sends shivers down the spines of American Jewish leaders. According to some surveys, an Ameri-can Jew is now statistically more likely to marry a non-Jewish per-son than to marry a Jew. For those who believe that Jewish identity is dramatically enhanced by a Jewish home in which both parents are Jewish (and there is more than ample data to support that contention), the implications are chilling. Even in families in which both parents are Jewish, there is cause for concern. Jewish families are having fewer children, not even enough, according to some estimates, to preserve their present numbers.

But numbers are not the ultimate issue. The real concern is identity. Imagine the following experiment: if we hired a private investigator to tail a typical "committed" American Jew from Sunday afternoon through Thursday, what evidence would the private eye find of this person's Jewishness? Would the reading material on this person's nightstand be palpably Jewish? Would the conversations be—even occasionally—about Jewish con-cerns? Do Jewish magazines arrive regularly in the mail? Would any Jewish religious or cultural events fill the calendar?

It would be interesting to see what our PI would witness at children's bedtimes. The concluding moments of a child's day, after all, are deeply impressionable ones. Bedtime is a moment in which we make choices about which stories to read, and have the option of including Jewish stories in the repertoire. But do we? Bedtime is the part of the day when we often sing, and can thus choose to include Jewish songs, perhaps a song in Hebrew. Jewish tradition recognized that going to sleep is a time when children feel tremendous vulnerability, so it created a custom of reciting the *Shema* with our children, filling that spiritual space with Jewish substance.

But why, so often, would our PI see none of this? Why, in bedtime moments so filled with ritual—just how far the door should be open, which lights should be on and which should be off, which stuffed animals should be where in the crib or on the bed—do we feel that *Jewish* ritual is out of place? And to what extent is this bedtime phenomenon true of most of our lives? All too often, the PI would return without much evidence of Jewishness, at bedtime or at any other moment from Sunday through Thursday.

Our hypothetical investigator would certainly find evidence of this person's professional life. He would find plenty of evidence to indicate the person's gender, and he would probably notice some American convictions or behaviors. These are central to our identity; they are an integral part of who we are, a critical element of how we define ourselves. But what about Jewishness? The irony now so familiar—that it was easier to maintain Jewish identity in the face of a menacing anti-Semitic world than it is in a free and welcoming society—raises serious questions about the wisdom of our strategy of trying to become just like the world around us.

The irony is painful. Back in the "good old days," when Jews were singled out, mistreated and prevented from participating fully in the culture around us, we didn't have to make a conscious choice to remain Jewish. Others did that for us. But now, in the much more tolerant environment of the end of the twentieth century, Jews are slowly fading into a background in which a generic form of liberalism has become a universal "religion," in which the pursuit of wealth and happiness seems to unite all ethnicities.

Some Jews sensed that this would happen, long before it actually started. Tradition has it that when Napoleon was attacking Russia in the midst of the Franco-Russian War, Shneur Zalman of

Lyady (1745–1813), the first Lubavitcher Rebbe (the leader of an ultra-traditionalist sect now commonly called Hasidism), was asked by his devotees whom they should support: the Czar, who had long oppressed them, or Napoleon, who might ultimately emancipate them. The Rebbe is said to have responded that they should support the Czar, because "the Czar will destroy your bodies, but Napoleon will destroy your souls."

AILING PARTNERSHIPS AND RESIDUAL FEAR: NEW CHALLENGES TO JEWISH IDENTITY

Deep in our hearts, we know that the Lubavitcher Rebbe was right. In principle, we recognize that we shall probably have to stand out if we want to matter and if we want to survive in any meaningful way. In response to this realization, Jewish parents are sending their children to Jewish day schools (mostly on the elementary and junior high school level) in unprecedented numbers. Many Reform congregations have restored the *kippah* and even the *tallit*. Jewish couples are giving their children more noticeably Jewish names, and in some cases have their children call them *Ima* and *Abba*, Hebrew for Mommy and Daddy. The common denominator? These are all an effort to begin to move Jewishness back to the core of our identities.

But then why not move full steam ahead? Why limit our steps to names, to some synagogue ceremonies? Why not begin to rebuild lives that are Jewish day in and day out, in which Jewishness is at our very core, and through which we could raise a new generation of newly committed and learning Jews?

There are many reasons, some of which we've mentioned. We don't know our tradition well enough to do this ourselves, and even in big cities, there are often not enough people to show us how. Even more fundamental, being different runs counter to everything we've been taught about how to succeed in America.

But beneath the surface, there lurks a more ominous reason as well. It is fear. Despite all our discussion of America's openness and tolerance, American Jews are not as confident as our rhetoric would suggest. We know that this country is very different from others in which we lived in the past—and much better for us—but we suspect that there are still some similarities. We fear that some residual resentment against Jews remains; we hesitate to stir up that resentment by being overly noticeable, making ourselves a *shanda fur de goyim*. When we consider the possibility that the world in which we live is not as friendly as we might have hoped, standing out seems less and less like a good idea.

We pride ourselves on living in a land more hospitable to Jews than any in our history, but we also look over our shoulder. Woody Allen captured this sensibility best when in *Annie Hall* he depicts a Jewish character becoming very agitated when he overhears someone else ask the question, "Did you?" To Allen's fictional character, "Did you?" sounds a lot like "Jew" and he grows both nervous and angry.

Allen is obviously ridiculing those American Jews who hear anti-Semitism at every corner and turn. But his image is funny precisely because it rings true. In that absurd scene, we see ourselves. We still do fear anti-Jewish sentiment. Sometimes that fear is warranted, while at other times our imaginations may work too hard. But either way, we have that fear.

To make matters worse, our fear is a complicated one, in some ways more complex than the fear of anti-Semitism that our ancestors had. For our ancestors knew exactly where the "battle lines" were drawn. It was generally clear who was the enemy, and who could be counted on for support. Today, however, matters are less simple. In fact, one of the factors that make our nervousness so painful is that we have become suspicious of some of those groups that were once our greatest allies.

A New Black Anti-Semitism

For many Jews brought up in the 1960s and 1970s, supporting civil rights was not simply something one did *as* a Jew; it was precisely what being a Jew meant. For these Jews, the prophetic tradition of reaching out to the underprivileged and the poor (to the widow and to the orphan in biblical language) was the very essence of Jewish work. That alone, many Jews believed, could suffice to make Judaism worth preserving. That alone, they believed, gave Judaism a valuable mission.

Of course, decades later, we find it more difficult to explain what made that agenda *distinctly* Jewish. Yes, these social sensibilities are deeply rooted in the Bible's prophetic tradition, but that tradition is now sacred for Christianity as well. Jews doing civil rights work in the South worked arm in arm with Christians who shared the same values. On university campuses, Jewish students find hundreds of non-Jews just as socially conscious as they are, often motivated by *their* various religious traditions. Decades ago, we were too excited to wonder what made these universal causes sufficient as raisons d'être for Jewish survival.

Today, we are not as certain what makes these causes distinctly Jewish. And to add to our discomfort, we're aware that some of these partnerships have not withstood the test of time. We never dreamed that our alliance with African-Americans would falter so quickly. But it has. Indeed, the newly radicalized African-American movement and its undeniably anti-Jewish vitriol add to our pain, to our lack of certainty about what our role in the world should be.

To be sure, much of the black community in the United States harbors deeply positive feelings about the Jewish community and about Jewish tradition. Many of the feelings of mutuality remain. But there are also new dimensions of the "black pride" movement that are profoundly disturbing to Jews.

In our somewhat romanticized memories, the very early days of the civil rights movement were times filled with hope and possibility. We recall—with sadness but with pride—Michael Schwerner and Andrew Goodman, two young Jewish civil rights workers who were murdered along with James Chaney, a black civil rights volunteer-activist, by racist whites in the South in the summer of 1964. We treasure our images of Rabbi Abraham

Joshua Heschel—a traditional rabbi who was the most outspoken Jewish voice in the 1960s in support of the civil rights movement—marching arm in arm with the Reverend Martin Luther King, Jr. in Selma, Alabama. Today, many Jews are justifiably pleased at the work being done by Michael Lerner, an important Jewish social activist, and Cornel West, a prominent African-American intellectual.

But as the title of Lerner and West's book, *Jews and Blacks: The Hard Hunt for Common Ground*, suggests, the relationship between blacks and Jews is not what it once was. Indeed, even in its heyday, it was more complicated than many Jews wanted to admit. Proud as we are of the image of Heschel and King, we have been less keen on recalling that at approximately the same time that they were walking arm in arm, Leslie Campbell, vice president of the African-American Teachers Association, read the following poem on New York's WBAI radio with unabashed praise:

> *Hey, Jew boy, with that yarmulke on your head*
> *You pale-faced Jew boy—I wish you were dead;*
> *I can see you Jew boy—no, you can't hide,*
> *I got a scoop on you-yeh-you gonna die.*
> *I'm sick of seeing in everything I do*
> *About the murder of six million Jews;*
> *Hitler's reign lasted only fifteen years. . . .*
> *My suffering lasted for over 400 years, Jew boy.*

If incidents such as those are unfamiliar to today's young Jews or seem like irrelevant "ancient" history, there are new ones to take their place. When the African-American rap group Public Enemy released their album *Fear of a Black Planet*, they included a song, "Welcome to the Terrordome" (1990), which referred to Jews as the "so called chosen, frozen." A line or two later, Public Enemy says of the Jews that "they got me like Jesus"—a reference to the accusation that the Jews killed Jesus, a claim that even the Vatican has given up.

The problem that songs like this pose for Jews is that they are not simply anti-Semitic writing, but rather, emerge from a movement with which Jews have long sympathized. For decades now, many American Jews have supported the values that lie at the very core of the black pride movement. We have long felt that part of our mission should be to support groups that have been oppressed, wherever and whoever they may be.

But what, then, should be our reaction to lyrics that refer to Jews as "so called chosen, frozen"? Do we keep trying to "blend in," ignoring the hostility (and knowing full well that were the tables turned, the African-American community would certainly not be silent), or do we "call it like we see it" and stand out, assailing this new anti-Semitism and demanding that society's political and religious leadership condemn it absolutely and immediately? Jews are not sure; we are uncomfortable, unsettled. We sense that it's time to stand up and assert our own interests, but we fear the backlash. And that makes Jewish identity profoundly uncomfortable. It makes some Jews wonder: is Judaism just a shame that must be borne?

Had anti-Semitism in popular music been limited to the rap world, most Jews would not have noticed. But it has spread far beyond. The most notorious example was Michael Jackson's song "They Don't Care About Us" on his *HIStory* album (1995). Again in the context of a song about black pride, Jackson saw fit to use the word "kike" and the phrase "Jew me," and though some objection was subsequently raised, the response from the Jewish community was relatively muted. Why was the Jewish reaction so tame? Because Jews feel trapped. How can one object to this song without being seen as objecting to black pride? For many young Jews, the bind in which they find themselves makes Jewishness distinctly uncomfortable.

Anti-Jewish sentiment as part of the black pride movement has hardly been limited to the world of music. Leonard Jeffries, professor of Afro-American Studies at City College of New York, has alarmed Jewish and non-Jewish Americans alike with his vicious anti-white and anti-Semitic vitriol. Yet although Jeffries is now a pariah in the academic community and has lost his administrative position, he remains in high demand as a speaker, packing auditoriums wherever he lectures. Even more disturbing is the hate-filled rancor that has become the trademark of Louis Farrakhan, a minister in the Nation of Islam. What disturbs many Jews about Farrakhan is not simply Farrakhan's blatant anti-Semitism. While Jews do not enjoy seeing their tradition described as a "gutter religion," that is not new, though it has been rather unusual in American history. What is more problematic is that Farrakhan's anti-Semitism is a linchpin of his program of advocating black pride. Anti-Semitism in the Nation of Islam is unfortunately central to a project that Jews could otherwise have endorsed and even supported—the resurgence of pride and dignity in a community that has for too long been victimized. Jewish ambivalence was perhaps at its height when Farrakhan's Million Man March was held in the fall of 1995. On the one hand, Jews endorsed many of the positive values espoused by the march and its participants. But having several hundred thousand people converge on the nation's capital at the behest of a rabid anti-Semite was beyond disquieting.

Even worse than Farrakhan has been his assistant, Khalid Abdul Muhammad. In 1993, Muhammad spoke to students at New Jersey's Kean College and accused "hook-nosed, bagel-eating, lox-eating Jews . . . from the synagogue of Satan" of "sucking our blood in the black community." But Jews find themselves in a most uncomfortable bind: should they object to Muhammad's right to give such a speech? American Jews have come to see themselves as intrinsically committed to the defense of American civil liberties! Which side should they advocate? Judaism? Or their liberal inclinations? This new situation is dizzyingly complex and profoundly discomfiting. That is why, though some Jews have spoken out, the response has been sporadic and uneven, at best.

What makes the situation even more complex is that mainstream members of the African-American community do not seem nonplussed by these developments. We find ourselves wondering if it is *we* who are hypersensitive, if the problem doesn't somehow lie with us. What should we have done, we wondered, when Andrew Young, a former ambassador to the United Nations, said that he disagreed with Farrakhan's anti-Semitism but insisted that he agreed with 90 percent of what Farrakhan had to say? Young, long perceived by Jews as a friend, said that the opinions expressed by the minister from the Nation of Islam should be seen as a "simple mechanism for survival for people who have been locked out of the economy."

Even the NAACP has disappointed us. When Farrakhan demoted Muhammad but affirmed Muhammad's claim that 75 percent of the slaves in the South had been owned by Jews (historians suggest that a more accurate figure is about .03 percent), the NAACP said that it was "satisfied" by Farrakhan's response. Should we assail the NAACP, an institution many of us had long supported? Should Jews rail against Andrew Young, a longtime ally? Though it's difficult for us to admit, we know what has happened: Jewish identity in America has clearly become extraordinarily complicated.

Modern Feminism and Its Challenge to Jewish Identity

African-American anti-Semitism is not the only issue that has made Jews question their once visceral assumption that being a Jew in America meant being society's cutting-edge mavericks. Another painful case in point is what has occasionally happened to the relationship between Judaism and feminism.

For decades, most American Jews have simply assumed that Judaism and feminism were natural partners. After all, many of this country's great feminist leaders have been Jewish (Betty Friedan, Gloria Steinem and Letty Cottin Pogrebin are some obvious examples), and the feminist movement did much to fuel the movement for increased women's rights in virtually all areas of Jewish life. Insofar as feminism seemed to be about enhancing the social, political and economic status of an enormous "underclass" (women, that is), it seemed that the social values expressed in the Prophets. These, after all, were the very values that led to the black-Jewish alliance and seemed to be a natural reason for Jews to befriend feminist causes as well.

Indeed, much of that is still true. But again, reality has been more complex than theory. There is a dark underside to parts of the women's movement, a dimension in which Jewish women have encountered painful and direct forms of anti-Semitism.

Some of the anti-Semitism of the feminist movement has political roots. The United Nation's Decade for Women began with a conference in Mexico City in 1975. At that conference, designed to address women's issues, delegates approved a resolution equating Zionism with racism, calling for the elimination of Zionism. Jewish women began to wonder who their real allies were. Was the world's women's movement growing hostile to Jewish women?

Five years later, in Copenhagen, another conference called for the eradication of the "evils" of Zionism, racism, imperialism and neocolonialism. To avoid a repeat of these incidents, Jewish women from the United States and Israel prepared for the 1985 Nairobi, Kenya, conference assiduously. Matters were better, but the conference did not pass wholly without incident. Sally Mugabe, the wife of Zimbabwe's prime minister, said in a public forum:

> The women of Palestine have suffered long enough. We call on the international community to work to end the Israeli aggression and the regime in South Africa. . . . Apartheid and Zionism are thorny problems and they are pricking women and children in South Africa and Palestine. If we women at this conference allow them to continue pricking the flesh of women, then we have not done our job at this conference.

The reference to Zionism and apartheid in one breath, when Jews throughout the world had joined the fight against apartheid, stung. So, too, did the reference to "Palestine," since by 1985, the State of Israel had been in existence for thirty-seven years, and no State of Palestine was to be found on the map.

Political anti-Semitism in feminist circles was primarily international, and not American. Furthermore, it has abated somewhat. Progress is being made on many of the political issues of importance to the women's movement, and anti-Jewish expressions are now deemed unacceptable in some circles. But this does not mean that the hostility to Judaism that Jewish women encountered in the women's movement has disappeared. Now that hostility often takes religious, rather than political, form.

Much of this subtle anti-Jewish sentiment is found in Christian feminist religious writings, including some from Americans. In many cases, the problematic views do not begin as attacks on Judaism. Rather, they start out as critiques of the patriarchal roots of Judaism and Christianity, as critiques of biblical attitudes to women. For many Jewish women, though, these critiques often go too far and sound like attacks on Judaism, not just on a dimension of women's status in the ancient Near East. For example, Mary Daly (an American feminist) argues that the scene in Genesis 19:1–11, in which Abraham's nephew Lot offers his daughters to a group of menacing men who want to attack his male guests, "illustrate[s] . . . the value placed upon women in the Old Testament."

But "Old Testament" (rather than "Bible" in general) suggests a focus on the *Jewish* origins of the "evil." And Daly's analysis is an obvious misreading of the text, by a woman more than capable of doing better. Lot is an obvious "bad guy" in the Book of Genesis. Time and again, he is compared to his foil, Abraham, and emerges severely lacking. The whole point of the story of Lot and his daughters is to show his moral inadequacy. Why, Jewish women began to wonder, would a fellow feminist associate Lot's behavior with the values of their tradition?

Still other feminists critique the idea of law, which is core to the Torah's promise to Abraham, Isaac and Jacob. In the words of one feminist very sensitive to Jewish women's issues,

> German feminists . . . stress that [God's] will and word are laid down in rigid laws which must be followed strictly and blindly. In their view, [God] legitimizes authoritarianism and "law and order," and is therefore anachronistic to feminist values which espouse autonomy and individuality.

Such attitudes often make Jewish women who want to take their own tradition seriously feel that they have to choose between the women's movement and their Jewish identity. Indeed, this problem has become widely discussed. Letty Cottin Pogrebin, a founding editor of *Ms.* magazine, wrote a much discussed article entitled "Anti-Semitism in the Women's Movement" in the June 1982 issue of *Ms.* Eight years later, the problem persisted, and Susanna Heschel, another well-known American Jewish feminist, wrote on "Anti-Judaism in Christian Feminist Theology" in *Tikkun* magazine. Is it any wonder that Jewish feminists have begun to wonder who they are, what they stand for, what Judaism is?

At times, issues of race and gender even conspire to exclude Jewish women from causes they want to support. Gloria Anzaldúa, a Chicana and radical feminist, clearly sees Jewish women as wholly Other, and suggests that they cannot understand the struggles her people have endured. In her introduction to a feminist anthology she edited, she refers to Jewish women as "white Jewishwomen," combining the "Jewish" and the "women" into one word. This little linguistic gimmick is an insidious attempt to suggest that Jewish women ought to be seen as "Other," the "enemy," and ultimately something other than women.

Anzaldúa says that "most of the white Jewishwomen" in one of her classes "felt isolated and excluded [and] felt that their oppressions were the same or similar to those of women-of-color." The exclusion her Jewish students must have felt in her classroom comes through when she writes that "the problem was that white women and white Jewishwomen, while seeming to listen, were not really 'hearing' women-of-color and could not get it into their heads that this was a space . . . about women-of-color."

Clearly, Anzaldúa is correct when she asserts that Jewish experiences and those of people of color are not identical. That is obvious. But if the issue is skin color, why distinguish between "white women" and "white Jewishwomen"?

To many Jewish feminists, vitriol like this seems to be searching for an excuse to dehumanize Jews, to deny that Jews, too, have suffered, and to suggest that Jews—even Jewish women—are essentially the "enemy" of women's causes because they have no need to battle oppression.

American Jewish feminists therefore frequently find themselves in a difficult position. For decades, they had argued that part of what motivated their feminist commitments was Judaism's devotion to the dignity of the individual, Judaism's commitment to social justice, the Jewish Prophets' admonition that Jews must protect the well-being of the dispossessed and the oppressed. For that reason, the values of Judaism and the values at the core of the women's movement have much in common.

Jewish women thus find themselves in a bind. For decades, they have worked to transform their tradition, to battle for women's roles in ritual, to recover women's voices in Jewish study, and to provide role models for young Jewish girls. In the midst of these battles, they have sought haven and support in the broader women's movement, certain that there they would find allies and supportive encouragement. But Jewish women have often found that the very movement to which they have devoted so much effort is often critical of a crucial dimension of their identity. Too frequently today, Jewish women wonder if they must choose between Judaism and feminism. They find themselves wondering what their Jewishness really means, asking "Who are we? What do we stand for? What might be a distinctly Jewish contribution to this feminist agenda?" Would asserting their Jewish identity mean that American Jews would have to take a step back from the "front" of feminism? American Jewish identity is complicated, more so than we would like to admit.

The New Christian Challenge to Jewish Identity

Paradoxically, these liberal social forces are not the only challenge to Jewish identity in America. Jews are also wary of the groups that *oppose* the new multicultural stream in American life. Now, even causes usually associated with the political right challenge prevailing assumptions about Jewish identity. One chief example is the Christian right.

In many respects, Jews have reason to welcome some of the rhetoric of the Christian right. Many Jews are concerned about what is called the Balkanization of our society; as a group that has struggled to make it into the mainstream, we're often alarmed at the rapid disappearance of that mainstream. We know that to many of those groups attacking the status quo, we appear to be part of the power structure. Thus, for some Jews, one of the attractions of the newly prominent Christian political structure is the hope of recapturing the sense of a distinct and unifying American culture. Even though the mere idea of supporting a group that is seen as conservative is instinctively strange for some Jews, they are attracted by the hope of a restored sense of shared cultural values. The role of the Christian right in combating modern American multiculturalism, therefore, sometimes seems like a welcome relief from the divisive onslaught of the left in our society.

But this is another example of Jews not being certain who our friends are. Much as many Jews applaud some of the traditional values of the newly activist Christian political forces in America, many are also nervous about the Christian right. For the Christian right may make it impossible to carry on with our agenda of becoming wholly American. Many of the Jews who believed (or still may believe) that key to our acceptance in this country is blending in, also believe that it will be easier to do so if religion becomes less of an issue in our society. "The less Americans focus on religion, and the more we completely exclude religion from the political arena, the better off the Jews will be," goes this argument. But the Christian right clearly wants to return religion to the very heart of American public discourse. There is little doubt that if the agenda of the Christian Coalition is successful, the country that emerges will be more emphatically and consciously "religious" than the United States has been in a long time.

Obviously, not all Jews are committed to blending in. For Chabad, the outreach wing of the ultra-Orthodox Lubavitch movement, "blending in" is a laughable notion. They would argue that no devoted Jew *could* blend in, and that even if we could, there's no reason to want to. After all, it was their ancestor who argued that the Jews should support the Czar rather than Napoleon. Thus, each December, it is Chabad that seeks to construct gigantic Hanukkah menorahs in public settings, trying to "even the playing field" with all the Christian symbols that appear at the same time.

But many other Jews, like those who are active in the ACLU, fight Chabad's efforts. While they usually build their case on constitutional foundations, what is at stake for them is often not the law. For many, whether they recognize it or not, the real issue is the public menorah and the way it threatens their whole agenda of guaranteeing Jewish survival by keeping a low profile. What horrifies them about Chabad is not Chabad's theology or even its politics, but its "different-ness." The ACLU Jews are Jews who were taught something along the lines of Dershowitz's family—"don't make a spectacle of yourself, and they'll leave us alone." When the Christian right seeks to make religion a more central facet of American social life, that strategy becomes ever more difficult to achieve.

The problems of the Christian right for Jews, though, go

much further. For groups like the Christian Coalition want more than to reassert traditional values. They are doing more than bringing religion as a force back to the town hall and city square. Their real agenda is to turn American society into a Christian society.

Now, we ought to be fair. The Christian Coalition is just that—a Christian organization. Its goal *is* to promote Christian values and to advocate for Christian expression in American society. But we have to ask: Do we want our children to have to face prayer in the public schools? Should Jewish graduates of elementary schools, public high schools and state universities have to listen to Christian prayer and Christian religious vocabulary during commencement ceremonies? Do we want "American" and "Christian" to gradually become synonymous?

There is nothing insidious about the work of the Christian Coalition. Its goals and objectives are clear to all. But the impressive power of the Christian Coalition is a wake-up call that our dream of a religion-free public square in America was just that—a dream. It will not come to be.

WHICH BRINGS Jews back to the question of identity. For almost two hundred years, we sought to become as American as possible. We believed that fitting into the mainstream of society would guarantee the liberties and opportunities that made America so alluring. But now, as we approach the twenty-first century, that sense of optimism and confidence is ebbing. The mainstream of America is not as benign as Jews imagined. It is a deeply conflicted mainstream, in which battles rage for the soul and direction of our society.

In these battles, Jews are only one of many combatants, and we are a small, vulnerable group. Those who battle against the status quo are often suspicious of Jews, sometimes even openly hostile. On the other side of the equation, whatever identifiable mainstream still remains in American life is predominantly Christian. So both the newly radicalized, "politically correct" left and the Christian right's response to it force Jews to ask: Who ought the Jews be? If being Jewish is going to make things more complicated, why bother?

Ours is an era of new and unexpected challenges to Jewish identity in America. The fundamental assumptions that defined an entire century of Jewish activity in this country are giving way. To survive another generation, we will have to reimagine American Jewish life; the version that we've built until now simply won't work.

America at large has begun to recognize that people are simply different. Thoughtful feminists like Carol Gilligan (in her book *In a Different Voice,* for example) and others have begun to argue that women and men *are* different in important ways. Absolute equality, some now say, is not the issue; men and women alike ought to demand an appreciation of their natural and important differences. Similarly, African-American leaders are issuing a new message: Black is not white. America is not a melting pot. Today's cultural ideal is not a bland mix of peoples in which differences either dissolve or are ignored, but rather, a multicultural mélange in which distinctiveness is acknowledged and even celebrated.

In theory, this new ideal sounds wonderful. But in reality, it poses serious problems for Jews. This new culture and ethnic assertiveness is unsettling for a people who are no longer certain how to define exactly who they are. This newfound focus on difference and distinctiveness is disconcerting for a community that has long prided itself on being as American as anyone else. As multiculturalism and ethnic pride sweep across the continent, American Jews are coming to realize that certain crucial questions can no longer be ignored: if every other group in America seems to be advocating its distinctiveness, how should Jews respond?

DOES THE WORLD NEED THE JEWS?

Jews today stand at a crucial crossroads, and have an important decision to make. For a long time, being Jewish was the natural part of our lives, and becoming American was our most important agenda. Now that Jews have become fully American, we realize that it is Judaism that often feels foreign. In a culture that is now focusing on identity more than ever before, we find ourselves utterly adrift. We need to clarify who we are and what we stand for.

When we are asked, "What is a Jew?" our common (and rather anemic) Jewish answer, "Someone who doesn't believe in Jesus," is wholly inadequate. If we are going to commit to Judaism, we will need to define ourselves in terms of what Judaism *is*, not what it is not. No longer can Hanukkah be a "non-Christmas." Purim cannot be our Halloween.

Perhaps, as Alan Dershowitz himself astutely suggests, it is time to stop worrying about being a *shanda fur de goyim*. Maybe we ought to cease hiding our Jewishness, and in this era of "pride in distinctiveness," we ought to begin proclaiming our differences. Perhaps if we did so we could make a case for Jews to care about Jewish life and to join in living its traditions.

Of course, some Jews are nervous about a campaign to assert Judaism's uniqueness. Some of us are afraid that speaking of Judaism's uniqueness will somehow verge on asserting Judaism's superiority. In our world, *that* is something many Jews understandably are not willing to do.

But this is not the real issue. The real impediment to proclaiming our uniqueness is that we just don't want to stick out. We are comfortable with the (false) notion that we can "watch" Judaism as a virtual spectator sport and see it survive, even thrive, in our children's generation. We want some Jewishness for our kids, but not too much. We are concerned that our children might—if exposed to the wrong camp or school—become "too

Jewish." We hear that strange phrase all the time, but what does it mean? Do we mean "too Jewish" or "too *noticeably* Jewish"? Or do we really mean "so committed to Judaism that being fully American and successful will no longer be the only thing that matters"?

In truth, we're not certain. We want to be able to answer yes to the question, "If humanity woke up and found a world without Jews, would it be impoverished?" but we're not sure how. So we begin our search. But a caution: whatever answers we ultimately offer to the question, "Why would the world be impoverished without Jews?" they must be more substantive than the simple claim that Judaism is one of the "colors" of the world's "rainbow" of religions and that it would be a tragedy for this particular color to disappear or slowly fade away. That view may be true, but it's dispassionate. No one will devote their life to being a shade in a color chart. Jewish kids will not understand why the rainbow requires that they spend weekday afternoons and Sunday mornings learning about a culture that neither their parents nor their friends live. Nice though the rainbow notion sounds, it will hardly be sufficiently compelling to get young, two-income couples to part with their hard-earned money and to share it with Jewish causes. No idea as ethereal as the rainbow will influence such critical decisions as whom to marry. If we're to find an argument that works, it will have to be more thoughtful than that.

Many people agree with environmentalists who insist that the spotted owl ought to be saved from extinction. It is easy, after all, to be a passionate environmentalist from afar. But meet a family dependent on a logger's salary, look into the faces of children wondering where their next meal will come from or the eyes of a couple humiliated by their inability to guarantee a certain future for their kids, and suddenly the spotted owl seems a little less important. When it comes down to choosing between the livelihoods of families who live off the logging industry and the survival of a bird that most have never seen, people quickly become somewhat more ambivalent. Theory is one thing; requiring personal sacrifice and hardship is another.

Jews think in exactly the same way. Purely theoretically, Jews probably *do* believe that it would be a tragedy for Judaism to disappear. They probably *do* believe that Judaism has a certain beauty to it, and that it would be awful for that beauty to vanish. Most Jews agree viscerally with Emil Fackenheim, one of this century's most important Jewish philosophers. Fackenheim argues that in the aftermath of the Shoah, in addition to the 613 commandments traditionally found in the Torah, there is a new one, which he calls the "614th Commandment." That commandment, says Fackenheim, is to refuse to give Hitler the "victory" of Jewish disappearance that he was not able to win with the Nazi army. Instinctively, when we wonder why Judaism ought to survive, we find ourselves reacting to Hitler; if *he* couldn't destroy the Jews, we say, our generation is certainly not going to bring about our own demise.

Yet as noble as that notion sounds, it is not much more compelling to modern Jews than the spotted owl is to most Americans. Few Americans would like to see the spotted owl become extinct, but even fewer are willing to do anything about it. Similarly, most Jews would agree that it would be sad if Judaism were to disappear. Yet it is one thing to claim that Judaism ought not disappear; it is quite another to make decisions about whom to marry, what to eat, how to spend our money and where to educate our children because of a commitment to a Jewish future.

Agreed: the disappearance of Judaism would be unfortunate. But if we are to work actively to ensure Judaism's survival and to make Judaism part of our lives, we'll have to find our authentic voice once again. We'll have to believe in our heart of hearts that God's promise to Abraham—that "the nations of the world will be blessed by your descendants"—can still become a reality.

JUDAISM AND SPIRITUALITY REVISITED

In the Introduction to this book, I distinguished between two very different sorts of arguments for Judaism's importance. Some arguments are inward, or spiritual. They explain how Judaism enriches us personally, helps us sense the presence of God, and assists us in defining a sense of who we are and where we fit in the cosmos. Other arguments, necessary for many contemporary Jews for whom such inward religiosity is either not an issue or not a sufficient argument, gaze outward. They address not what Judaism does for us personally, or spiritually, but what Jews and Jewish tradition bring to the world.

But as we prepare to turn to an examination of what Jewish tradition teaches about the role of Jews in the world, we ought to note that the answers we uncover may in the end prove deeply spiritual as well. Inward arguments and their outward counterparts are not mutually exclusive. Quite the contrary.

If spirituality means living with a sense of something transcendent in our lives, trusting that we make a profound difference in the cosmic scheme of things, then believing that Judaism can contribute to repairing the world can help make Judaism a deeply satisfying, spiritual experience. If spirituality involves sensing God's closeness, then living Jewish life as a tradition that helps repair God's world can come to mean living deeply, living fully, and even living spiritually.

Asking what Judaism does for the rest of the world does not mean walking away from the transcendent part of Jewish life. Most Jews interested in spirituality have never been taught that the spirituality they seek can be sought through a sense of Judaism's contributions to the world at large. Nor have most Jews committed to social action been taught to see their work as a reflection of Judaism's spiritual or "religious" tradition. The questions that modernity poses about Jewish identity afford us a chance to fuse spirituality and a commitment to the world.

Today, more than ever, as Jews seek reasons for deciding to be Jewish, as we wonder anew about what our message to the world is, Jews have reason to seek spirituality *and* to make their mark on the world around them.

A tall order, this new vision. It will require our reimagining American Jewish life. It will mandate that we create a new conception of Judaism in America in which either-or's do not exist, in which we can be both socially conscious as well as religiously and spiritually serious. This reimagined community will have to be one in which the basic commitment is not to hide, but to make a difference, where the goal is not to make Judaism more American, but rather, to plumb the depths of Jewish tradition in order to learn how Judaism might enrich American life. It is to that task that we now turn.

Part Two

WHAT IS
OUR
MESSAGE?

CHAPTER FOUR

"Not by Might and Not by Power"—The Message of Jewish Survival

Nothing about *Tom Sawyer* or *Huckleberry Finn* suggests that we ought to begin our search for a modern Jewish mission by reading Mark Twain. But Twain had, as we've seen, more than a passing interest in the Jewish people; Jews fascinated him. Probably unintentionally, Twain alluded to one critical element of the "blessing" that Jews might be in his famed article "Concerning the Jews":

[The Jew] has made a marvelous fight in this world, in all the ages; and has done it with his hands tied behind him. He could be vain of himself, and be excused for it. The Egyptian, the Babylonian, and the Persian rose, filled the planet with sound and splendor, then faded to dream-stuff and passed away: the Greek and the Roman followed, and made a vast noise, and they are gone; other peoples have sprung up and held their torch high for a time, but it burned out, and they sit in twilight now, or have vanished. The Jew saw them all, beat them all, and is now what he always was, exhibiting no decadence, no infirmities of age, no weakening of his parts, no slowing of his energies, no dulling of his alert and aggressive mind. All things are mortal but the Jew; all other forces pass, but he remains. What is the secret of his immortality?

Hyperbolic, to be sure. But as Jews search for an authentic and compelling identity in modernity, as we seek our authentic voice once again, Twain reminds us of an obvious but forgotten truth: our very survival is part of our message. It is not just that Jews need to survive so that we can subsequently say something to the world; our very existence speaks volumes.

This notion sounds surprising. Survival, we usually believe, is about history, not meaning. Staying alive is not the same thing as living with purpose. There has to be more.

Yes, there does have to be more. But for Jews, history and survival have their own powerful meaning, a meaning often lost on contemporary Jews. The reason we so seldom realize this is that we tend to ask the wrong questions about Jewish history. When Jews think about Jewish history, we often ask, why? Why did God allow us to suffer so? Where was God during the Shoah? When the Romans burned the Temple? When the Babylonians destroyed Jerusalem?

Jewish tradition, however, makes a rather odd claim about the tragedies that have befallen the Jews. It argues that struggling to survive is one of the most important ways in which Jews communicate their message to the world. Judaism suggests that part of the "blessing" that Jews can offer the world is a reminder that the weak can survive, that the outnumbered can persevere, and that the politically disenfranchised can endure by virtue of a tenacious commitment to the ideals for which they stand.

THE "MIRACLE" OF JEWISH SURVIVAL

It is ironic: at times, the non-Jewish world seems to understand this message better than the Jews themselves. Blaise Pascal (1623–1662), a Catholic Frenchman, both physicist and theologian, said of the Jews:

This people is not eminent solely by its antiquity, but is also singular by its duration, which has always continued from its origin till now. For whereas the nations of Greece and of . . . Rome and others who came long after, have long since perished, [the Jewish people] ever remains—in spite of the endeavors of many powerful kinds who have a hundred times tried to destroy it.

Similarly, when the eighteenth-century French writer—and notorious anti-Semite—Voltaire (1694–1778) discussed the possibility of miracles with the Prussian king Frederick the Great, the king challenged him to point to one authentic example of a miracle. "Sire," Voltaire is reputed to have replied, "the Jews."

Jews have often said the same of themselves. When the biblical prophet Malachi, speaking several hundred years before the common era, seeks to remind the Jews of God's power, he points to the fact that they had not disappeared in the face of adversity. In the midst of chastising them for their lapsed faith, he reminds them of miracles they do not appreciate: "For I am the Lord—I have not changed; and you are the children of Jacob—you have not ceased to be" (Malachi 3:6). The mere fact that the Jews have not "ceased to be" strikes both Voltaire and the prophet Malachi as virtually miraculous.

But this notion that Jewish survival is miraculous raises other important questions. Why should Jewish survival have to be a miracle? Is it coincidence? Do the Jews simply have bad luck? Or good luck?

As difficult as it might be for us to accept, the Torah offers a rather astonishing explanation. It suggests that facing adversity is part of the Jewish people's mission. Jews face these enormous challenges not despite their role in the world, but as part of that role.

The Torah makes that point even in Genesis, near the very beginning. Early in the Torah's story of Abraham's life, God makes him a promise:

Fear not, Abram,
I am a shield to you;
Your reward shall be very great.

(GENESIS 15:1)

But Abram is dubious. After all, he has no children, and thus asks, "O Lord God, what can You give me, seeing that I shall die child-less?" (Genesis 15:2). God's response is etched in the memories of Jews across the globe: "Look toward heaven and count the stars, if you are able to count them. . . . So shall your offspring be" (Genesis 15:5).

That, so to speak, is the good news. God promises Abram that his descendants, the Jews, will be numerous, far more numerous than their beginnings as one small family might have indicated. But there is a darker side to this promise. In an ominous turn, the Torah describes the continuation of this conversation between God and Abram:

> ¹²As the sun was about to set, a deep sleep fell upon Abram, and a great dark dread descended upon him. ¹³And [God] said to Abram, "Know well that your offspring shall be strangers in a land not theirs, and they shall be enslaved and oppressed four hundred years."   (GENESIS 15:12–13)

Egyptian slavery would become the crucible in which a family becomes a nation, the ordeal that transforms Abraham's great-grandchildren and their descendants into the Jewish people. Just as parents who give birth to a chronically ill child find that this experience transforms their entire perspective on life, slavery is destined to alter Jews' outlook. Slavery, Jewish tradition insists, was no accident; it had to be part of our history for us to play our role in the world. Thus, as we read the Torah—as we tell and retell our collective story—we recite a narrative that describes our national beginnings in slavery and ends with the Israelites still in the desert, still yearning to reach the Promised Land. Ours is a history rooted in adversity.

Other passages make the same point. Slavery and its horrors were a necessary precondition to the later greatness that God seems to promise. Consider the following passage from the Book of Deuteronomy, Moses' soliloquy to the Jews prior to his death on Mount Nebo. Summarizing their history and warning them about their future, Moses says that tenuousness is part of the Jews' inherent condition. Fragility, he suggests, is tied to their unique role:

> 32You have but to inquire about bygone ages that came before you, ever since God created man on earth, from one end of heaven to the other: has anything as grand as this ever happened, or has its like ever been known? 33Has any people heard the voice of a god speaking out of a fire, as you have, and survived? 34Or has any god ventured to go and take for himself one nation from the midst of another by prodigious acts, by signs and portents, by war, by a mighty and an outstretched arm and awesome power, as the LORD your God did for you in Egypt before your very eyes? 35It has been clearly demonstrated to you that the LORD alone is God; there is none beside Him. 36From the heavens He let you hear His voice to discipline you; on earth He let you see His great fire; and from amidst that fire you heard His words. 37And because He loved your fathers, He chose their heirs after them; He Himself, in His great might, led you out of Egypt, 38to drive from your path nations greater and more populous than you, to take you into their land and assign it to you as a heritage, as is still the case. 39Know therefore this day and keep in mind that the LORD alone is God in heaven above and on earth below; there is no other. 40Observe His laws and commandments, which I enjoin upon you this day, that it may go well with you and your children after you, and that

you may long remain in the land that the LORD your God is assigning to you for all time.

(DEUTERONOMY 4:32–40)

The story of the Jews, Moses insists, cannot be told without the story of slavery. Slavery is a critical element of the Jews' narrative because slavery tells us not only about their past, but about their purpose as well.

Even when Jews celebrate the end of slavery, their tradition effectively requires them to relive it, at least momentarily. The *Haggadah*, the text that Jews recite each year at Passover, says, "in each and every generation, each Jew must see himself as if he had personally been redeemed from Egypt." To forget our slavery would be to forget not only who the Jews were, but who we need to be. We "need" that adversity, says the tradition, not for the suffering it brings but for the growth and deepened perspective that comes from it.

Before we examine why that is, we should note how different this approach is from that taken by other communities. Quite understandably, most peoples do not wish to view their history this way. Leonard Jeffries has based a large part of his rhetoric on the (quite correct) assertion that African-Americans had a long history and rich culture before they were stolen from their native lands to suffer and die as slaves in America. As part of his campaign for African-American pride, Jeffries has sought to portray the period of American slavery as antithetical to the true identity of American blacks. "Being slaves," he essentially reminds his community, "is not what our culture is about."

Jews, however, have taken a different path. Our narratives describe our own slavery as ordained by God. The prediction of slavery is part of the same prophecy in which God promises Abraham's survival. Our festival of freedom mandates that we relive slavery as part of that celebration. Thus, though the question, Why do these things happen to us? is natural and unavoidable, it is not the question that helps us understand our mission.

The significant question for Jews is not *why* these things happen, but rather, *what* we become as a result of them.

The Torah has an answer. It claims that the experience of Egypt was designed to make the Jewish people forever more acutely aware of the needs of the socially marginal, the "stranger," as the Torah calls them. Dozens of times, the Torah ties our past experience in Egypt to our obligation to these "strangers." Consider these brief examples:

> [20]You shall not wrong a stranger or oppress him, for you were strangers in the land of Egypt. [21]You shall not ill-treat any widow or orphan. [22]If you do mistreat them, I will heed their outcry as soon as they cry out to Me.
>
> (EXODUS 22:20–22)

Shortly later, the Torah is even more explicit: "You shall not oppress a stranger, for you know the feelings of the stranger, having yourselves been strangers in the land of Egypt" (Exodus 23:9). The Israelites' experience in Egypt and their resulting sensitivity to the feelings of the outsider are supposed to create absolute intolerance for social inequality: "There shall be one law for the citizen and for the stranger who dwells among you" (Exodus 12:49, and similarly in Leviticus 24:22, Numbers 9:14, Numbers 15:15). The sense of devotion to humanity that is supposed to emerge from our experience in Egypt is so powerful that we cannot harbor a grudge even toward the people who originally enslaved us. Thus, "You shall not abhor an Egyptian, for you were a stranger in his land" (Deuteronomy 23:8).

Our slavery, therefore, was not an accident and is not even something to be bemoaned, because from our slavery came purpose. Part of our reason for being, an element of this authentic voice we're trying to recapture, is to become a watchdog, a defender of today's "strangers," wherever they might reside.

Yet, why the Jews? As many people have noted, anyone can do that. No one has to have been a slave to care about others' enslavement. No one has to have suffered any specific calamity to want to prevent others from meeting that fate. True. But at the same time, Jewish tradition asserts that the passion that comes from personal memory is the most powerful passion of all. Only a child raised in an abusive home can know the trauma and pain of that experience. Women who have been raped often speak of an unspoken bond they feel with others who have been through that horror. By making our past not just history, but living memory, our tradition wants to enable modern Jews to feel the plight of others as our own. Their experience is our experience, their memory is our memory. It is *our* memory because Judaism's way of life transforms the past and brings it to life in our own present.

That is why so much of the Jewish calendar is designed to make our communal memory come alive. Virtually all Jewish holidays relive these ancient occasions. Passover celebrates not just freedom, but the escape from slavery. The Ninth of Av, a little known day of fasting that usually falls in midsummer, brings back to life the devastation and hopelessness that followed the destruction of the Temple by the Babylonians in 586 B.C.E. and by the Romans in 70 C.E. Worshipers sit on the ground during this holiday, do not eat or drink for more than twenty-four hours, often sleep on the floor, and do not even greet each other by saying hello. In traditional communities, it is not unusual to see the person leading the service actually crying.

What is the point of holidays like these? What do these celebrations of Passover and the Ninth of Av accomplish? They turn ancient history into our personal story; what for others might seem like myth is for us an intimate and deeply etched memory. It is memory of our survival, but more than that. It is a memory of our own survival that invests us in the survival of others, of the "strangers" in our own world.

Survival in this sense is a strange notion for modern American Jews. Too often, we've been taught that Jewish history is about bemoaning our fate, about recalling how hard our history has been. Not so. To be Jewish today is to take our history and rather than view it in what Salo Baron, the premier Jewish historian of the century, called "lachrymose" terms, to see it as affording us the opportunity to share our message of triumph and perseverance with other peoples similarly afflicted.

No Jewish festival helps us make Jewish tradition come to life this way more clearly than Hanukkah, the "Festival of Lights." As we will see, though, we might better begin to think of Hanukkah not as a Festival of Lights, but as a Festival of Survival, in which survival has a unique Jewish twist.

HANUKKAH—THE FESTIVAL OF SURVIVAL

Because it almost always languishes in the shadows of Christmas, Hanukkah is the Jewish holiday that struggles most consistently for an identity of its own. For some Jews, Hanukkah has become the Jewish Christmas. Just as Christmas has lost religious significance for many Christians, so, too, Hanukkah is for many Jews simply a winter festival, a time for family to join together in the cold of December. As Christians decorate their homes and offices with lights, Jews kindle their own lights. As Christians exchange gifts with family and friends to add joy to the "season of brotherly love," Jews do the same thing. The erstwhile Jewish tradition of "Hanukkah *gelt*"—a Yiddish phrase that refers to the custom of giving a small, token amount of "Hanukkah money" to children and grandchildren—has now given way to a gift-giving practice that is virtually identical to the etiquette among Christians. Thus, even though many Jews point out that Hanukkah is most definitely not Christmas, they are not sure what it *is*. Ultimately, the single word that Jews associate most commonly with Hanukkah is—Christmas.

What, then, *is* Hanukkah? It is, in fact, a victory celebration. Hanukkah is the holiday that commemorates the Jews recapturing the Temple in Jerusalem from the Greeks (or to be more precise, the Seleucids) in 164 B.C.E. Outnumbered and seemingly overpowered, Judah Maccabee and his followers were somehow able to overcome the forces of Antiochus Epiphanes and to reassert Jewish hegemony over the Temple Mount, most of Jerusalem, and eventually—and for a short period—even some of greater Judea.

But even though Hanukkah originally celebrated a stunning military victory, Jews were never entirely comfortable with that theme for the holiday. In part, this discomfort with the celebration of military prowess was a product of their history. Jews lived without a country of their own, and hence without an army, for almost two thousand years. For millennia, military might was beyond Jews' reach, thoroughly out of the question. As a result, Jews turned adversity into principle; much of Jewish tradition became rather pacifist.

Even the classic talmudic discussion of Hanukkah, this "military celebration," avoids all mention of the Maccabees and their army. The Talmud relates:

> What is [the reason for] Hanukkah? For our Rabbis taught: On the twenty-fifth of Kislev the eight days of Hanukkah [begin], on which . . . lamentation for the dead and fasting are forbidden. For when the Greeks entered the Temple, they defiled all the oils inside, and when the Hasmonean dynasty prevailed against them and defeated them, [the Hasmoneans] searched and found only one cruse of oil which lay with the seal of the High Priest, but which contained sufficient oil for one day's lighting only; yet a miracle occurred there and they lit [the lamp] with [that one cruse of oil] for eight days. The following year these [days] were appointed a Festival. . . .
>
> (SHABBAT 21B)

In this version, Hanukkah has a more spiritual focus than in the earlier and more militaristic accounts found in the Books of the Maccabees. While the Talmud certainly does not deny the Maccabees' role in the victory, the real hero for the Talmud is God.

Though this account mentions the Hasmonean victory over the Syrian king (though we commonly call Antiochus a *Greek* king, that is not entirely correct), the more significant element in the Talmud is the miracle of the oil. By focusing on the oil (and not on the battle), the heroic credit is given to God (and not to humans). The subtle implication is clear: Jews ought to wait for God to bring about their salvation and should not presume to bring that redemption about themselves. After all, the rabbis remind us, Jewish revolts against Rome and other occupying powers usually resulted not in victory, but in utter and devastating disaster.

Despite our rather common conception of Hanukkah as a holiday for children, without much value for adults who may not believe in miracles of oil, Hanukkah is actually a time for serious reflection. It's not child's play, but serious adult engagement with fundamental Jewish questions. For the rabbis, Hanukkah was not just a celebration of military victory. Nor was it simply about the miracle of the cruse of oil, as important as that was to their conception of this festival. Rather, Hanukkah became a holiday about survival, about the spirit overpowering the sword, about goodness overcoming evil, and about the few—if their cause is just—ultimately vanquishing the many.

Judaism's claim is simple: Jews have a voice; it is the voice that reminds the world of the power of the weak. Hanukkah, a word that connotes "rededication," is our tradition's way of reminding us that we can rededicate ourselves to being the blessing of which God spoke to Abraham. "Just as we survived as a powerless minority," we cry out to the world, "so, too, can you."

"IN THOSE DAYS AND IN OUR OWN TIME"

But a word of caution: if our search for Jewish distinctiveness, for a Jewish message, is to be authentically Jewish, we have to be faithful to our history. The role we decide Jews should play in the world must emanate from a careful but fair reading of our tradition. It cannot simply be a role tailor-made for modern American Jews. It needs to be genuine, a reflection of the texts and traditions that have defined Judaism for more than two thousand years.

Therefore, we need to ask: is this reading of Hanukkah an authentic reading of this festival? Indeed, it is. Consider four texts associated with Hanukkah: the blessings over the candles, the *Al Ha-Nissim* prayer, the song known as "Rock of Ages" and the *Haftarah* (the prophetic reading) for the Sabbath of Hanukkah. All of these compositions, each in its own way, buttress our reading of Hanukkah as a festival of survival.

"In Those Days and in Our Own Time"— The Blessings over the Hanukkah Candles

As Jews around the globe gather to light the Hanukkah candles, they recite two blessings. The first, not unlike the blessing recited over the Sabbath evening candles on Friday nights, simply acknowledges God's commandment to kindle the Hanukkah lights. The second blessing, though, is more instructive. It reads, "Praised are You, Lord our God, Ruler of the Universe, who performed miracles for our ancestors, in those days and in our own time."

The final phrase of that blessing, *ba-yamim ha-hem ba-zeman ha-zeh*—"in those days and in our own time"*—is our first hint that Hanukkah focuses not only on the past, but on the present (and even the future) as well. Something about Hanukkah has to address the present—and the future as well.

The Miracle of Perseverance—"History" à la Al Ha-Nissim

What is that phenomenon that Hanukkah celebrates? It is survival, of course. This becomes even more apparent with another

---

* This blessing is most commonly translated as "who performed miracles for our ancestors, in those days at this season." But the Hebrew, *ba-zeman ha-zeh,* allows for both translations. The *Siddur Sim Shalom* translates it as "in those days, and in our time."

part of the Hanukkah liturgy, *Al Ha-Nissim*. The *Al Ha-Nissim* paragraph is added to the daily prayers and to the Grace After Meals during all eight days of Hanukkah. Recited three, four or even five times a day during the holiday, it becomes a central liturgical element of Hanukkah. Like the candle-lighting blessing, *Al Ha-Nissim* also stresses matters reaching far beyond the Hasmonean battles against the Greeks. In traditional prayer books, the passage reads as follows:

> In the days of Mattathias, the son of Yoḥanan, the High Priest, the Hasmonean, and his sons—when the wicked Greek kingdom rose up against Your people Israel to make them forget Your Torah and compel them to stray from the statutes of Your Will—You in Your great mercy stood up for them in the time of their distress. You took up their grievance, judged their claim, and avenged their wrong. You delivered the strong into the hands of the weak, the many into the few, the impure into the hands of the pure, the wicked into the hands of the righteous, and the wanton into the hands of the diligent students of Your Torah. For Yourself You made a great and holy Name in Your world, and for Your people Israel you worked a great victory and salvation as this very day. Thereafter, Your children came to the Holy of Holies of Your House, cleansed Your Temple, purified the site of Your Holiness and kindled lights in the Courtyards of Your Sanctuary; and they established these eight days of Hanukkah to express thanks and praise to Your great Name.

Hanukkah, if we read *Al Ha-Nissim* carefully, is not only about the Maccabees and their defeat of the Seleucid empire. It is about hope. It is about the faith that pure can triumph over impure, that the few can sometimes prevail against the many, that moral purity can triumph in an era of spiritual pollution. Our interpretation of the holiday *is* supported by the tradition: Hanukkah is about the tenacity of the Jews, but more broadly, it is about the persistence of good, the endurance of the weak. Hanukkah thus urges modern Jews to reflect on their survival, to wonder how we have persevered beyond all expectation, how it is that in spite of all the obstacles thrown our way, our history still inspired Voltaire—who hated Jews—to speak of us as a "miracle."

"Rock of Ages"—History and Hanukkah's Spiritual Dimension

Among American Jews, there is probably no Hanukkah song more familiar than "Rock of Ages." "Rock of Ages" is a rough translation of the Hebrew phrase *Ma'oz Zur,* a Hanukkah ode that was apparently composed in the mid-thirteenth century. But as is often the case when we sing songs so frequently that we ignore their texts and their meanings, most modern Jews are not aware of the real thrust of *Ma'oz Zur.* Is this well-known stanza the entire story, or is there more?

Not surprisingly, there is much more to the song than we commonly realize. Let's look at the full composition, in order to get a better sense of what the poet—and therefore our tradition as well—is trying to say:

> *O mighty Rock of my salvation,*
> *to praise You is a delight,*
> *restore my House of Prayer*
> *and there we will bring a thanksgiving offering.*
> *When You will have prepared the slaughter*
> *for the blaspheming foe,*
> *then I shall complete with a song of hymn*
> *the dedication of the Altar.*
>
> *Troubles sated my soul,*
> *when with grief my strength was consumed.*
> *They had embittered my life with hardship,*
> *with the calf-like kingdom's bondage.*
> *But with his great power*
> *He brought forth the treasured ones,*

Pharaoh's army and all his offspring
went down like a stone into the deep.

To the abode of His holiness He brought me.
But there, too, I had no rest
and an oppressor came and exiled me.
For I had served aliens,
And had drunk benumbing wine.
Scarcely had I departed [my land]
when at Babylonia's demise Zerubavel came—
At the end of seventy years I was saved.

To sever the towering cypress
sought the Aggagite, son of Hammedatha,
but it became a snare and a stumbling block to him
and his arrogance was stilled.
The head of the Benjaminite You lifted
and the enemy, his name You blotted out
his numerous progeny—possessions—
on the gallows You hanged.

Greeks gathered against me
then in Hasmonean days.
They breached the walls of my towers
and they defiled all the oils;
and from the one remnant of the flasks
a miracle was wrought for the roses.
Men of insight—days
established for song and jubilation

Bare Your holy arm
and hasten the End for salvation—
Avenge the vengeance of Your servant's blood
from the wicked nation.
For the triumph is too long delayed for us,

> *and there is no end to days of evil.*
> *Repel the Red One in the nethermost shadow*
> *and establish for us the seven shepherds.*

Ma'oz Zur is more than a folk song. It is rather a historical summary of many of the tragedies that have befallen the Jewish people. It begins (in the second stanza) with reference to Egyptian slavery, and then turns to the exile of the Jews at the hand of the Babylonians. The song then turns to Haman, the villain of Purim, whom it calls "the Aggagite, son of Hammedatha" (based on a reference in Esther 3:1). Eventually, in the penultimate stanza, the Hanukkah story itself appears, as the poet writes, "Greeks gathered against me then in Hasmonean days."

By placing Hanukkah in the fifth stanza, and not at the beginning of the song, *Ma'oz Zur* is clearly trying to claim that Hanukkah is part of a larger pattern. The Greek threat to the Jews, the poet suggests, continued an ongoing paradigm in which the Jewish people is somehow threatened, but seemingly at the very last moment, somehow escapes destruction. While the last stanza seems to cry out in anguish, praying for a messianic era in which Jews will no longer be threatened, most of the song has a different purpose: it is a reminder that Jewish survival is itself miraculous. Hanukkah wants us to be amazed and awed by Jewish history, by the sheer incomprehensibility of our survival; that is where Hanukkah's spiritual power comes from.

As we gaze at the flickering candles each evening of the holiday, our tradition wants one message to come through clearly: despite the number of threats to Jewish life and the tremendous imbalance of power between Jews and their foes, Jews are still here to tell their tale, to sing songs of their history, and to remind the world that the weak can, in fact, transcend the vagaries and cruelties of human history.

To the author of *Ma'oz Zur*, Hanukkah is not a children's holiday. Nor is it merely a winter festival, a holiday of light in a season of darkness. It is more than a holiday that commemorates the Jewish defeat of the Seleucids, whom we commonly call Greeks. For this poet (whose identity we do not know), Hanukkah was something much more substantive, far more compelling. Hanukkah, to paraphrase the *Al Ha-Nissim* prayer once more, is about the delivery of the "strong into the hands of the weak, the many into the few, the impure into the hands of the pure, the wicked into the hands of the righteous," and in distinctly Jewish terms, "the wanton into the hands of the diligent students of Torah."

"Not by Might and Not by Power"—
Hanukkah's Ultimate Spiritual Claim

There is one more brief passage we should examine as part of our discussion of the spiritual claim that the Jewish tradition has sought to associate with Hanukkah: the *Haftarah* the rabbis chose for the Sabbath of Hanukkah.

What is a *Haftarah?* In traditional synagogues, two different parts of the Bible are read each Sabbath morning of the year. One is a section from the Torah (the Five Books of Moses), while the other is a reading from the middle third of the Bible—the Prophets—designed to correspond in some thematic way to the Torah reading This reading from the prophetic literature is called the *Haftarah*.

Because Hanukkah is an eight-day holiday, there is always at least one Sabbath that falls on Hanukkah. Thus, the rabbis knew that at least one *Haftarah* would be read each year on Hanukkah. Though there are a number of passages in the Bible's prophetic literature that speak of war, and even victory over enemies, those are not the passages that the rabbis selected for Hanukkah's *Haftarah*. Rather, the rabbis chose a passage from the book of Zechariah. Toward the end of the *Haftarah*, this selection from Zechariah includes the very well known phrase, critical to the rabbis' reading of Hanukkah: "Not by might, nor by power, but by My spirit—said the Lord of Hosts" (Zechariah 4:6).

Here again, the tradition claims that Hanukkah is not about

military victory, but about a different sort of triumph. "Not by might and not by power"—it is about the survival of those who deem themselves too weak to survive, too disenfranchised to withstand the force of those who surround them. What a strange—but powerful—way to commemorate what was originally a military victory! It is a claim to all the world that Jews have a message for humanity—about the ultimate limits on the value of might, and on the timeless significance of the spirit.

Hanukkah is thus not only about Jews. It is about what Jewish history can represent to the rest of the world. The Jewish Festival of Lights is designed to bring light to those in need, whoever they may be, wherever they may reside. Hanukkah is not only a holiday on which Jews celebrate their own experience, but rather, a festival in which Jews seek to bring a message of hope to the disenfranchised everywhere. To return to the language of God's promise to Abraham, Isaac and Jacob, Hanukkah is about one of the "blessings" that it is our role to proclaim. On Hanukkah, Jews remind the weak and the impoverished everywhere that our own survival should give them cause for hope.

Not all Jews agree as to why we have survived. For some, it is due to God's direct intervention in history. These people believe that God has a covenantal relationship with the Jewish people, and that as bleak as things may sometimes appear, God will not let us vanish. For others, Jewish survival is a result less of God's action than of the way that Jews have lived and the ways they adapted their tradition to challenge. For still others, Jewish survival is inexplicable, but miraculous nonetheless. We cannot explain our survival, they say, but that does not prevent it from inspiring us.

Many of us experience that feeling with the birth of a child. No matter how much scientists and physicians can tell us about conception, pregnancy and childbirth, when we witness a birth we still sense a miracle. We may or may not believe that God played a role. We may or may not know a great deal about biology or physiology. But we are moved. And secular and religious alike, we speak of miracles. That two cells and nine months can combine to create a being that can smile is a phenomenon that fills us with awe, with gratitude and with hope.

We feel that hope not because we understand how a child is formed, but because the majesty of the frail but breathing child is so powerful. That is how Hanukkah can work, too. We need not understand *why* the Jews have survived. We may never know that. The simple fact, though, is that we have survived. We, too, frail but breathing at times, are still here. That message, says our tradition, is one we ought to use to fill the world with hope.

THE LIGHTS THAT STILL FLICKER—THE ROLE OF RITUAL IN HANUKKAH'S MESSAGE

While most Jewish holidays have many practices and customs, Hanukkah has only a few. Of those, the most central is obviously the lighting of the Hanukkah candelabrum, known in Hebrew as a *ḥanukkiah*. The custom, a familiar one for most American Jews, is to light one candle on the first night of the holiday. After the first night, we increase the number of candles each night until the full *ḥanukkiah*—with its eight candles—is lit on the final evening after the sky has grown dark.

When we think about it carefully, this is actually a strange custom. After all, if the purpose of lighting the *ḥanukkiah* is to re-enact the miracle of the oil in the Temple so many years ago, we appear to be lighting the *ḥanukkiah* in the wrong order. For when was there more oil—on the first day, or on the eighth day? Obviously, there was more oil on the first day, and it gradually diminished until there was none left (though new purified oil had since been prepared). If that is the case, we perform this ritual backward. Would it not make more sense to begin Hanukkah by lighting eight candles and then letting the number of candles gradually decrease throughout the eight days?

We are not the first to ask this question. The Talmud addresses the same issue in the following language:

> Our Rabbis taught: . . . the School of Shammai maintain: On
> the first day eight lights are lit and thereafter they are gradu-
> ally reduced; but the School of Hillel say: On the first day
> one is lit and thereafter they are progressively increased [up
> to eight on the last day].
>
> Ulla said: In the West [Palestine] two authorities, R. Yossi
> b. Abin and R. Yossi b. Zevida, differ [on the reasons for
> the dispute between the Schools of Shammai and Hillel]:
> one maintains that the reason of School of Shammai is that
> the number of candles ought to correspond to the days [of
> the holiday] still to come, and that of School of Hillel is that
> it shall correspond to the days that are gone; but another
> [view] maintains: the School of Shammai's reason is that [the
> number of candles] shall correspond to the bullocks of the
> Festival of Sukkot, while the School of Hillel's reason is that
> we go up in [matters of] sanctity but do not reduce.
>
> (SHABBAT 21B)

We learn a few interesting things from this brief passage. First,
we learn that our current custom of starting with one candle and
gradually increasing to eight was not always universally accepted.
This was the custom of Hillel and his disciples, a group known as
the "School of Hillel." But Shammai and his disciples—the
"School of Shammai"—took the opposite approach, arguing that
we should begin with a full *hanukkiah* and gradually lessen the
number to one candle at the end of the holiday. We learn something else, as well. We discover that the Sages were not entirely
certain why each of these two schools of thought took the positions that they did. In other words, we know *what* Hillel and
Shammai thought we should do, but we are not entirely certain
why they thought we should do it.

The Talmud gives two explanations for Hillel's position. The
first is that Hillel and his school felt that the number of candles
ought to correspond to the number of days of the holiday that

have already been celebrated (as opposed to the number of days remaining in the festival). The second is that Hillel was referring to a broad talmudic principle that in matters of sanctity, we strive to increase, and not to decrease. Thus, the argument goes, since the Hanukkah candles have their own sort of sanctity, it would be inappropriate to lessen the number during the holiday, and thus, we should commence the ritual by lighting one, and then progress to eight by the end of the celebration.

But neither explanation is fully convincing. The notion that the candles ought to represent the number of days already celebrated makes a certain degree of sense, but it is surely no more sensible than Shammai's suggestion that the candles should reflect the number of days remaining. If we keep in mind the fact that—at least on some level—the candles *are* designed to reflect the miracle of the oil, then Shammai's position may actually make more sense! With the second reason—that we increase in matter of holiness—we find weaknesses as well. For while it is true that this is a general talmudic principle, it is not entirely clear what the holiness in this situation is. Furthermore, the principle that "in matters of holiness we increase and do not decrease" was a generally accepted principle. Thus, had it been patently obvious that there is a sense of "holiness" to this ritual, how could Shammai and his disciples have disagreed with it? This reason, too, is a stretch.

Since the Talmud's explanations for the ritual are rather unconvincing, we need to look further. Indeed, the explanation for this ritual may lie not in complex talmudic reasoning, but in the simple visual and spiritual power of the ritual and its fire. Perhaps the tradition was trying to say something about the power of the weak, the perseverance of the oppressed. As they increase in number each evening, the flames are meant to reassure other peoples who worry that their own blazes will die out. The ritual responds by assuring them that the power of their community, their people, their culture and their tradition will not decrease, but will actually increase. The growing number of candles is the ritual's way of saying, "you will not dwindle, but rather, you will grow."

As each evening of Hanukkah comes, Jews around their *ḥanukkiot* (the plural of *ḥanukkiah*) are treated to a sort of ritual dance. It is not a dance of people, but a dance of flames and wicks. As the candles burn low, or as the oil in the *ḥanukkiah* gradually runs out, the fires do not simply disappear. For the last few moments of their burning, they flicker, seemingly ready to be extinguished, when suddenly they leap back to life. Just when it seems that the flame is gone, it suddenly revives. One moment there is darkness, and next, light reborn and renewed. There is a beauty, an almost magical quality, to this display. It is a quasi-desperate exhibition, a suggestion that the fire does not want to die. It struggles desperately to live. Though the flame will eventually die out, our response is to light the flames again the next evening, adding an additional candle or wick to the collection, making our point that we simply will not allow the lights to go out.

That is the point of Hanukkah. It is about lights, but not only the lights of the candles. Hanukkah proclaims and insists that the downtrodden, the powerless, the dispossessed and the all but vanquished are these flames. "We have survived, apparently against all odds," we say to the world, "and we believe that you can—and will—as well."

"PROCLAIMING THE MIRACLE"

But who hears all this? If the point of Hanukkah is to bring a message to the rest of the world, something is still missing. Our discussion of Hanukkah and its meaning would be incomplete if we did not mention one final dimension of the ritual of lighting the candles. Interestingly, Jewish tradition prescribes not only how many candles to light each night, but where the lit candles should be placed. The Talmudic discussion we have been quoting contains the following passage:

Our Rabbis taught: It is incumbent to place the Hanukkah
lamp by the door of one's house on the outside; if one
dwells in an upper chamber, he places it at the window near-
est the street. But in times of danger it is sufficient to place it
on the table. Raba said: Another lamp is required for its light
to be used.   (SHABBAT 21B)

The essential point of this section is that the lit Hanukkah
candles have to be situated in a place where they can be seen
from the outside. Jewish tradition calls this dimension of the ritual *pirsuma de-nissa,* "the proclamation of the miracle." Thus, the
Talmud states, one should ideally place the lit *hanukkiah* outside
the front door of one's house. If one lives upstairs, and cannot
place the lit candles at the doorway to the street (on the outside,
no less), one places them at a window where they can still be seen
by all who pass by. Furthermore, the rabbis mandate that if one
needs a light for reading or working, some other light must be
used. To utilize the Hanukkah candles for light would diminish
our sense that these lights are for one singular purpose—to proclaim a message.

The Talmud, of course, was realistic. It recognized that in
some places, such assertiveness might arouse the hostility of the
Jews' neighbors. Therefore, the Talmud said that if this custom
would be dangerous, it need not be followed. But the ideal was
clear. Today, therefore, it is the custom of traditional Jews to
place their Hanukkah candles at a window facing the street on
which they live. By making the Hanukkah lights a public ritual,
noticeable by all, Jewish tradition reminds us that Hanukkah is
not about us alone, but about peoples and nations everywhere.
That is why we do not allow the lights to go out; and that is why
we place them in a public place. The ritualized dance of the frail
and fragile flames is a tenacious struggle the entire world needs
to witness.

RETHINKING OUR QUESTIONS
ABOUT JEWISH HISTORY

With this conception of Hanukkah in mind, the questions we ask about Jewish history are not the "Why?" and the "Where was God?" with which we opened this chapter. No one can fully explain why the Jews have been the object of much of history's cruelty. But Hanukkah, when understood in this light, begs us to focus on a different set of questions. In light of Hanukkah, the question becomes not why those events took place, but how Jews have responded. What matters is not why our history has been painful, but whether we can transcend that pain and transform it into a message of healing and of hope for all humanity.

When we understand not only Hanukkah, but all of Jewish life, in this way, our conception of what it means to be a Jew begins to take shape. Suddenly, we find that modern Jews *do* have something to say to the world, to modernity, to other traditions. We have something to say not despite our history, but because of it. It is not, of course, that we have wanted to play the role of victim, or that we should seek it out now. Yet we are still here—to light candles, to sing songs that review our history, to place those burning flames in public view. Thus, the important question for Jews in modernity becomes not one of theodicy—evil in God's world—but one of mission.

To be a Jew thus becomes a matter of making a statement, of reminding the world of the possibility of survival for those who would seem to have no hope, of speaking with an authentic and distinct historical voice that has something of value to say to human beings wherever they may languish. *That* is a dimension of Judaism that is unique; it is authentically Jewish. And it does not make Jews out to be better or innately superior. It is a distinctly Jewish role, for it emerges out of an engagement with Jewish tradition and Jewish texts. And today more than ever, it is a role that matters, that can make a difference. That is the point of *pirsuma de-nissa,* the proclamation of the miracle.

DOES ANYONE HEAR THE MESSAGE?

But, we sometimes wonder, is anyone listening? Does anyone really notice our candles? After all, if this role for the Jew is only a matter of our intention, but has no bearing on how other people see us, what is the point? The proverbial question—Does a tree falling in the forest when no one is present make a noise?— comes to mind.

The reality, though, is that many people *do* hear. Mark Twain's image of the Jew as survivor is a classic example. But there are also many others. The image of the Jew as survivor has made its way into modern literary culture, as well. Consider Adrienne Rich's reflections on the condition of being a Jew:

> *It's an old fashioned, an outrageous thing*
> *to believe one has a "destiny"*
>
> *—a thought often peculiar to those*
> *who possess privilege—*
>
> *but there is something else: the faith*
> *of those despised and endangered*
>
> *that they are not merely the sum*
> *of damages done to them:*
>
> *have kept beyond violence the knowledge*
> *arranged in patterns like kente-cloth*
>
> *unexpected as in batik*
> *recurrent as bitter herbs and unleavened bread*

of being a connective link
in a long, continuous way

of ordering hunger, weather, death, desire
and the nearness of chaos.

"Bitter herbs" and "unleavened bread." Is there any doubt that Rich wants the reader to understand that "to believe one has a 'destiny' " is a Jewish matter? For Rich, "those despised and endangered" are clearly the Jews, a people who bring a message about "ordering hunger, weather, death, desire."

Still others have not only understood the message, but have even seen it in Hanukkah, much in the way we have described. We find a wonderful example in folk music, in the Peter, Paul and Mary song called "Light One Candle."

Light one candle for the Maccabee children for thanks that
their light didn't die.
Light one candle for the pain they endured when their right
to exist was denied.
Light one candle for the terrible sacrifice justice and
freedom demand.
But light one candle for the wisdom to know when the peacemakers'
time is at hand.

Don't let the light go out
It's lasted for so many years.
Don't let the light go out
Let it shine through our love and our tears.

Light one candle for the strength that we need to never
become our own foe.
Light one candle for those who are suffering the pain we
learned so long ago.

Light one candle for all we believe in that anger not tear
us apart.
Light one candle to bind us together with peace as a song in
our heart.

Don't let the light go out . . .

What is the memory that's valued so highly that we keep it
alive in this flame?
What's the commitment to those who have died when we cry out
"they've not died in vain"?
We have come this far always believing that justice will
somehow prevail.
This is the burden, this is the promise and this is what we
will not fail.

Don't let the light go out . . .

"Light one candle for those who are suffering the pain we learned so long ago"—again, the message of Hanukkah understood as being about more than the Jews themselves. Yet Adrienne Rich and Peter Yarrow are hardly the kinds of people to whom Jews are trying to convey their message. They are Caucasians in America, part of the power structure, or at the very minimum, hardly an oppressed minority. So, we ask, what about other groups that genuinely could find some inspiration in the Jewish story? Have we touched them?

Yes. Though the black-Jewish alliance in this country has sadly eroded in the last several decades, for a long time African-Americans did find solace in the story of Jewish liberation. Part of the power of the partnership and friendship of the Reverend Martin Luther King, Jr. and Rabbi Abraham Joshua Heschel stemmed from the fact that both were religious leaders of people who had lived in slavery, people whose stories often seemed uncannily to mirror each other's. Jews were undoubtedly drawn to the civil rights cause not only because they sensed that it was the "right thing to do," but because it spoke to their own history with harrowing parallels. Perhaps the most telling indication that the Jewish story has inspired the black community is to be found in the fact that material from Jewish history found its way into Negro antebellum spirituals. Consider the following well-known classic:

> When Egypt was in Israel land
> Let my people go.
> Oppress' so hard they could not stand
> Let my people go.
> Go down, Moses, way down in Egypt land.
> Tell ol' Pharaoh
> To let my people go.

African-Americans are not the only ones who have found cause for hope and source of inspiration in tales of Jewish survival. Some American Jews have found that peoples as far removed from the West as the Tibetans find Judaism's story compelling and instructive. In 1989, the year in which he was awarded the Nobel Peace Prize, the Dalai Lama is reported to have turned to the Jewish community and to have asked, "Tell me your secret—the secret of Jewish spiritual survival in exile." The following year, a group of American Jewish leaders traveled to Dharamsala to meet with the XIV Dalai Lama. Here is what Rodger Kamenetz, an American Jew and poet who accompanied those rabbis and other leaders on their visit to the Dalai Lama, learned about the Tibetans:

> [The Dalai Lama's] questions also revealed his own preoccupations with how to reform a religion while in exile. About 115,000 of his people are now living in a new situation, some in Dharamsala, more in the rest of India and in Nepal, others

scattered in Europe and North America. They are the first generation of a Tibetan diaspora, and . . . they face two crises at once—the crisis of exile and dispersion and the problems of modernity. . . .

As fascinating as the Tibetans' parallels to Jewish history are, what is most striking about this encounter is how this self-described conflicted American Jew came to see his own Jewishness as a result of the encounter. He notes:

> I was powerfully moved that Jewish history could be so relevant to another people. All the suffering, the martyrdom that had always been so bitter and difficult for me to accept, now appeared a lesson hard earned, and a precious knowledge, even a Jewish secret of survival. That was very exciting.
>
> I recognized that Rabbi [Irving "Yitz"] Greenberg's lifelong dedication to dialogue, within the Jewish world and with other religious leaders, is a key to renewing Jewish life, and keeping Jewish history alive. His belief that our history is meant to be—must be—a blessing for others is inspiring, unlocking old resentments and releasing the stored energy of our Jewish past.

That is precisely the point. The image of the Jew as the bearer of a story that matters can and does inspire. It is a voice that speaks to those outside the Jewish community, as well as to those within it. If Jewish history and its narrative of survival has touched African-Americans and Asian-Tibetans, we have every reason to believe that it can touch others, too.

And it has the capacity to touch us as well. Seeing our history as the story of a people that has a message of hope and of dignity to bring to other peoples is a profound starting point for a sense of Jewish identity in modernity. Emil Fackenheim notwithstanding, Jews will not choose Judaism simply so that Hitler not be given a posthumous victory. But Jews might well elect to take part in the enterprise we call being a Jew if they come to understand that the world needs them, that they are the bearers of a vital message and a sacred trust.

We will know when Jews have returned to this role. The signs will be obvious. Jews will have internalized the message of Hanukkah and the burden it places on them when they are no longer silent in the face of Bosnia. They will have internalized the role their tradition wants for them if, when President Clinton seeks to convince the American people that sending troops into Bosnia is in America's national interest, they respond, "national interest is not the issue. What is at issue is protecting those who need protection." American Jews will have moved beyond self-centeredness to a reconfigured sense of chosenness when they come to understand that if they want to harbor lingering animosity toward Franklin D. Roosevelt for not bombing the tracks to Auschwitz, then they have the obligation to speak loudly when they witness ethnic cleansing just half a century later. When Hanukkah speaks in chorus with Leviticus 19:16, admonishing Jews not to "stand idly by the blood of their neighbor," Jews will have recovered their voice. When a history of the "abandonment of the Jews" creates for Jews a sense of urgency about tragedies that befall others, the Jewish voice now so painfully silent will have been recovered.

To be sure, not all Jews or all Jewish organizations were silent on Bosnia. The Joint Distribution Committee sent medicines and worked to evacuate Jews as well as non-Jews. Many Jewish leaders spoke out, as well. But was Bosnia a source of angst for most Jews? Hardly. It wasn't a major issue even for Jews who care deeply about their Jewishness. And *that* is the issue.

When the churches of African-American communities began to burn across the South and beyond, how many committed Jews saw that as a genuinely Jewish issue? How many religious Jews felt compelled to stand guard, to rebuild, or to offer assistance? How many Jews understood that this was a Jewish concern not because it was a liberal or American concern, but because it reflected our own experience on Kristallnacht, and for hundreds of years before? Some, but too few.

Too few Jews experience Hanukkah this way. Too few sense the profound link between Jewish ritual and Jewish social vision. But why is it so hard for us to hear that call? Why is it that Hanukkah can be made to speak to transcendent issues, but so few Jews have experienced it that way?

MOVING BEYOND ETHNICITY

These are difficult questions to address, not because the answers are elusive, but because honest responses cut to the very core of the sort of Judaism that Jews have created in America. When we think carefully about what we have seen throughout this chapter, we gradually realize that the new elements to which we have been exposed have emerged from the ritual, religious dimension of Jewish life. Hanukkah simply celebrated as a winter festival, in which we light candles and exchange gifts, may be pleasant and enjoyable, but it is not profound. The profundity of Hanukkah begins to emerge through its liturgy, its quasi-liturgical songs and the talmudic arguments behind the various customs associated with lighting the candles.

To most American Jews, the details—of how and why one lights the candles, of where one places the *hanukkiah,* and about the recitation of blessings and *Al Ha-Nissim*—seem arcane, out of place in modern life. Such sense of commitment to detail seems counterspiritual. Contemporary Jews want a Judaism that can speak powerfully without details, without blessings, without prayers that can—at least at first—be difficult to learn and to understand. They seek a religious experience that is accessible, undemanding and powerful at the same time. Their goal is simple transcendence, spirituality without too much effort.

We must, then, encounter the elements of Jewish life that we have for too long cast aside. It is no accident that Rodger Kamenetz, the American Jew who learned so much about his tradition from a visit to the Dalai Lama—and who subtitled his book, "A Poet's Rediscovery of Jewish Identity in Buddhist India," rediscovered the power of Jewish life in the presence of not simply Jewish leaders, but Jewish religious leaders. The rabbis with whom he traveled came from very diverse places on the Jewish spectrum. But they all took the spiritual and religious components of Judaism seriously. None of them, no matter how liberal or how experimental, would have suggested that Judaism as a mere ethnicity or an ethnic version of secular liberal humanism could have anything substantial to say. In the company of these disparate individuals, the poet became a listener. He rediscovered his own tradition—and himself—perhaps even more than he learned about Buddhism.

Our choices are already becoming clear. We can have an American Judaism fashioned with comfort, autonomy and a generic American liberal sensibility at its heart, or we can have a powerful, compelling form of Jewish life that begs us to become part of something transcendent, of cosmic importance, of ultimate value. The two may well not intersect.

CHAPTER FIVE

Distinctiveness, Spirituality and Moderation—The Role of Law in a Renewed Chosenness

Why does survival matter? What is the meaning of defeating the Greeks, or of escaping Egyptian slavery? There is no point, Jewish tradition suggests, unless we know what to do with that freedom, unless we have a vision of what to make of our survival. It should therefore not surprise us that the Jewish calendar year contains not only Hanukkah, a holiday to celebrate survival itself, but Passover as well, a holiday on which we begin to define what we ought to do with the gift of freedom. It is in Passover that we may find the next major element of the Jews' message, the next characteristics of the authentic voice we are struggling to recover.

To most Jews, Passover is a celebration of freedom. It is about rejoicing over the exodus from Egypt, and by implication, about acknowledging other groups' need for similar liberation, their own quests for survival. There are feminist *Haggadot,* Passover rituals that focus on Soviet Jews, and even some (very controversial) proposals that Jews use the Seder to recall the Palestinians and their need for liberation. Ironically, Passover in the American Jewish mind is rather similar to Hanukkah. Freedom, like survival, is a powerful theme for this post-Shoah generation.

But Passover goes much deeper than that. Buried in the ritual of the Seder lies a hint about the second major contribution that Jews could see themselves making to the world. This hint begins on the second night of the holiday, when Jews outside Israel celebrate the second Seder. Toward the end of the *Haggadah,* there is a ritual called the "Counting of the *Omer.*" The *Omer* is the seven-week period between the start of Passover and the holiday of Shavu'ot (which celebrates the giving of the Torah at Mount Sinai). Jews count the *Omer* each night of those seven weeks, beginning with the second night of Passover, often at the Seder table.

The original command to count these seven weeks is found in the Torah itself:

> [15]And from the day on which you bring the sheaf of elevation offering—the day after the sabbath—you shall count off seven weeks. They must be complete: [16]you must count until the day after the seventh week—fifty days. . . .
>
> (LEVITICUS 23:15–16)

Because the Torah's language is rather ambiguous, the rabbis spent a great deal of time deliberating the passage, adding details to the practice of this ritual. They decided that in this case, "the day after the sabbath" meant the day after the beginning of Passover. While the Torah says nothing about how to count these seven weeks, the rabbis added very specific details. They stipulated that Jews should count the *Omer* in the evening, usually during *Ma'ariv* (the evening service).

Thus, each evening, traditional Jews recite a brief introductory paragraph, and then include two critical elements in their counting: first, a blessing, and second, a formula that enumerates the specific day:

> Praised are You, Lord our God, Ruler of the universe, who has sanctified us with Your commandments, and has commanded us to count the *Omer.* Today is the so-and-so day of the *Omer,* which is equivalent to so-many weeks and so-many days in the *Omer.*

So far, there is nothing particularly striking about this ritual. It seems like one more arcane Jewish custom, of no particular relevance to Jews' figuring out what they might have to say to the world on the eve of the twenty-first century. But there is more here than meets the eye. We just have to look more carefully.

Usually, in Jewish life, if a person accidentally forgets to perform a certain commandment, there is no perceptible punitive result. A person who forgets to pray in the morning can pray in the afternoon, and the next morning as well. A person who forgot to light Sabbath candles could certainly light candles the next week. And so on. But not so with the *Omer*.

According to one major view in the *halakhah* (traditional Jewish law), a person who misses more than one day of counting the *Omer* may not recite the blessing on any of the subsequent days that year. Here, unlike with other traditions, Jewish law implies, "If you forget more than one day in a row, you're out. You're excluded from the remainder of the ritual. So be very sure you don't forget!"

But why? Why "raise the stakes" by penalizing someone who forgets to count for a few days, forbidding them from performing the ritual for the remaining days?

One possibility: by heightening our awareness of the importance of counting the *Omer*, the rabbis were trying to highlight the link between Passover, which celebrates freedom and survival, and Shavu'ot, which celebrates Torah and the giving of the law. By creating a "countdown" from Passover to Shavu'ot, Jewish tradition suggests that mere freedom is not enough.

What is Judaism's response to the challenge of taking survival and making it substantive? To move from Passover to Shavu'ot. To progress from freedom to law. To Jews, meaningful living requires law. And that law has to be real. It is a law that commands. It governs our behavior. It even limits our very instincts. And in law lies another component of Judaism's message.

MODERN JEWISH LIFE WITHOUT JEWISH LAW?

Most modern Jews recoil at the idea that law ought to be a critical feature of Jewish life. Law in Jewish life strikes us as "too religious." Indeed, it seems virtually "un-American." Recall: as part of our process of blending into American life and trying to secure a place for ourselves here, Jews in America sought to internalize the very essence of American values. For many, those values were summed up by one school of thought: liberalism. For countless Jews, Judaism *became* liberalism. Liberal values were Jewish values. Liberal causes were Jewish causes. Liberal priorities became Jewish priorities.

In this scheme, Jews internalized the commitment to individualism and autonomy that often characterized liberalism in America. The more Jews equated Judaism with liberalism, the less law in their religion made sense. If American life is about freedom and autonomy, Jews wondered, why should they care about a constraining religious tradition that erodes their autonomy?

So American Jews moved further and further away from the halakhic (Jewish legal) piece of their tradition, and (like Andersen's mermaid) gave up that part of their voice so they could join the culture that so attracted them. But Andersen's mermaid disappeared into the foam on the sea. And Jews are discovering that without law at its core, Judaism will not be very different from Christianity.

The Christian Comparison

If we want a compelling answer to the question If the world woke up one day and there were no Jews left, what would the world be missing? Jews cannot be just like everyone else. If Jews are no different from the dominant culture in which they live, they have nothing to offer. That is why Judaism's focus on law becomes even more critical. After all, the culture in which Jews live today (outside Israel, of course) is Christian. American culture is Christian culture. For Jews to be substantively different from most Americans, Judaism cannot be the same as Christianity. And Judaism without law is not that different from Christianity without Jesus.

Yet what really distinguishes Judaism from Christianity? In part, of course, the answer is Jesus. But there has to be more. Judaism accepts the notion of human prophets, even human beings who become Messiahs. In the seventeenth century, many very traditional Jews believed that a Jew named Shabbetai Zevi (1626–1676) was the Messiah. When he apostatized and converted to Islam, his followers were devastated. Even today, the notion that a human being will someday reveal himself to be the Messiah is not as foreign to Judaism as many modern Jews (influenced by their life in a Christian society) want to believe. When the Lubavitcher Rebbe died in June 1994, thousands of his followers refused to believe he was gone, many claiming he would return to reveal himself as the Messiah. How different is that from what early Christians said about Jesus?

Thus, though the figure of Jesus is the most obvious difference between Jews and Christians, something else must be at play. That factor is law. While Exodus 19 says that Jews will be God's "chosen people" only if they observe the covenant and its commandments, Christianity sees the world very differently.

Consider the writings of Paul, the man who essentially fashioned early Christian theology. As Paul (or St. Paul as he is known to Christians) defined his emerging faith as distinct from Judaism, he felt compelled to repudiate the centrality of *halakhah*. In the Book of Romans, Paul explained that after the death of Jesus (also a Jew), something dramatic had changed in the way people should achieve holiness and seek a relationship with God:

> 6. . . Now we are rid of the Law, freed by [Jesus'] death from our imprisonment, free to serve in the new spiritual way and not the old way of a written law. 7. . . . What I mean is that I

would not have known what sin was had it not been for the law. If the [Torah] had not said [in the Ten Commandments] "You shall not covet," I would not have known what it means to covet. [8] . . . When there is no law, sin is dead.

(ROMANS 7:6–8)

Notice how different this is from the Torah's viewpoint! The Torah suggests that observance of the commandments (or law, as Paul calls it) will lead to holiness; Paul believes, however, that law somehow leads to sin. This disparaging attitude to the law is reflected in numerous examples in many books of the Christian Bible; we'll refer to only two others, both of which are very well known.

Later in Romans, Paul discusses circumcision. In a radical departure from Judaism's worldview, Paul insists that what really matters is not physical circumcision, but a spiritual condition:

The real Jew is the one who is inwardly a Jew, and the real circumcision is in the heart—something not of the [law] but of the spirit. A Jew like that may not be praised by man, but he will be praised by God.   (ROMANS 2:29)

In the Gospel of Matthew, Jesus makes a similar claim about the Torah's dietary restrictions. He insists that it is not the actual law that matters, but the idea behind the law that is truly important: "What goes into the mouth does not make a man unclean; it is what comes out of the mouth that makes him unclean" (Matthew 15:11).

Early Christians understood something that many Jews today fail to appreciate—Commitment to the value of law is part of the core of Jewish life. To live a religious life without command, without *halakhah,* is to destroy one of Judaism's most important claims to uniqueness. If Jews want to recapture an authentic voice with a message for the world, some serious engagement with Jewish law is going to be indispensable.

A "serious engagement with Jewish law," incidentally, does not mean Orthodoxy. Our quest for a renewed American Jewish identity has avoided discussing the Reform, Reconstructionist, Conservative and Orthodox movements. The challenge to reimagine American Jewish identity is one that faces the entire width and breadth of the Jewish community; no segment of the community is immune, and none has all the answers. Each of the movements, even the most liberal, could formulate its own way of engaging Jewish law seriously. Would a Reform conception of Jewish law and an Orthodox conception be the same? Obviously not. But serious engagement could happen in any of the movements, if people chose to embark on this journey.

The Spiritual Contributions of Jewish Law

Jewish tradition would carry our argument for the importance of law in Jewish life even further. It would claim that the value of law for modern Jews is not only to distinguish Judaism from Christianity, but to offer the world an example of how to make spiritual growth possible. Though we're not used to thinking of command or limitation this way, Judaism insists that law offers a powerful way of giving meaning to human life. It is not accidental that traditional Jews follow their celebration of freedom at the Passover Seder with the *Omer*—a countdown to the giving of the "law." Nor is it unimportant that the Hebrew word "Torah"—the source of our communal memory—actually means "law" or "instruction." A sense of command, or even obligation, is central to Judaism's conception of how we fill our lives with meaning and purpose.

Judaism suggests that having a relationship with God (or even trying to build one) is in some ways not unlike having relationships with people whom we love. Just as significant love relationships necessarily involve an element of obligation and of standards, the same is true of a relationship with God. We know from our human encounters that relationships do not survive unless we commit to them, unless we express our devotion to the people we love and care about in concrete ways, on a regular basis. Jewish tradition would ask: if these behaviors are so crucial in human relationships, with people we can touch, whose faces we can see and who can hold us when we feel alone, shouldn't a relationship with God—a God we cannot touch, whose face we cannot see—require at least as much from us? Jewish law is the way Jews make that commitment, the way they express the importance of that relationship.

Another reason for the importance of law in Jewish life has to do with Judaism's assessment of human nature. Jewish tradition believes that human nature requires law. While it might sound nobler to allow people to act kindly out of a sense of supererogation—the term Christians commonly use for "going beyond what the law requires"—Judaism has a different view of human nature. Instead of assuming that Jews will be inclined to give charity (thereby running the risk that they won't actually give it), Judaism *obligates* them to give it. Jewish law dictates how often to visit the sick, what and how to teach our children, and even how to treat the people to whom we're making love. While in an ideal world these standards might not be necessary, Judaism insists that our world is far from ideal. It believes we cannot be left exclusively to our own devices; it believes that we need a legal tradition to guide us.

Significant portions of the Christian Bible accuse the Jews in the time of Jesus of being preoccupied with matters of law (Acts 15:5 and Luke 5:17 are two famous examples). Many Christians have argued that this focus on law is a narrow, almost mean-spirited approach to life. The Jewish response, however, is that the issue is not theology, but a basic assessment of human motivation and of the needs of society. It is not only theology that makes law important, they could have said, but human nature itself. Here, too, a Judaism with law at its core would give Jews a sense that they had something to contribute, a model to offer, a blessing to share.

JEWISH LAW AS A FORCE FOR MODERATION

Yet beyond even all this, law plays another critical role in Jewish life. Judaism believes that law repairs society, bringing to reality the tradition's assertion that "all the nations of the world will be blessed" through Abraham's descendants. How does this happen? It happens, the tradition asserts, because Jewish law acts as a force for moderation in a world that desperately needs it.

It might seem strange that Judaism would see law as a tool for moderation. In our world, courts too often seem interested in politics more than justice, and litigation has replaced conversation. In a world torn virtually asunder by radicalism on the left as well as on the right, Jewish tradition invokes law as a means of reminding the world that no one has complete access to truth. Jewish law insists that passion for our most deeply held convictions must be tempered with a sense of humility—a constant awareness that we might be wrong.

Though this may sound surprising to many Jews, that is actually one of the most central commitments of Jewish law. *Halakhah,* Judaism's legal system, tries to offer answers to complex questions in a way that acknowledges that we can never be certain that we know "the truth and the whole truth." It tries to be committed to certain distinct behaviors and yet to create respect for other positions that may disagree. It does this not only in theory, but in practice as well. Let's look at two examples. One is taken from a traditional text, and the other from a well-known ritual.

The Mishnah—Preserving Minority Opinions

After the Bible, the first major text to become central to Jewish life was the Mishnah. Other texts had been composed and collected between the Bible and the Mishnah, but none achieved the canonical status that the Mishnah did when it was codified by Rabbi Judah the Prince in approximately 220 C.E. Rabbi Judah did

not "write" the Mishnah. Rather, he collected, selected and organized hundreds of individual oral teachings from among many
more, creating the first formal collection of these teachings.

Because so much of the Mishnah deals with legal matters,
many people consider the Mishnah a work of Jewish law; they
are largely correct. But before we accept too blithely this notion
that Mishnah is "simply" a law code, we ought to look more carefully at its style. Consider the very first passage of the Mishnah:

> From what time may they recite the *Shema* in the evening?
> From the hour that the priests enter [their homes] to eat their
> heave offerings, until the end of the first watch—[this is the
> view] of Rabbi Eliezer. But the sages say: Until midnight.
> Rabban Gamaliel says: Until the rise of dawn. [Rabban
> Gamaliel's] sons returned from a banquet hall [after mid-
> night]. They said to him: We did not [yet] recite the *Shema*.
> He said to them: If the dawn has not yet risen, you are obli-
> gated to recite [the *Shema*].
>
> (BERAKHOT 1:1)

For a law book, this is a very strange opening passage. After
all, the Mishnah assumes that the reader knows what the *Shema* is
and what its various components are. The Mishnah also takes for
granted that the reader understands that the *Shema* must be said
in the evening (and in the morning as well), and that the reader's
only question is by when in the evening the *Shema* must be
recited. Furthermore, it is not entirely clear why a law book
would include the brief anecdote contained in the second half of
the paragraph.

But even more perplexing is the Mishnah's failure to tell the
reader which of the three legal positions is actually the "correct"
one. After all, there are three opinions in the first paragraph.
Rabbi Eliezer says the *Shema* can be recited until the end of the
first watch, the Sages say until midnight, and Rabban Gamaliel
says until dawn! Who is "right"?

There is no simple answer to that. The *Shulḥan Arukh,* the premier code of Jewish law, says that ideally one should recite the *Shema* as soon as the stars have appeared, but that technically, one *may* recite it as late as the early rise of dawn (*Shulḥan Arukh, Oraḥ Ḥayyim* 235:3). Already, compromise begins to emerge clearly as a Jewish legal value.

But there is something even more important here than this "compromising" position. The Mishnah—and the Talmud which followed it several hundred years later—make a consistent practice of recording "unaccepted" views. Rabbi Eliezer and the Sages are ultimately not the legal bottom line in this case. But their opinions are studied by all who open the Mishnah. The Talmud is filled with literally thousands of "losing" opinions, each of which is recorded alongside the "winning" position, and each of which is accorded the same degree of respect and seriousness as the opinion that ultimately prevails.

This phenomenon continued throughout Jewish legal history, long after the Mishnah and Talmud were produced. Indeed, it even became an issue of serious contention some eight hundred years later. When Moses Maimonides (1135–1204) compiled his great legal work, the *Mishneh Torah,* in 1180, he was trying to create a concise legal reference that would provide the answers that proved so evasive in the Mishnah and Talmud. But he was assailed by major critics for having omitted the "minority" opinions. Even though hundreds of years of history had eradicated any possibility that these positions might prevail, Maimonides's *Mishneh Torah* was rejected out of hand by some authorities simply because it failed to preserve the debates found in the Mishnah and the Talmud. While the *Mishneh Torah* did go on to become one of Judaism's most important legal compilations, the objections to that work remain important.

Why? If the purpose of a legal system is to tell someone how to act, why preserve the opinions that are not ultimately codified?

Judaism's answer: we preserve these opinions because no one has exclusive access to the truth. Judaism worries that a sense of certainty can cause disregard and contempt for the other. Absolute certainty is the root of tyranny, the tradition claims. We need ambiguity in order to generate respect for other possibilities. While it is not only unavoidable, but even desirable, that we will become passionate about positions we hold, the unique nature of Jewish legal debate forces us to maintain respect for the other even in the face of passion.

The Mezuzah—A Pervasive Mark of Compromise

This fundamental Jewish belief, so at odds with the prevailing view of secular society, is reflected not only in Jewish texts but in ritual as well. Though many Jewish rituals suggest the importance of validating conflicting positions, the most classic example is the *mezuzah*.

The *mezuzah* is a small container that is affixed to doorposts and that contains sacred texts (including the above-mentioned *Shema*) inside. The practice of affixing a *mezuzah* to doorposts is as old as the Torah, and is commanded in a part of the *Shema* itself:

> 4Hear, O Israel! The LORD is our God, the LORD alone. 5You shall love the LORD your God with all your heart and with all your soul and with all your might. 6Take to heart these instructions with which I charge you this day. 7Impress them upon your children. Recite them when you stay at home and when you are away, when you lie down and when you get up. 8Bind them as a sign on your hand and let them serve as a symbol on your forehead; 9*inscribe them on the doorposts of your house and on your gates.*
>
> (DEUTERONOMY 6:4–9)

But how should we affix these words to doorposts? On which side? In what position? Here, the Torah is silent. Over the course of time, Jewish tradition decided that the *mezuzah* should be affixed to the right side of the doorway, approximately two thirds of the way up. It is also our custom to affix the *mezuzah* on a diagonal, with the bottom end of the *mezuzah* facing toward the outside and the upper end facing in. But as was true with the *Omer*, this seemingly innocuous practice actually has profound implications.

Interestingly, our current custom of placing the *mezuzah* diagonally on the doorpost does not follow either of the two major positions on this question. The first view was offered by Rashi (1040–1105), perhaps the greatest biblical and talmudic commentator in all of Jewish history. According to Rashi, the *mezuzah* should be placed on the doorpost in a completely vertical position. But Rashi's grandson, Rabbenu Tam, disagreed. Rabbenu Tam (1096–1171) was one of the most important legal authorities of the Middle Ages. He argued that the *mezuzah* should be affixed to the doorpost horizontally. What is significant about modern Jewish custom is that it follows neither the position of Rashi nor the suggestion of Rabbenu Tam. Indeed, the custom that we currently follow is at variance with everyone. None of the important classical authorities argued for placing the *mezuzah* diagonally. Thus, on one level, modern Jewish practice is essentially wrong!

But this seemingly "incorrect" custom has its own wisdom. The *mezuzah*, which greets Jews as they enter buildings and rooms, serves as a symbol of compromise and moderation. Hung in a position that satisfies neither major opinion but that takes both seriously, it becomes a ritual that invokes the ideal of compromise. It urges us to follow its example, to temper passion with humility, to balance conviction with openness. That is clearly the point of the following Mishnah:

And why do they record the opinion of Shammai and of Hillel [if the law follows only one of the two]? To teach the generations to come that a person should not be stubborn about his opinion, for lo, the patriarchs of the world were not stubborn about their opinion.

And why do they record the opinion of an individual

along with that of the majority, since the law follows the opinion of the majority? So that, if a court should prefer the opinion of the individual, it may decide to rely upon it.

(EIDUYOT 1:4–5)

Even cases that seem to be settled, the Mishnah suggests, should never be seen as totally resolved. There was undoubtedly wisdom and some truth in the position that did not prevail; a balanced and caring world needs to preserve those insights, as well. That moderation is a value to which an authentic reading of the Jewish tradition is passionately committed.

One well-known talmudic text reflects these values almost poetically:

> R. Abba stated in the name of Samuel: For three years there was a dispute between the School of Shammai and the School of Hillel. The former asserted, "the *halakhah* is in agreement with our views," while the latter insisted, "the *halakhah* is in agreement with our views." Then a heavenly voice announced, "both are the words of the living God, but the *halakhah* is in agreement with the rulings of the School of Hillel."
>
> Since "both are the words of the living God," why was the School of Hillel entitled to have the *halakhah* fixed in agreement with their rulings? Because they were kindly and modest, they studied their own rulings but also those of the School of Shammai, and were so humble that they mentioned the actions of the House of Shammai before their own.

(ERUVIN 13B)

Yet text and ritual are not enough. If these values in Jewish tradition are to make any difference to our lives, they have to find a place in the agonizing decisions that often shape us. Theory is fine for scholars, but we need a place where we can feel this moderation, where we can sense the tradition struggling inside our own consciences. Judaism has to urge moderation not only in the library, but in the questions that arouse our passion, that keep us awake in the dark of night.

But does that happen in Jewish tradition? Indeed, it does. Ours is a tradition of the mind, but also of the heart. In many critical areas, Judaism moves out of theory and into practice, bringing this value to bear on the real-life issues that confront us. No issues are more agonizing and divisive in our society than those of abortion and capital punishment. As we'll now see, Judaism's belief in the importance of moderation even in the face of passion clearly colors its pronouncements on both these issues.

ABORTION—JUDAISM'S EFFORT AT MODERATION

Few issues polarize modern American life more than that of abortion. Once a religious and moral question, abortion is now the subject of heated social and political debate. No candidate for major public office can hope to be elected without committing to some position on the subject, and for many voters in the United States, the abortion issue alone is sufficient reason either to endorse or to oppose a given candidate.

Yet abortion is more than polarizing. It is agonizing. We are torn between the precious and innocent life just beginning, and the harsh realities of the world just outside. Rape. Incest. Poverty. Shame. How are we to balance these with the sanctity of the life taking form? Women who have felt a child kicking inside them know that this is more than theory. Men who have placed their hands on their wives' abdomens, sensing the movement of a child that they know they created, understand that the choice for others can be horrific. What is right? And what would be horribly wrong?

The notion that Jews or Judaism might have something distinct to contribute to the abortion discussion strikes many people as surprising, at best. When asked, most Jews respond almost automatically that Judaism is "pro-choice." They might agree with Judaism's position, or they might disagree. But very few Jews have a sense that Judaism has a unique—and critical—contribution to make to this debate.

Interestingly, the Torah actually says nothing about abortion. But one section about miscarriage is almost always cited in discussions of the Jewish view of abortion:

> [22]When men fight, and one of them pushes a pregnant woman and a miscarriage results, but no other damage ensues, the one responsible shall be fined according as the woman's husband may exact from him, the payment to be based on reckoning. [23]But if other damage ensues, the penalty shall be life for life, [24]eye for eye, tooth for tooth, hand for hand, foot for foot, [25]burn for burn, wound for wound, bruise for bruise.
>
> (EXODUS 21:22–25)

It is clear from the Torah's language that the loss of the fetus is not considered a loss of actual life. The phrase "no other damage ensues" means that the mother did not die. If the fetus is lost but the mother is not killed, then compensation is given exclusively in monetary form.

How does this prove that the fetus is not a life? Is it not possible that even compensation for loss of life would be given in the form of money? No, it is not. For later in the same passage, when the text reads "but if other damage ensues," the biblical punishment for causing loss of life is clear—it is eye for eye, tooth for tooth, life for life. If the fetus were "life," the punishment would be life for life. But it is not. From this early biblical source, it is obvious that Judaism does not consider the fetus a full-fledged human being.

It might seem, therefore, that Judaism is "pro-choice," if only by implication. But we need to read on. Explicit discussion of abortion emerges in the Jewish tradition somewhat later, in the Mishnah. There, we read about a woman whose life is in danger because of a very difficult delivery:

> The woman who is in hard labor—they dismember the child in her womb and they remove it limb by limb, because her life takes precedence over his life. If its greater part has gone forth, they do not touch him, for they do not set aside one life on account of another life.
>
> (OHALOT 7:6)

Here, too, even at nine months (for the woman is already in labor in this instance), the fetus is not a human being in the fullest sense. If the delivery threatens the mother's life, the fetus must be removed from her "limb by limb"—quite obviously causing its death—in order to save her. The woman in this case does not make a decision. She does not choose between her own life and the life of the fetus; the fetus simply must be aborted. Judaism, therefore, is not "pro-life," because it does not believe that the fetus is a full human being. And as we have begun to see, it is not "pro-choice," because the woman does not choose. If anything, Jewish tradition occupies a middle position. Might we call it "anti-choice"? It's not a phrase that Madison Avenue would promote; but it does capture the essence of what Jewish tradition says.

Other sources clearly reject the "fetus as part of the woman's body"—or "pro-choice" argument. The Talmud (*Yevamot* 69b) specifically notes that until forty days after conception, the fetus is considered *maya be-alma,* or "mere water." By obvious implication, the Talmud is also suggesting that after forty days, the fetus is not "mere water." It is something much more significant. It may not be accorded the full status of a born person, but neither can its potential humanity be denied. Subsequent Jewish law outlawed nontherapeutic abortion. Although some important halakhic (Jewish legal) authorities interpreted "therapeutic" rather broadly (including emotional distress as well as physical danger), their basic point was clear: abortion is not a "right" and it is not a Jewishly permissible form of birth control.

Traditional Jewish law ends up saying something much subtler than either of the two basic American positions. It rejects out of hand the "fetus as human being" claim. It not only permits abortion when the mother's life is in danger (originally, for physical reasons, and later, for reasons including mental health), but actually commands abortion in such cases. No Jewish woman whose life is in danger from a pregnancy and who could be saved by abortion has the right to choose death over abortion. The Torah's perspective is best summarized by the phrase "therefore choose life, that you and your descendants may live" (Deuteronomy 30:19).

But our tradition also rejects the "fetus as part of the woman's body" argument. No traditional Jewish sources speak of abortion in terms of the woman's right. None reflect the notion that a fetus is simply a "thing" to be disposed of at will. Judaism typically permits abortion only in the narrowest of circumstances— when the mother's life is endangered.

As we consider the differences between Jewish tradition's perspective and the two basic modern American positions we outlined above, it becomes clear that Judaism could, in fact, become a significant and distinct voice in American life. A Jewish community less interested in equating Judaism with generic liberalism and more intent on a serious encounter with Jewish tradition and its sources would have a great deal to add to the debate. It would suggest that the fetus might be seen as neither a "thing" nor a "person." It might argue for a public policy (unpopularly called "anti-choice") that involved neither blanket prohibition nor complete sanction, but that argued for a more thoughtful middle position.

Most importantly, a Jewish community aware of its own tradition's sense of conflict could try to temper the stridency of American society's debate. It could point, with great Jewish authenticity, to the real goal: the recognition of complexity. A Jewish voice would not *solve* the issue for American society. That is not the goal. But it *could* suggest to both the "pro-life" and the "pro-choice" movements that they are equally mistaken in having reduced a subtle and painful issue to slogans.

We ought not confuse Judaism's compromise or ambivalence with apathy. A tradition that both commands abortion in certain cases but that forbids it in many others is not a tradition predicated on a lack of interest; it is a tradition committed to recognizing complexity. Judaism insists that the value of religion ought not be in providing pithy theological positions that make intricate questions facile. Its real value is in sensitizing human beings and society to the profound intricacies raised by issues such as abortion. Some people want absolute answers. They think that what matters is *resolving* questions, not dwelling on them without end. That may or may not be true, but Judaism disagrees.

As 3 or 4 percent of the American population, Jews are not going to determine the political outcome of this debate one way or the other. If a tide of American opinion developed in either direction, Jews—even if united—could do little to change it. The American Jewish community, however, needs its own voice for a different reason: it needs to recognize that it has something valuable to say. We need to be able to participate in the debates currently filling the American public square as Jews, with an authentic Jewish voice.

Yet how characteristic of Judaism is this abortion discussion? Is all of Jewish legal tradition committed to this delicate balancing of passion and moderation? Important as the style of the Mishnah, the position of the *mezuzah* and this approach to abortion may be, more evidence of this policy of moderation would be useful. Capital punishment provides it.

CAPITAL PUNISHMENT IN THE JEWISH TRADITION—
A STUDY IN UNRESOLVED AMBIVALENCE

Like abortion, capital punishment tears at the heart of American life. We watch accounts of horrific kidnappings and murders of young children, and we believe in our heart of hearts that the murderer should die. Neighborhoods are gripped in fear as stalkers terrorize them, and they vow that if the person is caught, there will be no mercy.

But then life gets complicated. We read of how the criminal was victimized as a young child, how he grew up without love, in constant terror. We read that African-Americans get sentenced to death at much higher rates than whites. And we wonder, what is fair?

Unlike abortion, which is discussed only scantily in the classic sources, capital punishment is addressed in countless instances in both the Bible and later rabbinic literature. Indeed, the Bible virtually opens with a clear suggestion that punishment by death is a vital part of its system of justice. Even before the Torah begins telling the story of the Jewish people, it describes God's commands to Noah and his children after the ark settles at the end of the primordial flood. In this passage, known in later Jewish tradition as the "Seven Noahide Commandments" (seven basic rules that apply to all human beings, Jewish or not), capital punishment figures prominently. When Noah and his sons have departed the ark after its settling on Mount Ararat, God says to them:

> [3]Every creature that lives shall be yours to eat; as with the green grasses, I give you all these. [4]You must not, however, eat flesh with its life-blood in it. [5]But for your own life-blood I will require a reckoning: I will require it of every beast; of man, too, will I require a reckoning for human life, of every

man for that of his fellow man! ⁶Whoever sheds the blood of
man, by man shall his blood be shed; For in His image did
God make man.

(GENESIS 9:3–6)

There is a profound irony in this passage. Human beings, the
Torah suggests, are unlike other animals. We are unique in that
we are created in God's image. For that reason, spilling human
blood has to be punished in the severest possible manner. Ironically, however, spilling human blood is punished by perpetuating
the "crime": more blood must be spilled.

The irony notwithstanding, however, the Torah is not
ambivalent about capital punishment. Time and again, it mandates capital punishment for a whole host of transgressions. In
one passage, for example, the Torah prescribes death for a variety
of transgressions in rapid succession:

¹²He who fatally strikes a man shall be put to death. . . .
¹⁴When a man schemes against another and kills him treach
erously, you shall take him from My very altar to be put to
death. ¹⁵He who strikes his father or his mother shall be put
to death. ¹⁶He who kidnaps a man—whether he has sold him
or is still holding him—shall be put to death. ¹⁷He who insults
his father or his mother shall be put to death.

(EXODUS 21:12–17)

Nor is that all; the list of capital crimes in the Torah is far
more extensive. The Torah mandates death for, among many
others, approaching Mount Sinai as Moses prepares to ascend it
(Exodus 19:12), bestiality (Exodus 22:19), violations of the Shabbat
(Exodus 31:14–15), adultery (Leviticus 20:10) and worshiping foreign gods (Leviticus 20:2). The list goes on. In the five books of
the Torah alone, the phrase "put to death" appears forty-four
times. In the entire Hebrew Bible, it appears sixty times.

But as much as the Torah insists on capital punishment, it is also concerned that the punishment not be abused. In Deuteronomy, the Torah discusses the punishment of a man or woman who has engaged in idolatry:

> 5You shall take the man or the woman who did that wicked thing out to the public place, and you shall stone them, man or woman, to death.—6A person shall be put to death only on the testimony of two or more witnesses; he must not be put to death on the testimony of a single witness.—7Let the hands of the witnesses be the first against him to put him to death, and the hands of the rest of the people thereafter. Thus you will sweep out evil from your midst.
>
> (DEUTERONOMY 17:5–7)

Suddenly, the picture becomes somewhat more complex. Though the Torah enumerates an enormous list of transgressions punishable by death, it also prohibits excessive use of the punishment. Not only must crimes punishable by death be witnessed, the witnesses must also commence the execution. Did the Torah intend this to somehow limit the number of executions that would take place? It is difficult to know. Do we find, already embedded within the Torah's commands about capital punishment, some deeply rooted ambivalence?

Perhaps. But perhaps not. Maybe the Torah has no ambivalence about capital punishment. Maybe its requirements about witnessing and the witnesses' throwing the first stone are simply designed to make the process as fair as possible. But if the Torah itself reflects no ambivalence, the same cannot be said for sections of the rabbinic tradition that followed.

The rabbis' ambivalence about capital punishment is most evident when they discuss witnesses. The Torah mandates (Deuteronomy 17:6) that there be at least two witnesses before capital punishment is invoked. But it says nothing about what those witnesses must actually see or do. That "omission," however, is addressed in a rabbinic work very much like the Mishnah, composed somewhat later:

> As for anyone liable to the death penalty [when] imposed by a court, they convict them only on the testimony of witnesses, after warning, and after they inform him that [what he is about to do] subjects him to liability to the death penalty in court. Rabbi Yosé bar Rav Judah says: "Only if they will inform him specifically of the sort of death penalty to which he will be subjected." . . . [If] they warn him and he was silent, or if they warn him and he nods his head, even though he says: "I know,"—he is exempt—unless he will say: "I know it, and it is with that very stipulation that I am doing what I am doing!"
>
> (TOSEFTA SANHEDRIN II:1–2)

Note what the Tosefta says here. It says that the witnesses must not only see the crime, they must actually communicate with the criminal. They must tell him that what he is about to do is a capital crime (and according to Rabbi Yosé bar Rav Judah, they must even know—and tell him—to which of the four forms of capital punishment he will be subjected). Moreover, the Tosefta continues, the perpetrator-to-be must hear the witnesses, acknowledge them, and even claim that it is specifically for the purpose of being executed in that fashion that he is about to commit this crime!

What has happened here? While the Torah stipulates the death penalty for a whole host of offenses, the rabbinic tradition made carrying out the death penalty virtually impossible. How conceivable is it that such a conversation between two witnesses and a murderer (or adulterer) could actually take place? How many executions could there possibly be with these requirements?

The answer, of course, is few—if any. While the Torah commands capital punishment, the rabbinic tradition seems to forbid it. What greater demonstration of ambivalence could there possibly be? The common question, What does Judaism say about capital punishment? is even more impossible to answer than the question, What does Judaism say about abortion? Judaism says many things, contradictory things. It says that there are certain crimes so heinous that the person who commits them deserves to die. But it also says that taking human life is enormously complicated, for the destruction of a human being is the destruction of a reflection of God's image. It says not only that the judicial process must be fair, but that real fairness may be impossible. Is it even saying that capital punishment can never be implemented fairly?

Again, the incongruence of such opposing claims is precisely the point that the Jewish tradition makes. When people become wholly convinced that their position is airtight, the tradition suggests, something has gone awry. Capital punishment ought to be an agonizing issue. The person no longer agonized about her position, the tradition says, has lost that crucial sense of the complexity and profundity of the issue. From a Jewish perspective, social policy and the discourse of the public square are not benefited by the strident quarrels between Robert Dole and Edward Kennedy, or Rush Limbaugh and Howard Stern, or even the NRA and the ACLU. When discourse on society's most pressing issues becomes a cacophony of two opposing positions, each thoroughly convinced of its correctness, Jewish tradition would assert that we all lose.

We live in an era of left-wing and right-wing journals, in which the positions advocated in articles are often predictable based on just the name of the magazine. That, of course, is partly unavoidable and is to a certain extent the result of marketing necessities. But the rabbis of the Talmud would have been saddened—and profoundly disconcerted—to find a society in which people primarily chose to read positions with which they agreed. Most books in modern society reflect the views of the author, and the author alone; in contrast, each page of the Talmud is an argument, a debate. Not a single page contains just one person's view. The difference between these American and Jewish "pages" speaks volumes.

It is not accidental that the Talmud, essentially the "transcripts" of debates that took place in the lively rabbinic academies of old, is effectively a twenty-volume-long argument. While Hollywood caricatures of traditional rabbis often involve "on the one hand . . . and on the other hand" stories, the tradition is not ashamed of that characteristic. People may chuckle at images of the traditional rabbi unable to make up his mind because both sides of a dispute seem legitimate to him, but Judaism sees that as a virtue. In a much remembered scene, Tevye, in *Fiddler on the Roof,* speaks to himself and vacillates between different decisions, saying "on the one hand . . . but on the other hand . . ." He's an adorable character at that moment, and most of us resonate to his feelings. We've all been there. But in truth, Tevye is more than adorable. He represents an important dimension of Jewish tradition.

One last Mishnah on the subject of capital punishment should make that clear:

> A Sanhedrin [high court] which imposes the death penalty once in seven years is called murderous. Rabbi Eleazar ben Azariah says, "once in seventy years." Rabbi Tarfon and Rabbi Akiba say, "if we were on a Sanhedrin, no one would ever be put to death." Rabban Simeon ben Gamaliel says, "then you would multiply the number of murderers in Israel."
>
> (MAKKOT 1:10)

Rabbi Eleazar ben Azariah says that even one execution in seventy years is too much. Rabbi Tarfon and Rabbi Akiba say that any execution ever is too much. But Rabban Simeon ben

Gamaliel has no patience for what he considers their naïveté. "Stop executing murderers," he says, "and you'll only make matters worse. Society must simply be rid of people who kill."

Rabbinic literature has no tolerance for a society that no longer engages in serious debate. Ours is a world, the Talmud would have said, in which complex issues are too often oversimplified, in which the agonizing is too frequently reduced to the easily resolvable. Judaism insists that the world needs more; the genius of Judaism's tradition is its devotion to training Jews to think that way.

LAW AND THE POSSIBILITY OF SAFE PASSION

Why is moderation so important to Jewish life? There are many reasons, of course, some of which we've mentioned. But one additional factor is important.

Jewish tradition knows that religion without passion is meaningless. A tradition that resides only in our minds and never pulls on our heartstrings does not touch us where we live most deeply. That, for many American Jews, is precisely the problem with contemporary Jewish life. It is sometimes interesting but too infrequently passionate, energized and compelling.

But therein lies a problem. If religion without passion is lifeless and unimportant, religion with passion can sometimes be dangerous. It can lead to extremes, to zealotry. One of Judaism's great insights has been that religious law is one way of reining in that potentially explosive passion, without destroying it altogether.

In Chapter One, we examined God's command on how to treat Amalek, the tribe that the Torah says attacked the Israelites on their journey from Egypt to the Promised Land. What is to be our reaction? The command is clear:

> Therefore, when the Lord your God grants you safety from
> all your enemies around you, in the land that the Lord your

God is giving you as a hereditary portion, you shall blot out
the memory of Amalek from under heaven. Do not forget!

(DEUTERONOMY 25:19)

The Torah is rather unforgiving in its insistence that Amalek be
destroyed. Indeed, in I Samuel 15, King Saul commits what is
described as a sin by failing to kill all the Amalekites' cattle, and
for that, the Bible says, he ultimately lost his throne.

Couple this insistence on revenge against Amalek with
Purim, the holiday on which Jews recall the Amalekites (because
Haman, the villain of Purim, is said to have been a descendent of
Amalek), and it suddenly becomes somewhat less difficult to
understand how Baruch Goldstein could kill Muslims at prayer in
their mosque on Purim in 1994. Most Jewish observers were horrified at this display of violence and hatred, and said that Goldstein's sentiments had no place in Jewish life or tradition. But
wasn't Goldstein simply acting in accordance with the thrust of
the command in Deuteronomy? How can Jews read that passage,
and then condemn Goldstein?

The answer—Jewish law. There is, whether we like it or not,
an element of Jewish tradition that *does* seek revenge against the
enemies of the Jews for what they have done. But while such passion is viewed as either natural or even potentially positive, it cannot remain ungoverned. Jewish thought *might* countenance
Goldstein's anger at his enemies (though why those people sit-
ting quietly in prayer were his enemies is far from clear); Jewish
law, however, rejected absolutely his right to kill them. That is
what even the most right-wing religious groups in Israel and
throughout the world said after the murders, and they were
right.

When politically left-wing and even moderate Jews
responded to Goldstein's attack by saying that the feelings that
gave rise to his actions have no place in Jewish life, they were mistaken. (They would have done better by noting that even the
Bible says [in I Chronicles 4:43] that Amalek no longer exists.) We

may be embarrassed by Goldstein's feelings, and we certainly
might not share them. But an honest reading of our tradition
does not support the contention that Goldstein's views had no
basis in Jewish tradition. The more correct assertion would have
been that while the tradition resonates to some of his feelings, its
legal component simply forbids his actions.

Why did many Jewish observers not make this distinction? In
part, they were so humiliated by Goldstein that they simply
wanted to assert that the tradition had no place for anything that
he stood for. But beyond that, many of those observers represent
streams of Jewish life in which Jewish law has become marginal-
ized, if not irrelevant altogether. American Jews, in their effort to
make Judaism "fit" better into suburban America and the West's
focus on autonomy, have moved far away from law as a critical
dimension of Jewish life. For them to begin to make fine legal
distinctions at a moment like that would have been the height of
irony, and they knew that. The tragedy is that because law is so
foreign to most American Jews' conception of what Judaism is,
they had to either err (and say that the tradition did not reflect
any of Goldstein's sentiments) or be silent. Ironically, the only
ones who could intelligently condemn Goldstein based on Jewish values were the religious right. Because most of the Jewish
world had nothing to say beyond a platitudinous (and incorrect)
assertion that Judaism forbids killing, the world got a skewed
image of what Judaism's options are. And Jews lost a profound
opportunity to illustrate the complexity and profundity of their
tradition.

But this only points to the challenge that searching for an
authentic Jewish identity will present us. A Jewish role in the modern world that is not platitudinous but that is also not elitist, that
is both distinctly Jewish and intellectually sophisticated, may well
require more than thought. It may actually demand of us new
commitments to Jewish behavior. There is no reason to believe
that standing for something should be easy, or that it should be
unrelated to who we are and how we live. Jews will have to

decide—honestly and forthrightly—whether or not Judaism without law at the center is either meaningful or authentic.

OURS IS A world too often painful, too frequently frightening. It
is an unforgiving world, a world in which the very fabric of social
convention is frayed to the point of seeming irreparable. It is a
world in which no matter how secure one's neighborhood, a dangerous locale seems to lurk immediately around the corner. It is
a world in which the more complex problems become, the more
simplistic and boisterous are the solutions offered.

Judaism does not pretend that it can resolve these issues. But
Jewish tradition does have a unique contribution to make to the
discussion. In Jewish discourse, certainty is taboo. Judaism—in its
rituals, its literature and its legal arguments—insists that intelligent debate is never easy, and that simple solutions are probably
illusions.

Sadly, most Jews are not aware that this is our model. We have
internalized America's sound-bite mentality, so that our most
common questions about Judaism are usually no more thoughtful than, What does Judaism say about. . . ? When they ask those
questions, most Jews want a quick answer. More often than not,
they want to be assured that what Judaism has to say is in keeping
with what they already believe. When Jews ask what Judaism says
about abortion, they typically want reaffirmation that their personal views are endorsed by their tradition. The same with capital punishment, attitudes toward illegal immigrants, welfare
reform and on and on. Too often, they ask those questions to
avoid struggle rather than to engage in it.

American Jews have reveled in this "greatest hits" approach to
Jewish life not only because it allowed Judaism to confirm positions we already held, but because this sort of encounter with
Jewish life demanded nothing from us. We could ask others what
Judaism said, without having to consider the possibility that the
tradition was so complex that we needed to learn and to
encounter it ourselves.

But that will no longer work. If Judaism is to matter, American Jews need to let it speak. We've seen that much of Judaism's distinctive content appears only through its texts and its law. Thus, the American Jewish community has to decide if it is serious enough about mattering to reengage these texts—and their law—once again. When the People of the Book, a name first given to the Jews as a compliment by the Muslims, become strangers to their own books, that people has no choice but to remain silent.

Because so many of Judaism's texts are legal, it will be virtually impossible to reencounter Judaism's texts without an openness to its law. It is no accident that Talmud and other traditional texts tend to be studied in the traditional community infinitely more than in the nontraditional community. For nontraditional Jews, committed to the centrality of individual autonomy, the consistent study of texts that speak in terms of "ought" and "must" and "are commanded to" creates a painful cognitive dissonance. Why study texts that speak in a language you have consciously rejected?

To recapture the richness of our tradition and the sophistication of our message, we have to return to those ancient texts, the tomes that Allan Bloom called "wise old books." But in order to do that, Jews will have to be willing to consider once again the centrality of law in their tradition. That means that in a viable American Jewish future, the significant dividing lines will not be between Orthodox, Conservative, Reconstructionist and Reform. They will not be between right wing and left wing, or between politically liberal and conservative. The dividing lines that will matter in American Jewish life will be between those communities that engage in serious dialogue and encounter with Jewish law, and those that don't. The lines will be between Jews willing to cede part of their autonomy to a tradition that demands allegiance, and those who will not make that concession.

Who will survive? Who will have a message worth hearing?

The answer is clear: those parts of the community that have not divorced themselves from the reservoir of substance that had always characterized Jewish life until the sirens of Western liberal American society proved too alluring. How many of us will that be? Our survival may depend upon the answer.

CHAPTER SIX

Standing Uncomfortably Outside the Mainstream—Reclaiming Our Subversive Heritage

*I*n 1914, Woodrow Wilson told a group of immigrants to America, "You cannot become thorough Americans if you think of yourself in groups. America does not consist of groups. A man who thinks of himself as belonging to a particular national group in America has not yet become an American."

Woodrow Wilson was hardly the only person to feel this way. Blending in was *the* American ethic of that time. In the early 1900s, workers at the Ford Motor Company were all but required to attend an Americanization school. At this school, they studied proper English, learned American manners and were taught to shed the distinctive characteristics they had brought with them to this country. Ford even created rituals to drive the point home. As they completed their studies, the students participated in a graduation ceremony, in which

> all the men descend from a boat scene representing the vessel on which they came over; down the gangway . . . into a pot . . . which represents the Ford English School. Six teachers, three on either side, stir the pot with ten foot ladles representing nine months of teaching in the school. Into the pot 52 nationalities with their foreign clothes and baggage go and out of the pot after vigorous stirring by the teachers comes one nationality, viz. American.

Today, in the radicalized multicultural and multiethnic society that is America, the Ford ceremony seems both insensitive and contrived; President Wilson's admonition seems naive, almost absurd. It is simply not true that "America does not consist of groups." Life in America is all about groups. Admittedly, this society might be simpler (and more pleasant at times) had Wilson's vision become reality, but it simply never did.

The fault lines between groups in America are many. Ours is a society divided by race, place of origin, socioeconomic status, political philosophy, sexual preference and orientation and—no less important than any of these—religion.

Paradoxically, while most of America has ignored Wilson's admonition, Jews have taken it rather seriously. Eager to play a major role in the creation of this "boundary-less" society, the American Jewish community did exactly what Wilson implicitly encouraged. We concentrated on being Americans, and in a predominantly Christian culture, we focused on the similarities between Christianity and our own religion.

Of course, American Jews never argued that there would no longer be different religions. That would have spelled the end of Judaism. Rather, the American Jewish dream was simply that religion could become a relatively private matter, and that instead of focusing on the differences between us and others, we might pay attention instead to the many similarities between faiths.

It sounded wonderful, at least in theory. But as we've noted before, this position has undermined Jews' ability to explain why Judaism matters. Attention paid almost exclusively to the values they share with the Christian world has confused a younger generation of Jews; ours is a generation no longer certain what a Judaism so similar to Christianity offers to the world. Would the world be worse off if we disappeared?

Nor is this just a theoretical confusion. American Jews have bought into Wilson's implied vision so wholeheartedly that they often seem to believe that Judaism *is* Christianity, or at least, that the differences between Judaism and Christianity are meaning-less. Sound absurd? Consider the following story about the Jew-ish National Fund (JNF), the international organization that collects money from Jews around the world and then plants trees throughout Israel.

In 1996, the JNF announced that it had agreed to plant a forest of ten thousand trees for the Messianic Jewish Alliance of Amer-ica and the Union of Messianic Jewish Congregations, mission-ary groups that seek to convert Jews into followers of Jesus. These groups—not just Christian, but Christians committed to converting Jews to Christianity—would have raised approxi-mately $50,000 for the JNF. To be sure, $50,000 is a substantial sum, but it would hardly have changed the financial condition of the JNF in any serious way. Nonetheless, the JNF agreed to plant the forest and to install a permanent expression of thanks to the missionary organizations. The JNF, an international organization that had long been the pride of Jews throughout the world and a symbol of the rebirth of the Jewish state, saw nothing wrong with honoring missionizing groups by planting a grove in their honor in the Jewish homeland. For generations, Jewish families had placed coins in *pushkes* (little charity boxes) each week for the JNF to rebuild the land of Israel. The JNF was, at one point, vir-tually symbolic of our hope for a Jewish future. But now, deeply influenced by the prevailing American Jewish worldview, its lead-ers accepted the forest project with the proviso that the word "messianic" not be used, "apparently in deference to protests from Orthodox groups."

When the *Forward,* a New York–based Jewish newspaper, ran the story about the JNF decision, many people were outraged. Ultimately, the JNF was pressured into rescinding the plan. In an official statement, it said, "The Jewish National Fund, in response to a strong outpouring of protest . . . acknowledges that it made a mistake."

"Made a mistake"? That is like saying the *Titanic* had a leak! For hundreds of years, Jews have seen missionizing Christians as a grave danger. They understood that Judaism was not Christianity. They understood that Judaism and Christianity had split over serious issues, and that the attraction of Jews to Christianity had been a serious threat to Jewish thriving ever since. But, apparently, no longer. American Jews' inability to insist that Jews are not Christians, that Christians who missionize to Jews are threats to the Jewish people, has reached almost absurd proportions. The JNF decision was no simple mistake; it is evidence of a cancerous illness in the American Jewish psyche, a frightening universalism so pervasive that it knows almost no bounds. It is not, of course, that the trees were a danger or that non-Jews ought not be allowed to participate in building Israel. But this was not so simple a case; those who missionize Jews are a threat to the Jewish people, and the JNF decision was effectively an agreement to look the other way.

The JNF decision, thankfully, is hardly typical. Those sorts of egregious errors are rare in American Jewish life. But other indications of our inability to distinguish Judaism from Christianity are much more common. One of these is the ubiquitous phrase "Judeo-Christian ethic," a phrase Jews love to use but seldom think about clearly.

THE TRAP OF THE "JUDEO-CHRISTIAN TRADITION"

American Jews are deeply enamored of the idea of a "Judeo-Christian" tradition. Why? Because the words "Judeo-Christian" suggest that Jews in this society are not peripheral, but mainstream. When they hear that American culture is derived from both Christianity *and* Judaism, Jews feel welcomed—not only as outsiders but as insiders as well. Our attachment to the phrase "Judeo-Christian" enabled us to see ourselves not as welcome guests, but as essential founders of this republic and its system of values.

But there is a danger to this appealing idea. For if Jewish survival is going to require a unique Jewish voice, a distinct Jewish message, doesn't the suggestion that Judaism and Christianity are so similar actually undermine what we need most?

But that's really only part of the problem. Ultimately, the phrase "Judeo-Christian" just means "Christian." It pays lip service to Christianity's Jewish roots, but little more. After all, what is "Judeo" about the Judeo-Christian ethic that is not also Christian? What, in other words, is distinctively Jewish about that tradition? Why is it not simply a "Christian ethic"?

The Hebrew Bible is clearly part of that tradition, but Christians consider the "Old Testament" sacred. The Christian Bible (which Christians call the "New Testament") is also part of that tradition, but it is not sacred to Jews. In humanities courses at universities across the country, syllabi on the origins of the Western world and its great ideas typically include the Hebrew Bible, the Christian Bible, the writings of St. Augustine or St. Thomas Aquinas. But what about the Talmud? Rabbinic Midrash? Maimonides? Almost never. And why not? Because *those* texts are foreign to Christianity. Texts that are foreign to Judaism *are* included in the popular definition of the Judeo-Christian "core." Texts foreign to Christians are not. The bottom line: in America, "Judeo-Christian" is a polite way of saying "Christian," and American Jews so desperately wanted to be included that we never noticed.

This is not to suggest that Judaism and Christianity do not share profound roots. That Jewish values lie at the very core of Christianity, and therefore at the very core of American life as well, is beyond doubt. Jesus and his first disciples were Jews, and apparently well-educated Jews. Jesus' famed "last supper" was clearly a Passover Seder. Even the rituals of the two traditions often seem similar. While Judaism has a *mikveh* (a ritual bath for purification purposes), Catholic tradition has baptism. In the sacrament of communion, wafer and wine are central; at the Shabbat table, to name just one ritual, wine and challah are critical. Judaism and Christianity are both monotheistic traditions. Their ethics systems have much in common. And the list goes on. Judaism and Christianity *do* share much.

But that similarity is precisely our problem. Because Judaism and Christianity seem so alike, Jews who live in Christian cultures often cannot explain how their Jewishness sets them apart from the culture around them.

All of this unsettles us. We do not want to hear, after decades of trying to be indistinguishable from those around us, that becoming more comfortable in America is antithetical to Jewish mission, or undermining of Jewish survival. That is precisely the opposite of what we have been taught to believe. So we try denial: "What's so bad about being like the culture around us?"

To a certain extent, of course, nothing at all. Indeed, it is the shared values of Judaism and Christianity that have made the Jewish success story in America possible. But these similarities are also dangerous. They also contribute to a vision of Jewish life that is deeply inauthentic. Strange though it sounds to American Jews, Jewish tradition has always claimed that Jews need to be different in order that they might play a quasi-subversive role in society.

"Quasi-subversive," of course, does not mean that it is Jews' role to overthrow society! Rather, the goal is to be a contributing and respectful "thorn in the side" of society. But at the same time, our aim is not to be just like the world around us, but rather, to improve the world around us. Jews' role is not to second every motion in society, but to second-guess society's priorities. It is not only that Jews have an alternative position to espouse; the tradition occasionally insists that Jews have to be prophets, outcasts, harsh critics of prevailing social mores.

A KINGDOM OF PRIESTS AND A HOLY NATION—AGAIN

The idea that Jews are intended to be different emerges most clearly in a passage we have already examined. As we saw in Chapter Two, as the Children of Israel leave Egypt and begin their arduous trek across the desert, God explains their unique role in history with the following words:

³And Moses went up to God. The LORD called to him from the mountain, saying, "Thus shall you say to the house of Jacob and declare to the children of Israel: ⁴'You have seen what I did to the Egyptians, how I bore you on eagles' wings and brought you to Me. ⁵Now then, if you will obey Me faithfully and keep My covenant, you shall be My treasured possession among all the peoples. Indeed, all the earth is Mine, ⁶but you shall be to Me a kingdom of priests and a holy nation.' These are the words that you shall speak to the children of Israel."

(EXODUS 19:3–6)

Earlier, we focused on the conditional nature of Israel's place in the world; Jews will be God's treasured people, the Torah says, if and only if they uphold their share of the covenant. But there is another point to this passage, a subversive element to God's message. That element is expressed through the seemingly simple phrase "holy nation," a phrase that is important because of the unique characteristics of the word "holy" in Hebrew.

The word that the Torah uses for "holy" in this passage is *kadosh*, a term familiar to many Jews from the *Kaddish* (a memorial prayer) and the *Kiddush* (the prayer sanctifying the Sabbath or holidays, said over wine). But buried in the meaning of *kadosh* is not only the sense of "holy," but "separateness" as well. When the *Kiddush* speaks of making Shabbat holy, it means that Shabbat is sanctified specifically *because* it is somehow separated from the rest of the week. The liturgy that ends the Shabbat, the *Havdalah* service, makes that eminently clear:

Blessed are You, Lord our God, Ruler of the Universe, who separates the holy from the profane, light from dark . . . [and] the seventh day from the six days of creation. Praised are You, Lord, who separates the holy from the profane.

Havdalah suggests that for Jewish tradition, holiness is closely related to separateness or distinction.

Marriage is another example. In rabbinic Hebrew, one of the terms for marriage is *kiddushin,* a term based on that same root. Why? The tradition wanted to claim that the man and woman in question are now "separated" from the remainder of the community and linked distinctly to their spouse.*

Throughout Jewish tradition, holiness and separateness are related. And since chosenness and holiness are also related, chosenness is intrinsically bound up with separateness. Not an easy pill for American Jews to swallow. But our tradition is clear. Jewish tradition wants the Jews to matter, and it believes that in order to do that, Jews need more than a unique voice. We need to be distinguished from society, separate, even occasionally at odds with it.

Consider the liturgy again. Because *kadosh* means separate, we can retranslate one of Judaism's best-known phrases. The most commonly recited blessing formula in Jewish life reads *asher kiddeshanu be-mizvotav ve-zivannu . . .*

That phrase is almost omnipresent in Jewish life. We recite it as part of the blessing prior to lighting the Sabbath candles, before kindling Hanukkah lights, at the beginning of the wedding ceremony, at a *bris* and on dozens upon dozens of other occasions. Usually, prayer books translate that phrase as "who has sanctified us with commandments, and has commanded us to. . . ." But since *kadosh* also means "separate," the blessing actually has another meaning; it also means "who has made us distinct through the commandments, and has commanded us to. . . ." For Jews, to be "sanctified" means to be made distinct, even separated. Could that be a dimension of what chosenness means on the

---

*Prior to the Middle Ages, Judaism allowed men to marry more than one woman. Therefore, though our contemporary sensibilities differ, the classic rabbinic tradition would say it was actually the *woman* (and not the man) who was "set apart."

eve of the twenty-first century? Is it possible that for us, the issue is not betterness but separateness?

Havdalah, the ceremony that concludes Shabbat, makes the same point. The last time we looked at *Havdalah,* we omitted a portion. Consider it now in full:

> Blessed are You, Lord our God, Ruler of the Universe, who separates the holy from the profane, light from dark, *Israel from the other nations [of the world* and] the seventh day from the six days of creation. Praised are You, Lord, who separates the holy from the profane.

There are countless other examples, but Jewish tradition's claim is clear. Separateness is not a modern notion fashioned in an era of declining Jewish allegiance. It is not a recent invention with which Jews can respond to multiculturalism or a frightening rate of assimilation. It is an idea thousands of years old. This idea is as ancient as Exodus 19, as fundamental to Jewish life as the Torah that defines us.

COMFORT DOES NOT MAKE FOR SIGNIFICANCE

As central as this idea is to Judaism, American Jews do not want to hear it. We resist the notion of being outsiders in part because America was to be the land where there simply would be no outsiders (though that has clearly not happened), but perhaps more importantly, because being an outsider is uncomfortable. Many American Jews are actually pleased that there are some Jews committed enough to Jewish life to dress differently and live wholly different life-styles. But most would recoil at the idea that *they* themselves dress like that. Who, they wonder, would want to endure the stares, the changed and strained relationships with colleagues, neighbors, friends? It's not just a matter of dressing like Hasidim; for the vast majority of Jews in America, even wearing a *kippah* in public is a dramatic and profoundly uncomfortable statement of belonging. Jews in this society have been taught that a rich and fulfilling Jewish life could also be a distinctly comfortable one. Our tradition, we're beginning to see, disagrees.

Many of Judaism's greatest contributions in the past were due to our willingness to be different. In a pagan polytheistic world, Judaism introduced monotheism. In a world characterized by Hammurabi's code, the Torah was radical. It insisted that parents did not have the right to kill their children, that killing the stranger or a poor person was no less a crime than killing a rich person. To a world that all too often treated women as chattel, our tradition introduced the *ketubbah,* the traditional Jewish marriage document. The *ketubbah* guaranteed the woman that in the case of divorce, her husband would have to provide her at least a modicum of financial security. And other examples abound; many of our greatest moments have emerged when we dared to be different.

But to make Judaism compatible with American liberalism, Jews in this country (primarily on the left end of the Jewish religious spectrum) focused on the social message of the biblical prophets. Those prophets, we insisted, advocated compassion for the widow, concern for the orphan and commitment to the poor. Spreading *that* message, we said, would be our role.

But spreading a message is not always simple. What most Jews in America were not taught was that the biblical prophets never suggested that a prophetic people could be socially comfortable. Indeed, in many cases, the significance of the prophets' message was in inverse proportion to their own personal comfort. Isaiah, we are told, was compelled to walk naked to symbolize both his estrangement and his dedication to his calling:

> ²Previously, the LORD had spoken to Isaiah son of Amoz, saying, "Go, untie the sackcloth from your loins and take your sandals off your feet," which he had done, going naked and barefoot. ³And now the LORD said, "It is a sign and a portent

for Egypt and Nubia. Just as My servant Isaiah has gone
naked and barefoot for three years, 4so shall the king of
Assyria drive off the captives of Egypt and the exiles of
Nubia, young and old, naked and barefoot. . . ."

(ISAIAH 20:2–4)

The same was true of the prophet Hosea as well. Hosea
opens with an astounding demand: "When the Lord first spoke
to Hosea, the Lord said to Hosea, 'Go get yourself a wife of
whoredom and children of whoredom' " (Hosea 1:2). Why?
What was the point of God's command that the prophet marry a
prostitute? In part, God wanted Hosea to experience the disloy-
alty that God experienced when the Israelites worshiped other
gods. But in addition to that, the image clearly evokes a sense of
being a social outcast. The social alienation that results from
marrying a prostitute would be almost unbearable for most of
us. *That* is God's point; there is nothing easy about being
"prophetic." Bearing a message, "being a blessing," requires an
element of Otherness.

This notion that we cannot be completely integrated into the
surrounding society if we want to stand for something was made
perhaps most poignantly by the biblical exegete Isaac ben Judah
Abrabanel (1437–1508), who in his commentary on the Passover
Haggadah, penned the now famous phrase: *ein navi be-iro*—no
one can be a prophet in his or her own city (*Zevaḥ Pesaḥ* 54b).
There is something about comfort that denies the possibility of
prophecy. Somehow, feeling too much at home undermines our
ability to see what is wrong with the world in which we live.

The British poet and critic Matthew Arnold (1822–1888) once
remarked that the purpose of Greek philosophy was to make the
Greek comfortable in Athens, while the Hebrew prophet sought
to make the Jew uncomfortable even in Jerusalem. Perhaps the
time has come, if Jews are serious about Jewish survival and Jewish relevance, to become less comfortable in this surrogate
Jerusalem. Perhaps the critical Jewish question is not how Jews

can become ever more American, but how Jews armed with their tradition can contribute to America by critiquing some of its values. Can we learn to be both loving of our American setting and grateful for all it has provided us, while maintaining a distance from some of its values and priorities? The answer to that question may contain the key to whether or not we matter.

The Midrash was already aware that being part of the Jewish people might well mean being at odds with some of the world around us. Referring to the first time that Abraham was called a "Hebrew" (Genesis 14:13), it makes a play on the meaning of that word. For the root of *ivri*, the word that the Torah employs, can mean either "Hebrew" or "side," as in side of a river. Based on that, the Midrash remarks, "Abraham was on one side of the river, and the rest of the world was on the other" (*Genesis Rabbah* 42:8). About a millennium ago, the rabbis understood that there were times we and the rest of the world would be—and would need to be—on opposite sides of the river.

We know today what previous generations of American Jewish leaders may not have known; it is a delusion to think that being thoroughly American leads to being thoroughly Jewish. Quite the contrary. Wholesale Americanization of Judaism must eventually lead to the emasculation of Jewish life. Martin Luther King, Jr. made this claim perhaps most poignantly and pithily when he remarked, "If you don't stand for something, you'll fall for anything."

The challenge for contemporary American Jews is to begin to ask what a modern Jewish "prophetic" message might be. In many ways, the specific results of this investigation matter less than that it takes place. Different groups of Jews might well arrive at differing conclusions as to what the message should be.

But whatever its conclusions, the search needs to be sophisticated. Jews need to do justice to both Jewish tradition and the culture in which they live. The conversation cannot be based on a view of the best of Judaism and the worst of America. That is neither fair nor intellectually honest. The search for Judaism's meaning needs to reflect Judaism's best *and* America's best. But it cannot whitewash Judaism or Jews. It requires honesty, not delusion. Reality, not myth.

Similarly, the case for Judaism's relevance cannot come at the expense of respect for the society in which Jews live. To claim that Judaism is a clarion call to justice in a society rooted in iniquity is wrong. It is unproductive and unfair to suggest that only Jewish tradition urges respect for human life even in a world in which human life is cheapened. Jews do not have monopolies on those commitments. This is a world in which Jews are regularly exposed to the very best of what the non-Jewish world teaches. Jews today know that we are not the only ones seeking goodness, or working for justice. Sophisticated and wondering Jews will commit to Jewish life not because it is better, but because even in a world of many valuable and insightful traditions, it is unique.

But to many Jews, this notion is far-fetched at best, and outrageous at worst. For some, the mere suggestion that we have a message for the world smacks of *chutzpah*. It sounds audacious to claim that Jews have a message that the rest of the world needs to hear. After all, Jewish tradition explicitly states that it is *Jews* who were to fulfill the commandments; non-Jews have no such obligation. Why should America at large care what 3 or 4 percent of its population might think? Is it not hubris to assume that our message deserves to be heard by everyone?

No, it is not. If contemporary Jews bring their message to the society around them, they will do so as one voice in the chorus of traditions that make up our culture. We would offer our message not as "truth" or as the only way to see the world, but as *one* important way to see the world. We would suggest not that everyone ought to *do* what Jewish tradition demands of Jews, but rather, that the way in which we think about important issues and complex problems might enrich the debates our society has.

BEGINNING THE SEARCH: JUDAISM'S IMPLICIT
CRITIQUE OF AMERICAN EDUCATION

There is perhaps no arena of American life that Judaism's tradition critiques more strongly than the way our society thinks about education. On a multitude of levels, Judaism would argue (if Jews only knew enough about Judaism to let it) that the values and priorities of American education are skewed and unhealthy. One area of particular concern to Jewish tradition is what has happened to our society's sense that there are certain things that everyone should learn, certain ideas to which we ought all be exposed. Jewish tradition, as we will now see, is deeply committed to the idea of education as the glue that binds a community; Jewish values, as reflected in the texts of our tradition, are wholly at odds with much of the educational world around us.

Building a Society of Shared Values:
The Need for a Unified Curriculum

In modern America, the pressures of multiculturalism have destroyed virtually any remaining sense of a communal core of learning, any belief that there are certain things everyone in our society should know, books we should all have read. In theory, of course, the multiculturalism argument is about what should be in the core; in practice, though, the core is disappearing. The current sense in our society is that everyone should be able to choose what they wish to study, what they wish to know. If that results in fewer shared realms of knowledge, the argument goes, that is a necessary price of a higher value—the expression of each group's intellectual and cultural interest. Arthur Schlesinger has perhaps put it best:

> Cultural pluralism is a necessity in an ethnically diversified society. But the motives behind curriculum reform sometimes go beyond the desire for a more honest representation

of the past. "Multiculturalism" arises as a reaction against Anglo- or Eurocentrism; but at what point does it pass over into an ethnocentrism of its own? . . . Can any historian justify the proposition that the five ethnic communities into which the New York state task force wishes to divide the country had equal influence on the development of the United States? Is it a function of schools to teach ethnic and racial pride? When does obsession with differences begin to threaten the idea of an overarching American nationality?

Because of their traditional commitment to civil rights, and because of an abiding desire not to "rock the boat" of social acceptance in America, Jews have by and large been relatively silent on the multicultural assault on the core curriculum of American culture. It's also a matter of fear, of course. We have already seen that some of these multicultural forces—certain segments of the African-American community and some streams of the feminist movement as well—are overtly hostile to Jews. That hardly makes Jews comfortable with the idea of defending the educational or intellectual status quo, even those parts of it that we might *want* to defend. We face an uncharted terrain in this realm, and are therefore inclined to sit the battle out.

Why would Jewish tradition insist on maintaining a core? First, because Judaism does not believe that there is a clear boundary between education and behavior. The Talmud discusses the relative merits of religious study and religious practice, and concludes that study is more important:

Rabbi Tarfon and the Elders were once reclining in the upper story of Nithza's house, in Lydda, when this question was raised before them: Is study greater, or practice? Rabbi Tarfon answered, saying: Practice is greater. Rabbi Akiba answered, saying: Study is greater, for it leads to practice. Then they all answered and said: Study is greater, for it leads to action.   (KIDDUSHIN 40B)

This is hardly the conclusion we might have expected. Judaism is, after all, a tradition that takes behavior very seriously. It is a way of life that has something to say about virtually every facet of our daily life. Surely we would have expected the concrete values of practice and behavior to outweigh the amorphous benefits of study. But the tradition insists overwise.

This association between study and action has far-reaching implications in Jewish life. Jewish tradition has never accepted the notion that there could be such a thing as pure learning without any implications for behavior or society. Judaism would argue that if a society no longer studies the same material, it cannot behave in any united way. It cannot ultimately have shared values. For that reason, Jewish law is quite clear about what ought to be learned and when. Indeed, one well-known source actually provides a curriculum for the entire Jewish people, tying different sorts of learning to different ages. The passage, from the Mishnah (in *Ethics of the Fathers*), reads as follows:

> [Rabbi Judah ben Tema] used to say: five years [is the age] for [the study of] scripture, ten—for [the study of] Mishnah, thirteen—for [becoming subject to] commandments, fifteen—for [the study of] Talmud, eighteen—for [getting married under] the [bridal] canopy, twenty—for pursuing [a livelihood], thirty—for [full] strength, forty—for understanding, fifty—for [ability to give] counsel, sixty—for mature age. . . .
>
> (AVOT 5:21)

This source, of course, is more prescriptive than descriptive. This is what the Mishnah says *should* happen, not necessarily what *did* happen in the Jewish community. But even the ideal is instructive. The point? Learning certain material—religious, value-laden material—is considered as basic to a life well lived as getting married or earning a living. The notion that a society can survive if what one learns is entirely a matter of communal taste or of private consideration is—from Judaism's point of view—absurd.

In Judaism's perspective, literacy and knowledge of text are the tickets of entry into society. With them, everyone has a chance to debate a society's critical issues. Without them, a person is doomed to being an outsider. That is partly why it never occurred to Jewish immigrants to the United States in the early 1900s that the public schools ought to offer classes taught in Yiddish, or that election ballots ought to be printed in Yiddish as well as English. They understood what some current immigrant groups do not—that to be part of this society one must learn its language. Bilingual ballots reflect an approach dramatically different from Judaism's; but most Jews who think about the issue are more influenced by American civil liberties advocates than by the substance of their own tradition.

To many American Jews, this approach sounds uncaring, paternalistic. To some, it might even sound racist. But the issue here is not the exclusion of immigrants from political and educational progress; rather, it is recognition of what constitutes making one's way in a new society. Judaism's approach says that learning necessarily precedes participation. That is why the Tur (a relatively early legal code published in 1475) even prescribes details about a child's first learning experiences:

> It is a positive commandment for every Jew to teach his child* Torah, as it is written, "and you shall teach them to your children (Deuteronomy 6:7)" . . . and if his father did not teach him, he is obligated to teach himself. . . .
>
> And from when does he begin to teach his son? From the time that the child can speak. He begins by teaching him, "Moses commanded us [regarding] the Torah, as an inheritance of the community of Jacob" (Deuteronomy 33:4) and the first verse of the *Shema*. After that, he teaches him some

---

*The original text is probably best translated as "son." Sadly, women were long excluded from the best that Jewish education had to offer. Though that has thankfully changed, the gender language in these texts still reflects that earlier reality.

verses, until he is about six or seven years old. Then he must take him to a teacher. If it is the custom of that city for the teacher to charge, he must pay the teacher until [the child] can read the entire written Torah.

(TUR, YOREH DE'AH 245)

Jewish tradition does not leave critical issues of education up to the parents. The Tur stipulates when the child should begin learning (from the moment he can speak), the age at which he needs a teacher (six or seven), and even that the father must pay the teacher if that is the local custom. Simply put, the education of children is society's business, not the parents' or any other sub-section of society.

Before we go on, let's return to the Tur. What are the verses that the Tur says the child should learn? The very first verse the Tur prescribes, "Moses commanded us [regarding] the Torah, as an inheritance of the community of Jacob" (Deuteronomy 33:4), speaks of command, of obligation, of community. The Torah is described not as ethnic history, or as culture, but as command ment. Children, the tradition says, need to be taught to see them-selves not simply as individuals or members of a certain ethnicity, but as members of a larger community, in the case of Jewish life, "the community of Jacob." In keeping with the centrality of law that we discussed in Chapter Five, Jewish tradition asserts that any useful education needs to inculcate in every child a sense of obligation, of ought, of responsibility. The very essence of edu-cation, Jewish tradition insists, is to create a sense of being part of something bigger than ourselves, a community that spans gener-ations and continents, a community dedicated to living lives that matter.

The notion that education should function this way may sound rather natural, but as numerous people have noted, Amer-ican education at most prestigious institutions hardly seems to agree. Allan Bloom's critique of American higher education, *The Closing of the American Mind,* has become a virtual classic. In it,

Bloom's prescription for what a university ought to be reflects the deep influence Jewish texts had on him:

> It is childishness to say, as some do, that everyone must be allowed to develop freely, that it is authoritarian to impose a point of view on the student. In that case, why have a university? If the response is "to provide an atmosphere for learning," we come back to our original questions. . . . Which atmosphere? Choices and reflection on the reasons for those choices are unavoidable. The university has to stand for something.

Bloom and Jewish tradition agree. For communities to survive, there are certain things that simply must be learned. Education needs to communicate certain attitudes. Bloom and Jewish tradition share a conviction that concern about the collective ought to shape the education of each individual. Asserting this view clearly and loudly would, indeed, make Jews uncomfortable in many American settings. But that, the tradition responds, may be exactly why the Jews are here. That, it claims, may well be part of what Jews were "chosen" to do; it is what Jews ought to "stand for."

No Right to Teach—Judaism's Perspective on Pedagogy

If Jews were committed to the idea that being Jewish in America meant standing for values that are sometimes at odds with those of the larger culture, we would have even more to say about education in America. If American Jews began to internalize Jewish tradition's attitudes to learning, our critique would range far beyond the issue of curriculum. Because Jewish tradition sees education as a moral issue, it has also developed different standards for who ought to be able to teach.

Two brief statements from the same section of the Tur that we saw above make the point very clearly. The first discusses the instructor's behavior, and says, quite simply:

[if there should be] a master who does not behave appropri-
ately, even though he may be a great scholar and the people
need his [learning], one may not learn from him until his
behavior changes, as it is written, "for the lips of a priest are
observed, and rulings are sought from his mouth, for he is a
messenger of the Lord of Hosts" (Malachi 2:7).

(TUR, YOREH DE'AH 246)

Jewish tradition does not recognize a "right" to teach or absolute
freedom of expression for teachers. The verse from the prophet
Malachi cited at the end of the passage makes it clear that to the
author of the Tur, what was most important was the impact of
this teacher on society at large. If the teacher's behavior was
deemed dangerous or distasteful, all the knowledge in the world
could not guarantee him a right to maintain his teaching. Faculty
who are world-renowned but who mistreat their students are
guaranteed nothing by Jewish tradition.

Indeed, the needs of the community so outweigh any right a
person might have to teach that it doesn't take heinous behavior
to be removed from a teaching position. In fact, if a person is
doing a perfectly fine job but an even better teacher comes along,
society is *obligated* to hire the better teacher:

It is not appropriate to appoint someone to teach children
unless he is pious, fluent [in his field] and exacting [in his
scholarship]. If someone were teaching children and another
[teacher] became available who was better than [the first], we
dismiss the first for the sake of the second.

(TUR, YOREH DE'AH 245)

How to implement a policy like this in modern America is not
clear. After all, the dignity and self-sufficiency of the "former"
teacher needs to be protected, and all teachers need some sense
of security. But in its insistence on safeguarding the public good,
Jewish tradition argues that the rights of individuals must be cur-

tailed. The tradition does not suggest that individuals should be disregarded, or that they do not matter. Quite the contrary.

But Judaism does believe that given a choice between the community and the individual, the community takes precedence. Professors who get tired and uninterested, or teachers who take unacceptable liberties with students, quite simply have no right to teach. They may teach only so long as their service in that role enhances and enriches their community.

Matters in American higher education could hardly be more different. In Western universities, academic tenure is a virtual sacred cow. Much of that is for good reason. Tenure protects diversity of opinion and safeguards faculty rights to teach material or ideas that may be unpopular. But these rights—and a concern for academic freedom—have become so entrenched that once a professor receives tenure, virtually nothing can undo that "right" to teach. Sexual misconduct between a faculty person (in a position of authority and power) and a student often goes on for years before the system can respond. And the same is true of the abuse of free speech. When Leonard Jeffries accused Jews of having played a major part in the colonial slave trade (which they did not) and further pointed to what he said was a

> conspiracy, planned and plotted and programmed out of Hollywood [by] people called Greenberg and Trigliani . . . Russian Jewry [who] had a particular control over the movies . . . put together a financial system of destruction of Black people. It was by design, it was calculated. . . .

he lost his administrative position. But he retained his tenure, and with it, his right to teach and to continue to influence students. Apparently, this right trumped any obligation on his part to back up his claims with data, or to maintain a level of discourse that avoided inciting hatred. When Arthur Butz, a little known professor of electrical engineering at Northwestern University, published his now infamous *The Hoax of the Twentieth Century* (denying the Shoah) in 1976, he did not lose his position, for he was tenured.

It would be absurd for modern American Jews to argue for the elimination of tenure. Much about the system is critically important. Tenure is one of the ways American universities protect the rights of unpopular ideas to be heard, and Jews have also benefited from that system. But there can also be no denying that a serious encounter with Jewish tradition yields a harsh critique of many of the current values implicit in tenure. Many of these issues are much broader than education itself. Taking the focus on rights too far erodes the sense that a society is about shared enterprise and responsibility. A stable and survivable society, Jewish tradition argues, requires a different set of priorities. Modern Jews versed in their tradition would have much to say about the world we inhabit. Ours could be a message the world needs to hear.

THE IMPORTANCE OF SACRED SYMBOLS

Why are American Jews so reticent to give voice to these Jewish values? Why is such a successful and educated community so silent? In part, of course, many American Jews have not been taught enough about their tradition to know what its deeply held values are. But the issue is more complex. We have worked too hard to make our way in to "take on" American society and its values. But being outsiders—at least in part—is one element of what recovering this voice would require.

Why? Because Judaism's critique of American values is not a mere policy issue. It is about much more than one aspect of education or another. It is about the way we view the world, about the role we believe individuals play in society. It is about fundamental conceptions of responsibility, of the life well lived. It is about what ultimately matters, and too often, Judaism would say that in American culture, not enough really matters.

One place where Jewish values virtually collide with popular

American culture is in a realm we might call "reverence." We live in a society that virtually eschews reverence. Almost nothing in our contemporary secular setting is considered sacred; very little demands our allegiance or respect. This is true with public institutions and public figures (for whom respect is considered almost laughable), and with the human body. Whereas Jewish tradition prohibits tattoos out of respect for the body (based on Leviticus 19:28), American youth are growing up in a culture of body piercing, in which social acceptance is gained through self-mutilation.

The issue of reverence is also at play in the concrete symbols that supposedly represent the values our society values. There is no longer anything that we are not allowed to destroy. The mere notion that an item might be described as sacred, limiting our right to modify or demolish it, is considered an invasion of our right to self-expression. We see that issue at play in countless ways, but perhaps most obviously in discussions of a constitutional amendment that would ban the destruction of the American flag.

For most liberally inclined Americans, destruction of the flag is distasteful. But the mere idea that this destruction might be prohibited bothers them, for it cuts against the very grain of their sense of constitutional liberties. Most American Jews feel the same way. We are often uncomfortable when we see images of the flag being burned, torn and made into a T-shirt or, as in some recent museum exhibitions, even being stuffed into a toilet. America has been too good to Jews for this not to touch some raw nerve. But as much as American Jews might wish this didn't happen, we do not feel it would be appropriate to forbid it. Ultimately, like the culture around us, many Jews today believe it is more important to protect the values of freedom of expression than to protect a symbol by calling it sacred.

But how important is freedom of expression? Strange though that question may sound, Jewish tradition would have us pause for a moment before asserting that such liberties are our most important concern. Judaism would acknowledge that one can be angered—even revolted—by Jewish tradition. Jews have every right to be angry with God, to argue about the Torah's morality, to question whether ideas like chosenness make sense. The Jewish tradition never demands intellectual surrender from Jews, even from traditional Jews. We can all dispute it, argue with it, even urge its emendation.

But despite that intellectual openness, no Jew, under any circumstances, would be permitted to destroy the Torah—or any other sacred book, for that matter—no matter how objectionable she or he found it. We can wrestle with the ideas in those books, and even reject them; we're forbidden, however, from ever destroying the book itself. Why? Because Jewish tradition asserts that to be part of any culture is to acknowledge that it has certain symbolic representations that outweigh even our need and desire for self-expression. That is why in Jewish memory, it is only our enemies who burn our books and our sacred objects. We have never allowed ourselves that liberty. Nazis burn Torahs; Jews don't.

Jewish literature is replete with examples of Sages arguing with God and disputing their tradition. But destroying the Torah—the very symbol of the people to whom they had committed their lives—would have been unthinkable. Quite the contrary. Torah scrolls that can no longer be used have to be buried. In some Jewish communities, the burying of a Torah scroll is astoundingly similar to the funeral for a person. Though Jewish law certainly does not equate the value of a scroll with the value of human life, Jews have been known to risk their lives to save Torahs from fire or other danger. Why? Because they have long recognized that distinguishing between a community's values and the symbols of those values is not easy. Ultimately, Jewish tradition believes, a loss of reverence for the symbols leads to cheapening the underlying values themselves.

Judaism's limitation on self-expression would probably extend far beyond the flag. Jewish tradition would urge moderns to ask whether pornography advances the goal of seeing all human beings as created in God's image. If pornography actually undermines that goal and objectifies women, the Jewish tradition would ask, why would self-expression possibly be more important than those concerns? And what has happened, it would want to know, if when Congress sought to restrict pornography on the Internet, it was the Family Research Council (a conservative, largely Christian group) that advocated the restrictions, and the ACLU (which lists many prominent Jews on its rolls) that successfully got the legislation overturned in June 1996?

These are not simple issues, and there is no one position that will satisfy all legitimate moral and social agendas. But why is the Jewish voice so lopsided? What has happened to Jewish consciousness in America? Why do Jews automatically assume the positions of American liberalism without even a glance to the sometimes subversive or critical dimensions of their own tradition?

CHILDREN—THE ULTIMATE EXPRESSION OF PUBLIC INTEREST?

Before moving on, we ought to examine one last area in which Jewish sentiments and those of American culture are at odds. This example touches on the "holy of holies" of American life. It is a couple's decision about whether and when to have children.

For those of us raised on American values, decisions about having children are exceptionally personal and private. They are our classic example of "it's no one else's business." The birth control revolution of the 1960s gave us much more control over these decisions, and most Americans would be incredulous if someone suggested that these matters were anything other than completely private.

In fact, American courts are deeply committed to protecting that privacy. In 1972, in *Eisenstadt v. Baird,* the Supreme Court ruled that "[i]f the right of privacy means anything, it is the right of the individual, married or single, to be free of unwarranted government intrusion into matters so fundamentally affecting a person as the decision whether to bear or beget a child." Courts aside, our contemporary social consciousness suggests without qualm that this is a purely personal decision, and no one—no court, no family member and not even any religious tradition—should dare to tell us otherwise.

But consider Judaism's attitude to this question, as reflected in the Mishnah:

> A man shall not abstain from procreating unless he already has children. [As to the number], the House of Shammai ruled: two males, and the House of Hillel ruled: a male and a female, for it is stated in Scripture, "male and female [God] created them" (Genesis 5:2).
>
> (YEVAMOT 6:6)

The Mishnah's focus is not on rights, but on obligations. Strange (perhaps even offensive) though it may seem to our modern sensibilities, Jewish tradition does not share the Supreme Court's sense that family decisions are exclusively private ones. What interests the tradition is not the family's rights, but its obligations. Why? Presumably because Jewish tradition argues that a foremost responsibility of every adult who is able to do so is to preserve her or his culture for future generations. That means, in part, making sure that there will be enough people to sustain that culture in the future.

American Jews shudder at the notion that children might be an obligation. And we act out our rejection of this idea by simply refusing to have the numbers of children it would take to preserve current Jewish numbers. It takes approximately 2.2 children per couple to maintain a steady population. American Jewish couples have fewer. Often, this is not because American Jews do not care about the future of Jewish life, but rather, because

Judaism in America has become so equated with liberalism and its emphasis on individualism. The mere notion that couples ought to consider such issues in their personal decisions sounds absurd, even offensive.

But the rabbis of our tradition felt that the welfare of society depended upon people having children, upon children learning trades, and upon young men marrying young women. Those actions, they believed, were part of what it would take for their community to survive. Those actions, therefore, became matters not of rights, but of responsibilities. That is why the Sages even regulated what a father must do for a son:

> A father is required [to perform the following] for his son: to circumcise him, to redeem him [from service in the Temple], to teach him Torah, to marry him to a wife and to teach him a craft. Others say, also to teach him how to swim.
>
> (KIDDUSHIN 29A)

Obviously, a Jewish community committed to this perspective would have to be very careful and consciously sensitive. Decisions about whether to have children and how to raise them *are* deeply personal. There are couples who are unable to have children, or who are unable to have as many as they would like. There are people who have experienced such grave trauma in their pasts that they cannot bring themselves to conceive children. People have many complex, subtle and very private reasons for making the decisions that they do. Jewish tradition does not deny that, nor does it nonchalantly seek to invade people's most intimate musings. It simply asks that as we make these sorts of decisions, we also consider the appropriate place of the individual in society, the necessary balance of rights with responsibilities and obligations.

RETRIEVING OUR MESSAGE—RIGHTS OR
RESPONSIBILITIES, INDIVIDUALS OR COMMUNITIES?

Part of the fundamental Jewish critique of American society, therefore, will probably revolve around the issue of community versus individual. Jews are uniquely poised to offer a collective perspective on this issue, a view that emerges directly from their sources, that is authentically and distinctively Jewish. And it is a critical corrective.

At the core of America—the democracy that has been most hospitable to Jews—lies a commitment to the supreme value of the individual. European and American political philosophers like Locke, Hobbes, Rousseau, and Thomas Jefferson celebrated the individual virtually above all else. America has long prided itself on a commitment to what many have called "rugged individualism." It is a culture of the individual against the world, the lone human being struggling to preserve autonomy and dignity by achieving self-sufficiency. It is an environment that gave rise to Ayn Rand's *Atlas Shrugged* and her many memorable characters, each of whom—decent people though many were—viewed life through a thoroughly individualist lens. Describing the culture that has emerged in this country, Robert Bellah, a sociologist and an astute observer of American society, writes:

Individualism lies at the very core of American culture. . . . We believe in the dignity, indeed the sacredness, of the individual. Anything that would violate our right to think for ourselves, judge for ourselves, make our own decisions, live our lives as we see fit, is not only morally wrong, it is sacrilegious. Our highest and noblest aspirations, not only for ourselves, but for those we care about, for our society and for the world, are closely linked to our individualism.

Judaism, it is now clear, does virtually all it can to downplay the centrality of the individual. True, the Jewish tradition grants inestimable value to each human being. It claims that all people are created in God's image and that anyone who "saves a single person is deemed . . . to have saved an entire world" (Mishnah *Sanhedrin* 4:5). Nonetheless, Judaism is fundamentally oriented to the community, not to the individual.

Jewish tradition takes numerous steps to argue that communal life is the critical issue for Jews. That is why certain parts of the service, including the mourner's *Kaddish,* may be recited only if a *minyan* (a minimum prayer quorum) is present. That is why the *Viddui* (the well-known Confession recited on Yom Kippur that begins *ashamnu, bagadnu, gazalnu*—"*we* have been guilty, *we* have betrayed, *we* have robbed . . .") is written in the plural.

Even as each individual Jew confronts her or his own short-comings, the language of the High Holiday liturgy is more communal than individual. Thus, for instance, in the famed *al ḥet* section (each line of which begins "For the sin *we* have committed before You by . . ."), the language is once again plural. Even though many in the congregation (most, we hope!) have not committed some of those sins (such as murder and the like), the tradition reminds the Jew that she is part of something larger, a community of interconnected and interdependent individuals.

The same values emerge in Judaism's implicit rejection of the word "charity." The Hebrew word *tzedakah* ranks among Judaism's most familiar terms. Most Jews commonly translate it as "charity." In the Western tradition, charity implies a sense of beneficence; to behave charitably is seen as going beyond the call of duty. Charity suggests supererogation, doing more than what is required of us. In our largely Christian, largely secular culture, charity is considered a private act, one that emerges out of our own sense of what we feel is appropriate.

Jewish tradition's perspective, however, could not be more different. Judaism does not suggest charity; it demands *tzedakah,* telling Jews when to give and how much to give. Though modern Jews are tempted to rebel against this assault on our autonomy and wonder aloud, "Who says I *have* to give?" there is no denying the clarity of Judaism's perspective. *Tzedakah* is actually a word that comes from the root *ẓdk*, from which the Hebrew word *ẓedek*, or righteousness, comes. *Tzedakah* therefore means not "charity," but "righteousness." In Jewish life, failing to give charity is not a matter of personal decision, but a matter of unrighteousness. That is why, strange though it may seem to a Westerner, Jewish tradition insists that *tzedakah* can actually be compelled and that recalcitrant individuals can be forced to give.

Indeed, the Torah commands that a person harvesting a field may not cut and harvest the corners of the field. Nor may he go back to collect gleanings that have fallen. Those corners and gleanings, and grapes that have fallen in the vineyard, the Torah says, do not belong to the farmer, but to the poor (Leviticus 19:9–10). Jewish tradition is not willing to wait for the farmer to be charitably motivated; "charity" is built into the system. It is a system that mandates the poor be provided for. Maimonides, in fact, goes much further than the Torah:

> You are obligated to give to the poor person in accordance with what he is lacking. If he has no clothes, you must clothe him. If he has no furnishing for his home, you must purchase them for him. If he does not have a wife, you must [provide him the money he needs] to get married. If she was a woman, you marry her to a man. Even to the following extent: if it was this poor person's nature to ride on a horse and to have a slave running before him, but he became poor and lost his money, you must purchase him a horse and a slave to run before him. . . . [But] you are only obliged to restore him to his former condition, and not to make him wealthy.
>
> (HILKHOT MAT'NOT ANIYIM 7:3)

There is much about Maimonides's claim that is unclear. How does one distinguish between buying a horse and a slave for a poor person (which, if the person had previously had such things, we are required to do) and making the person rich (which we are not required to do)? How can anyone determine what the poor person legitimately lacks? What if the poor person lost his money as a result of personal habits of his own making? Are Jews still obligated to restore him to his former place?

These are all important questions, but even more important is Maimonides's central claim: we are obligated to give money to the poor. This, after all, is not charity. It is a tax system. Living as part of the Jewish community means being part of that tax system. Indeed, following the Talmud's claim (*Sanhedrin* 17b), Maimonides declares as a matter of law that no Jewish scholar may reside in a place that does not have a mechanism for collecting and distributing *tzedakah* funds (*Hilkhot De'ot* 4:23). The *Shulḥan Arukh,* Judaism's classic code of Jewish law, stipulates that one must give no more than one fifth of one's income to charity (so as not to exacerbate society's problem by impoverishing yourself), but that at the same time, each person must give at least one tenth of his or her gross earning to *tzedakah* (*Yoreh De'ah* 249:1). Again, this might be more prescriptive (stating what *should* happen) than descriptive (stating what *does* happen), but our traditions, values and the ways in which they're different from the culture around us are clear.

Judaism is not interested in one's motivation for giving. Nor is it concerned that by commanding *tzedakah* it might rob people of the opportunity to give on their own and thus gain a special feeling of satisfaction. Judaism's perspective is simpler. It is more concerned about public welfare than it is about individual self-congratulation. It says simply that the hungry must be fed, the naked must be clothed and the endangered must be protected. That is all that matters.

There is hardly a person in America who has not walked down the street and seen beggars with hands outstretched. Coming to the bottom of highway exit ramps, we find homeless people, individuals or even families, asking for money, food or shelter. Often, the sheer numbers of these people are simply overwhelming. We ignore them, because the enormousness of the problem makes us feel powerless. And we reassure ourselves that as sad as it is, this is really not our problem. We pay our taxes, we give when we can, we're decent people. More than that, we tell ourselves, no one can ask.

Judaism disagrees. We can't impoverish ourselves, so we surely cannot give to everyone. But it *is* our problem. We don't have the right to walk by, to ignore the plight of people who sleep in cartons and who beg for food at freeway off-ramps. Even in this shift of attitude, Judaism has something to say that is dramatically different from a focus on individuals and their rights. It gives Jews a voice that is prophetic in the classic sense of the word.

If Jews could recover the voice we gave up when we decided to join this society completely and at all costs, we would know what to say: the *rugged* individualism of America has become *rampant* individualism. The stories that our two systems tell about desert travels make the point clear. In the American tradition, the paradigmatic characters are those who forged westward, facing dangers alone. It is the "lone cowboy" who is the quintessential image of the American prairie experience. But the quintessential Jewish image in the desert is that of six hundred thousand Jews leaving Egypt together, wandering en masse as they make their way to the Promised Land. That is not to suggest that there are no Jews who wander in the desert alone, for there are, or that no early Americans moved west in groups, for they surely did. But the fundamental difference in the stories that we tell about ourselves is nonetheless revealing. Western liberalism is a culture of individualism, of rights virtually above all. Jewish tradition is a culture of community, and of the obligations needed to enable that community to survive.

RECOVERING A JEWISH SUBVERSIVE MESSAGE

The evidence is in: the distinction between Jewish values and Jewish living is specious. For generations now, American Jews have argued that religion could be optional, that they could transmit Jewish values while not insisting on too demanding a way of Jewish life. But life has proven more complicated than American Jews expected it would. At every turn, whether in prayer or in *tzedakah,* whether with regard to tenure or academic institutions, Jewish tradition conveys its fundamental commitments and beliefs through ritual and religious expression. An American Jewish community not rooted in those expressions will not know what Judaism's commitments are. *That* sort of community, it is now clear, will have no idea why it should try to survive.

A Jewish community willing to reencounter the ritual and religious dimension of its tradition would understand that advocating community over individualism, asserting obligations over rights is part of what Jews could come to represent, part of the way we might answer the question of what the world would be missing if the Jews were to disappear. The search for a unique Jewish message is no search for a holy grail; it is a search that simply leads back to a tradition that has long been ours.

Yet at the same time, a necessary note of caution. If we are to recapture this element of Jewish tradition and shape it into a "subversive" message of critique, it must be loving critique, not gratuitous criticism. Cultural influence is almost always mutual, and Jews have also benefited profoundly from the West's focus on individuals and rights. Not only Jews, but Jewish tradition as well, have profited from our exposure to America's way of thinking. In almost all walks of Jewish life, the status of women is improved over what it was a century ago. That would not have happened were it not for the sensibilities and sensitivities we learned from rights-based American culture. To the extent that the Jewish community is now more open to Jews with disabilities, to unmarried Jews, to couples who cannot have children, to gays and lesbians, and to many others, that is due in part to what we have learned from the best of what America has taught us.

No thoughtful observer of the Jewish community would ever deny this debt to the world in which Jews live. At the same time, however, this indebtedness and profound sense of belonging to that world cannot blind Jews to the fact that we need to remain distinct. Woodrow Wilson was simply wrong. What makes America great is precisely the fact that there *are* groups in America, each with its own tradition and its own insights to bear. That is what makes this country exciting, and it is what *could* give Jews in America the sense of purpose they have lost.

Can we rediscover a unique voice and share it with a world desperately groping for moral moorings? Armed with fortitude and with renewed openness to the tradition they turned away from, the potential is almost limitless. What remains to be seen is whether contemporary Jews still have that courage.

Part Three

BRINGING

THE MESSAGE

TO LIFE

CHAPTER SEVEN

"Exile" or "Diaspora"?— Is Jewish Life in America Illegitimate?

*A*lmost immediately after I was born, my grandfather left his family in America and moved to Israel. He had vowed to make *aliyah* (as moving to Israel is called) ever since the Depression had eroded his faith in America, and eventually he did. He waited for me, the eldest child of his only daughter, to be born, and left to begin a new life. He said good-bye to my grandmother, my mother and her older brothers, picked up and was gone.

Shortly after he arrived in Israel, he had a rubber stamp made up, which he used at the top of every air letter that he wrote for the next fifteen years. It was in Hebrew, but translated into English, it read: "Jews! Come to Israel, so that you may live and we may live."

Not particularly subtle, this little message. But my grandfather's message is one that American Jews hear from a variety of corners: life in America is a dead end for Jews. According to this view, the real future of the Jewish people is in Israel, and those American Jews who genuinely care about Jewish life and intensive Jewish living will decide to make *aliyah*.

This claim is made more compelling and urgent by all the challenges to Jewish identity in America that we've been discussing. "If Jewish life in America is so difficult to maintain," many American Jews wonder, "why bother?" Perhaps, many of us muse, the issue is more complex than the simple fact that Jewish identity in America is difficult to preserve. Perhaps, indeed, Jewish life outside Israel is doomed, not only because of America and its unique challenges, but because Diaspora Jewish life is fundamentally illegitimate. Should we not even bother?

There is a parallel notion, propagated by some Israelis and by some readers of the Jewish tradition, which asserts that now that Israel exists, Jewish life there is "center stage" and Jewish life everywhere else is peripheral. There is a sense among many American and Israeli Jews that Israel is now the sun, and all other Jewish communities are somehow planets that are in varying degrees condemned to do little but revolve around Israel. But that notion is highly disheartening to American Jews. When we hear Israelis say that only Jewish life in Israel is authentic, we are not sure how to respond. When we hear religious Zionists argue that the tradition considers Diaspora living dysfunctional, we wonder: what does the tradition actually say? Suddenly aware of how little we know, American Jews often find ourselves even more disoriented, more dejected, more convinced that the enterprise of American Jewish survival may be fruitless—perhaps even wholly without merit.

This climate has created a strange schizophrenia among American Jews. At one moment American Jews love Israel, at another they detest it. Israel is either a land of democratic, peace-loving pioneers and brave generals, of beautiful teenagers who serve in the army and love poetry, or Israel is an anti-democratic, nonpluralist disappointment, a barbaric occupying military presence in which right-wing ultra-religious zealots refuse to serve in the army but determine foreign policy. These are caricatures, of course, but they are competing caricatures between which much of American Jewry swings in a predictable pendulum-like fashion. But these conflicting images of Israel contribute to our confusion about the role of Diaspora Jews and our relation to Israel. And that confusion fuels the fires of ambivalence about the very enterprise called American Jewish life.

This confusion is dangerous. It undermines American Jewish

commitment to Israel, and on the home front it saps the strength of those who would strive to make a difference in American Jewish life. This denigration of Jewish life outside Israel is a challenge, therefore, that must be addressed. No longer can we allow it to go unresolved, unanswered. We need to think deeply about these issues. First, we need to know what the tradition says about all this. Second, we need to ask ourselves what purpose, if any, our being here might serve. Then, and only then, can we begin to think clearly about whether American Jewish life has meaning, or even a future.

WHERE IS "CENTER STAGE"?
THE LAND OF ISRAEL IN JEWISH TRADITION

To address these questions, we proceed in our usual fashion. We turn first to the sources of Jewish tradition that for thousands of years have guided Jewish belief. We turn to those texts, biblical and beyond, that make up Jewish communal memory, that comprise the pages of the written tradition that tell our story. To many Jews, the centrality of the land of Israel in Jewish life seems so obvious that it is scarcely worth discussing. Obviously, they would respond, Israel is the ideal place for Jews. Everything in our master narrative says so.

Does it? At first blush, this attitude seems undeniable. In the world of Jewish prayer—the part of the Jewish tradition that Jews most commonly encounter—the tradition leaves little room for doubt.

Indications from the Liturgy

Perhaps the most obvious indication of Israel's centrality in the world of Jewish prayer is how Jews stand when they pray. Regardless of where we may be, Jews face Jerusalem in prayer. In the United States and Europe, we face east. In Russia, Jews face mostly south. Jews in South Africa face north. And so on. Even in Israel, Jerusalem determines the way we pray. In cities like Beer-

sheba, in the south of the country, one faces north—toward
Jerusalem. In places like Ashdod, on the western coast, we face
east—again toward Jerusalem. Even in Jerusalem itself, the wor-
shiper faces the site where the ancient Temple stood in Jerusalem.

This implicit point becomes quite explicit in the words of the
liturgy. The middle paragraph of the *Shema*, a passage taken
from the book of Deuteronomy, speaks of the importance of
teaching the tradition to children:

> [18]Therefore impress these My words upon your very heart:
> bind them as a sign on your hand and let them serve as a
> symbol on your forehead, [19]and teach them to your chil-
> dren—reciting them when you stay at home and when you
> are away, when you lie down and when you get up; [20]and
> inscribe them on the doorposts of your house and on your
> gates—[21]to the end that you and your children may endure,
> in the land that the LORD swore to your fathers to assign to
> them, as long as there is a heaven over the earth.
>
> (DEUTERONOMY 11:18–21)

For Deuteronomy, mere survival is not enough. *Where* we survive is also important. What matters is not just survival, but survival on "the land that the Lord swore to [our ancestors] to assign
to them," survival in the Land of Israel.

Even the way that the prayer book introduces the *Shema*
makes this point. The prayer immediately preceding the *Shema*,
known as *Ahavah Rabbah*—"Abundant Love"—concludes with a
very telling plea. When we reach that portion of the service, Jews
who are wearing a *tallit* (prayer shawl) gather the fringes that are
tied to each of the garment's four corners, and say:

> And bring us in peace from the four corners of the earth, and
> lead us with dignity to our land. For You are a God who
> brings about salvation, and You have chosen us from among
> all people and tongues. . . .

"Lead us to our land" and "You have chosen us from among all people. . . ." Here again, the notion of a Jewish calling, a sense of mission, a claim of having been "chosen" to bring something significant to the world is inextricably tied to the land.

The *Shema* is hardly the only example of this in the liturgy. Consider now the *Amidah*, Judaism's most central prayer, recited three times daily. In the version recited on weekdays (all days except for Shabbat and holidays), Jews read:

> Sound that great shofar to [announce] our freedom, raise the banner to gather our exiles, and gather us together from the four corners of the earth. Praised are You, Lord, who gathers the dispersed of His people Israel.

Though this blessing does not specifically mention Israel, it alludes to the Jewish homeland when it speaks of gathering exiles from across the globe. From where will they be gathered? From wherever they may be, anywhere in the world. To where? To only one place—to Israel.

Then the *Amidah* continues, and shortly after, pleads:

> And to Jerusalem, Your city, may You return in mercy. May You dwell there as You have promised. Build it now, in our day and forever, and speedily reestablish the throne of David in her midst. Praised are You, Lord, who builds Jerusalem.

The angst the Jews feel about a Jerusalem unredeemed becomes most palpable on Shabbat, when traditional Jews yearn for a perfected and redeemed world. In the Sabbath morning *kedushah*, one of the most powerful moments in the service, we find a brief paragraph the translation of which scarcely reveals the poignancy and pain expressed by the Hebrew original:

> Appear from Your abode, Our King, and rule over us, for we await You. When will You rule in Zion, may it be speedily in

our day, and forever. May You be exalted and sanctified in
Jerusalem Your city, for generation upon generation, and for
eternity. . . .

Later on in the Sabbath morning service, as the *Haftarah* is completed, the person reading that prophetic selection recites a blessing that pleads, in part, "Have mercy upon Zion, for she is the
very source of our life."

Nor are allusions to Israel limited to the synagogue service.
They pervade traditional Jewish homes as well. The Grace After
Meals, seemingly recited as a simple expression of gratitude for
food, places Israel at its center, even when the food did not come
from Israel. One portion of the *Birkat Ha-Mazon,* this grace,
reads:

> We thank you, Lord our God, for having bequeathed to our
> ancestors, a desirable, good and vast land. . . . Praised are
> You, Lord, for the land and for the food. . . .
>
> Have mercy, Lord our God, upon Israel Your people, upon
> Jerusalem Your city, and upon Zion, the dwelling place of
> Your majesty. . . . And rebuild Jerusalem, the holy city, speed-
> ily in our day. Praised are You, Lord, who builds Jerusalem.
> Amen.

Thus, images of Jerusalem, Zion, Israel and the ingathering
of exiles to the Promised Land all play a significant role in the
synagogue liturgy as well as in prayers recited at home.
Jerusalem pervades the consciousness of Jews, wherever they
may be. It is a strange orientation, this preoccupation with a city
that most Jews never got to see. But it is not difficult to explain.
For since the very beginning of our people, Jews have had a virtual love affair with that land and that city.

Biblical and Rabbinic Views of the Land

It's not as strange as it sounds for a people to love a city, even when most of them have never been there. Muslims have that relationship with Mecca. There are immigrants to America, from Italy, from Ireland and elsewhere, who communicate a love and reverence for their homelands that is palpable for their grandchildren, even though those grandchildren have never seen those places. Generations of Italian- and Irish-Americans have fallen in love with places across the ocean because they were raised on myths of those lands, poetry and songs in those native languages, the styles of humor from that culture, food from those lands. The love in their grandparents' eyes as Italy or Ireland were mentioned planted the seeds of a love that overcame even huge geographic distances, even the absence of personal memory.

The same is true for Jews. The only difference is that for us, the wistful yearning for a land far away began not two or three generations ago, but two or three thousand years ago. This longing is as old as the Book of Psalms:

> 5If I forget you, O Jerusalem,
> let my right hand wither;
> 6let my tongue stick to my palate
> if I cease to think of you,
> if I do not keep Jerusalem in memory
> even at my happiest hour.
>
> (PSALMS 137:5–6)

The best-known poem that makes this point is the *Hatikvah* ("The Hope"), written in 1878, and which ultimately became Israel's national anthem. Amazingly, the anthem for the Jewish state still speaks of *a dream* of returning to Zion.

As long as deep in the heart
The soul of a Jew yearns
And toward the East
An eye looks toward Zion

Our hope is not yet lost
The hope of two thousand years
To be a free people in our land
The land of Zion and Jerusalem.

How did this love affair begin? Again, with the very story we tell about ourselves. The very first words that God utters to the very first Jew in the Torah are "Go forth from your native land and from your father's house to the land that I will show you" (Genesis 12:1). Where is that land? Though unnamed, it is clearly the place Jews ultimately came to call Israel.

Of the Torah's five books, almost four are completely devoted to the Jewish people's journey from Egypt to the Promised Land. This "diary," this book of national collective memory, is thus a chronicle of Jews' struggling to reach this one place, this home specifically chosen for their people. It is the story that Jews read annually, year in and year out, beginning the cycle anew as soon as it ends. It is the story that speaks not of Jews, but of *Israelites*, suggesting an almost inseparable relationship between the People of Israel and the Land of Israel. It is the story of a people that cannot imagine being anywhere else.

It is that history that gives the land its special status. As their journey ends, the Israelites are told:

> [10]For the land that you are about to enter and possess is not like the land of Egypt from which you have come. . . . [12]It is a land which the LORD your God looks after, on which the LORD your God always keeps His eye, from year's beginning to year's end.
>
> (DEUTERONOMY 11:10–12)

In Israel (but only in Israel?), God will care for this people, God will nurture them, God will love them. Indeed, the people and the land are so inseparable that the Prophet Joel, speaking in God's name, calls Israel "My Land" (Joel 1:6, 4:2).

Even the Torah's vocabulary communicates this love. The Torah's love for the land of Israel, and its view of the land as sacred, is expressed perhaps most beautifully, but also subtly, in the way it uses the Hebrew word *morashah*. As rough equivalents to the English word "inheritance," the Torah uses both the Hebrew word *yerushah* as well as the word *morashah*. While *yerushah* means inheritance of any sort, *morashah* has the quality of "sacred inheritance." Of what importance is that? Interestingly, the word *morashah* appears only twice in the Torah (Exodus 6:8 and Deuteronomy 33:4). In Deuteronomy, the word *morashah* refers to the Torah. In Exodus, it refers to the Land of Israel, as God promises, "I will bring you into the land which I swore to Abraham, Isaac and Jacob, and I will give it to you for a possession, I the LORD."

Judaism without Torah is unimaginable. Without Torah, there is nothing that makes Judaism Jewish. But the Torah seems to suggest that as central as Torah is, it alone is not enough. The Jews' *morashah*, their sacred inheritance, includes not only the Torah, but more. Their inheritance is the Torah—but also their land. Those two are the sacred bequests that set Jews apart and that give them purpose.

In later rabbinic literature, which speaks more theoretically, this Jewish love affair with the land of Israel continues. The Mishnah, the formative document of rabbinic Judaism, declares that "the Land of Israel is more holy than all other lands" (*Keilim* 1:6), and the Tosefta, a slightly later rabbinic work, claims that "dwelling in the Land of Israel is equated [in importance] to all the other commandments in the Torah" (Tosefta *Avodah Zarah* 4:3).

Perhaps most astounding is a passage from a portion of the Talmud known as the tractate *Ketubbot*. The passage begins with a Mishnah, which reads:

> [A man] may compel all [his household] to go up [with him] to the land of Israel, but none may be compelled to leave it. All [of one's household] may be compelled to go up to Jerusalem, but none may be compelled to leave it.
>
> (KETUBBOT 13:11)

Outside Israel, a man's power over his household is so great that he can compel them to go to the Land of Israel. But once there, even the head of the household cannot command them to leave. Similarly, within Israel, he may command them to go to Jerusalem. But again, once in Jerusalem, he does not have the power to require them to leave.

The yearning for the Jewish homeland is even more obvious in the discussion in the Gemara (the later rabbinic amplification on this Mishnah) that follows:

> Our Rabbis taught: One should always live in the Land of Israel, even in a town most of whose inhabitants are idolaters, but let no one live outside the Land, even in a town most of whose inhabitants are Israelites; for whoever lives in the Land of Israel may be considered to have a God, but whoever lives outside the Land may be regarded as one who has no God. For it is said in Scripture, "To give you the Land of Canaan, to be your God" (Leviticus 25:38). Has he, then, who does not live in the Land, no God? But [this is what the text intended] to tell you, that whoever lives outside the Land may be regarded as one who worships idols. Similarly it was said in Scripture in [the story of] David [who sought shelter from his enemy, King Saul, in the country of Moab and the land of the Philistines], "For they have driven me out this day that I should not cleave to the inheritance of the Lord, saying: 'Go, serve other gods.'" Now, whoever said to David, "Serve other gods"? [No one!] Rather, [the text intended] to tell you that whoever lives outside the Land may be regarded as one who worships idols.   (KETUBBOT 110B)

What a strong statement! Perhaps hyperbolically (but perhaps not), the Talmud says that Jews and their land are so inseparable that for Jews to be without the land would be to have no purpose at all. It would be, in the Torah's terms, to stray hopelessly and utterly away from God, away from the source of all meaning and security. It would be to pretend to be something we are not, to decide—like Andersen's mermaid—to give up a piece of the Jewish self in order to join another culture.

As poetic as these passages are, Judaism speaks most clearly and perhaps even most eloquently when it translates broad principle into action, when it moves from homily to law. It is in law—in the details of Jewish life that those who do not appreciate its spiritual power might call "minutiae"—that Judaism brings a love for the Land of Israel to the realm of the concrete and the quotidian.

Halakhic "Hints" About Israel's Status

In general, Jewish law forbids a Jew to ask a non-Jew to perform any action on the Sabbath that the Jew could not personally perform at that time. The rabbis believed that to tell Jews that they could not do something but to tell them that they could ask someone else to do it for them would make a mockery of the entire system. But interestingly, the *halakhah* makes a famous exception to this general rule. Based on a discussion in the Talmud (*Gittin* 8b and *Bava Kamma* 80b), Jewish law states that if a Jew wants to buy land in Israel, he can instruct a non-Jewish person to draw up the contract even on Shabbat (Maimonides, *Hilkhot Shabbat* 6:11). Jewish life in the Jewish land is so important that preparing a contract for the purchase of land in Israel overrides even a critical law of Sabbath observance.

The Land of Israel even affects the laws of *tzedakah*. In its "triage" of who should receive "charitable" funds before whom, the *Shulḥan Arukh* (the code of Jewish law) mandates that the poor of the Land of Israel should receive assistance before the poor of any other land (*Yoreh De'ah* 251:3).

Other examples abound. Many of the festivals stipulated by the Torah were originally one day in duration. Shavu'ot (the Festival of Weeks), the beginning portions of Passover and Sukkot (the Festival of Tabernacles), and Shemini Azeret (which effectively concludes Sukkot) are all described by the Torah as one-day celebrations. That, indeed, is how they are celebrated in Israel to this day. Outside the Land of Israel, though, these holidays are celebrated for two days. The original reason for this practice, introduced during the Second Temple period, was that it was impossible to inform Jews of foreign lands of the precise date of the holiday in a timely fashion, since the date depended on sighting of the moon in Israel. By adding a second day in the Diaspora, Jewish authorities could be relatively certain that the holiday would be celebrated by Jews the world over at the correct time.

But this custom of adding a day and observing the holidays for two days was maintained even after sighting of the moon was replaced by a mathematically calculated calendar. Why? Many commentators justify the continued practice as a matter of custom that has become so entrenched that it cannot change. But other authorities argue that the additional day is important for another reason: it reminds every celebrant across the world that there is a profound spiritual difference between being in Israel and being anywhere else.

Even the *halakhah* concerning the affixing of a *mezuzah* (the ritual we discussed in Chapter Five) is affected by this desire to distinguish Israel from all other places. According to both the Talmud (*Menahot* 44a) and the *Shulhan Arukh*, only permanent residents need to affix a *mezuzah* to their doorposts. Since residences are considered temporary until Jews have lived in a certain place for thirty days, a *mezuzah* technically does not have to be affixed until thirty days have passed (*Yoreh De'ah* 286:22). In Israel, however, the law states that a *mezuzah* must be affixed immediately upon beginning to live in a house; presumably, the *halakhah* considers any act of dwelling in Israel permanent by definition!

No one made this point more clearly than Naḥmanides (1194–1270), one of the medieval period's most important biblical commentators and talmudic scholars. Commenting on the verse in Numbers, "And you shall take possession of the land and settle in it, for I have assigned the land to you to possess" (Numbers 33:53), Naḥmanides ruled that the word *vi-shavtem*—"and settle in it"—was no mere exhortation. Rather, he said it was an explicit command. For that reason, he included settling in the Land of Israel among his list that enumerated the 613 commandments, and in 1267 left Spain and settled in Israel, where he lived until his death.

A CLEAR PICTURE seems to be emerging. Jewish tradition seems unequivocal about the place of Israel in Jewish life. From everything that we have seen, from the liturgy, from biblical and rabbinic sources, and even from Judaism's legal tradition, there would seem to be no doubt that life in Israel is not only preferable, but, in fact, the only option for serious and committed Jews. Anything other than life in Israel, these sources suggest, is at best a compromise and may even be illegitimate.

Even the Hebrew language itself reflects this ambivalence. The most common word for Diaspora, *galut*, is also the word for exile. While English has distinct words for "diaspora"—a geographic condition, and "exile," a spiritual condition, the Hebrew *galut* doesn't distinguish. Geography affects the spirit; to be orphaned physically is to be unanchored spiritually as well.

While most American Jews do not know enough Hebrew to internalize this message, we have picked up strains of that music from numerous places. When we hear noted Israeli political scientist Shlomo Avineri use an international "pulpit" to demean Diaspora communities worldwide, we feel dismissed, almost cursed. If our Israeli counterparts think we're illegitimate, what's the point of going on? When Deputy Foreign Minister Yossi Beilin told a major international Zionist group in 1994 that they should cease fund-raising efforts on Israel's behalf and tend to their own crumbling Jewish communities, we felt rejected. What is our role, if not to support Israel? When these comments convince American Jews that Israel is center stage for all Jewish activity, the inevitable corollary is that Diaspora Jewish life ultimately does not matter.

UNLESS American Jews can find some reasonable response to this notion that Israel, and only Israel, occupies center stage, we will have no hope of reconstructing a meaningful identity in America. At this point, a majority of the world's Jews still live outside the Land of Israel. Does it make sense to suggest that their lives and their Jewish commitments are illegitimate, inauthentic, doomed to failure? Hardly! That's an absurd, self-defeating approach to the Jewish future. We need something very different. We need to ask once again whether the picture we have sketched of a Jewish tradition that validates only Jewish life in the homeland is, in fact, a full or correct picture. As we've seen, Jewish life is rarely simple. Not surprisingly, there is a very different side to this picture as well.

ANOTHER VIEW OF DIASPORA JEWISH LIFE

As much as the ideal of Jewish life is clearly to live in Israel, Jewish authorities from antiquity to the present have had to acknowledge that most Jews choose to live in the Diaspora. Even today, when there is a renewed State of Israel, most Jews have not gone to their homeland. Throughout history, those who have wanted to be brutally honest have had to admit that theory is just that—theory; Jewish reality, they understood, is not always as simple.

One of the classic admissions of this ambivalence about living in Israel is found in a work we first encountered in Chapter Two, the *Kuzari*. In the *Kuzari*, written at roughly the same time that Naḥmanides and Maimonides lived, Rabbi Judah Ha-Levi speaks through a fictitious rabbi who is illustrating the beauty—and truth—of the Jewish tradition to a gentile king. As part of his lengthy discussion of Judaism, the rabbi discusses the centrality of Israel in Jewish life, and actually summarizes many of the passages we examined above.

But the king is unimpressed. He responds to the rabbi that such a tradition seems hypocritical when so many Jews elect not to live in their allegedly sacred land. This is the second of the two times in the entire *Kuzari* that the rabbi finds himself unable to prove the king wrong. The rabbi acknowledges the inconsistency, and says, "You have embarrassed me, King of the Kuzars." He admits that when it comes to the Land of Israel, Jews do not take the words of their tradition seriously. In beautifully poetic language, he says:

> And our utterances of "bow toward His holy hill" (Ps. 99:9), "bow down to His footstool" (Ps. 99:5) and "Who restores His Presence to Zion" are little more than the chirping of a starling, for we do not think about what they mean, as you have duly noted, Kuzar King.
>
> (KUZARI 2:24)

The rabbi acknowledges what we all know. Jews are ambivalent. Though we have a Jewish homeland and have long prayed for its restoration, we have not made it our home. We pray for Israel's welfare, but we choose to do so from the comfort of America.

Yet while Rabbi Judah Ha-Levi might have seen Jews' decisions to live outside Israel as an unfortunate compromise with the legal reality, other authorities sought to place the majority of Jews on firmer legal ground. Earlier, we cited the famous passage from the talmudic tractate *Ketubbot* that argued that a Jew living outside the Land of Israel was so spiritually impoverished as to have "[had] no God." And while that is certainly the thrust of that particular talmudic discussion, a very different viewpoint appears at the bottom of the very same talmudic page. There, we read:

Rabbi Zera was evading Rav Judah because he desired to go
up to the Land of Israel while Rav Judah had expressed [the
following view:] Whoever goes up from Babylon to the Land
of Israel transgresses a positive commandment, for it is said
in Scripture, " 'They shall be carried to Babylon, and there
shall they be, until the day that I remember them,' says the
Lord" (Jeremiah 27:22).

(KETUBBOT 110B)

According to this story, Rabbi Zera, who wanted to make *aliyah*
and move to Israel, avoided Rav Judah because he knew Rav
Judah would tell him that he ought not go. Rav Judah, who
claimed that any return to Israel was a violation of God's desire
that the Jews languish in Babylonian captivity, surely represents a
strange and highly individualistic position, not echoed elsewhere
in the vast literature of the Talmud. But Rav Judah was an important authority, and his pro-Diaspora view has therefore been
recorded for eternity in the pages of the Talmud.

Rav Judah, however, was not the only one to claim that living
outside the Land of Israel was a legitimate choice for Jews. He
may have been one of the few talmudic authorities to make this
claim explicitly, but many others spoke with their actions no less
clearly that Rav Judah did with his words. Of the two Talmuds,
the Babylonian and the Palestinian, the Babylonian is by far the
more complex, sophisticated and imaginative work. Many of
the authorities quoted in the Babylonian Talmud lived, as the
name suggests, in Babylonia. They certainly had the option to
settle in Israel; moving there was not beyond the realm of the
possible. True, Jewish life was more comfortable in Babylonia
than in Israel. But many Jews *did* live there, and *these* Babylonian
scholars chose to live their lives and do their work elsewhere.

This phenomenon continued long after the talmudic period.
While Nahmanides argued that Numbers 33:53 clearly articulated
a command to live in Israel, Maimonides disagreed. Like

Naḥmanides, Maimonides also compiled a listing of the 613 commandments. But interestingly, in Maimonides's list, the command to settle in the Land of Israel does not appear. And while Maimonides did visit Israel in 1165, he chose not to remain there. He made a conscious choice to leave, and never apologized for it.

Ever since Maimonides, scholars have struggled to explain his decision not to include living in the Land of Israel as one of the 613 commandments. Most authorities have argued that though Maimonides did not specifically mention this particular commandment, he certainly intended it to be inferred from other parts of his work. But not everyone takes this view.

After Naḥmanides criticized Maimonides for not including the commandment to live in Israel in *Sefer Ha-Miẓvot,* his listing of the 613 commandments, Rabbi Isaac de Leon, author of the *Megillat Esther* (published in 1591), a commentary on Maimonides's work, defended Maimonides:

> It seems to me that the reason that our Master did not include the inheritance of the Land or dwelling in it [in his listing of the commandments] is that [this commandment] was in effect only from the time of Moses and Joshua, through [King] David, as long as they had not been exiled from their land. But once they were exiled from their land, this commandment [to live in Israel] will not be in effect until the days of the Messiah.
>
> (MEGILLAT ESTHER, POSITIVE COMMANDMENT NO. 4)

What a radical approach! Despite all the evidence in the tradition that speaks of living in Israel as the only legitimate option, Rabbi Isaac de Leon makes a courageous claim: theory is wonderful, he seems to say. But the Jews have been exiled for centuries, he reminds us, and it is time for the tradition to reflect what we know—most Jews simply do not and will not live there.

A similar perspective has emerged even in the most traditional circles of twentieth-century American Orthodoxy. The passionate Zionism of much of contemporary Orthodoxy notwithstanding, some Orthodox authorities have recognized the enormous incongruity between what the legal tradition advocated and what most religiously committed Jews actually do. Apparently uncomfortable with that cognitive dissonance, they have argued that remaining in America (or elsewhere outside of the land of Israel) is not, in fact, a violation of Jewish law.

Perhaps the greatest halakhic authority of the twentieth century was Rabbi Moshe Feinstein (1895–1986). Born in Belorussia, Feinstein eventually emigrated to the United States where he became internationally recognized for his voluminous knowledge and for his prolific composition of legal rulings on a variety of issues. In one of those rulings, he addressed the question of whether it is permissible to live outside the Land of Israel. Despite all the legal sources we saw earlier that argued for Israel's centrality and for the urgency of moving to Israel, Rabbi Feinstein ruled:

> As for your question whether there is a commandment to live in the Land of Israel as Naḥmanides believes . . . it is not a commandment at this time. True, most authorities hold that it *is* a commandment. But it is obvious that at this moment [in history] there is no such obligation . . . for if there were, we would find that it is forbidden to live outside the land of Israel, since [living there would constitute] violation of the positive commandment [of living in Israel]. . . . But we find no such prohibition, except for [the prohibition] that one who lives in Israel may not leave to dwell in the Diaspora. . . . It emerges that only for residents of Israel is it forbidden to live outside of Israel. . . . And since it is not a positive commandment, we should also be concerned . . . about whether we would be able to fulfill all the commandments "tied to the land."
>
> (IGGEROT MOSHE, EVEN HA-EZER, 102)

Rabbi Feinstein could not be clearer. Living in Israel is not required. Indeed, he goes further. He suggests at the conclusion of this brief argument that since we are not required to live there, we should be particularly concerned that going there might put us in the position of being obligated for the many (primarily agricultural) commandments that must be performed only in Israel and that are difficult to perform. Is Rabbi Feinstein thus suggesting that it is perhaps better *not* to be there? Is he subtly arguing *for* Diaspora life?

It is not clear how far we are to take Rabbi Feinstein's implications. But others have been much more direct, and have said explicitly that Diaspora living is better than living in Israel. In 1987, Professor Jacob Neusner, a prolific American scholar of Judaica, denied without embarrassment the very assumptions underlying the "denigration of the Diaspora." Writing in the *Washington Post,* he asserted:

> It's time to say that America is a better place to be a Jew than Jerusalem. If ever there was a Promised Land, we Jewish Americans are living in it. Here Jews have flourished, not alone in politics and the economy, but in matters of art, culture and learning. Jews feel safe and secure here in ways that they do not and cannot in the State of Israel. And they have found an authentically Jewish voice—their own voice—for their vision of themselves. . . . God alone knows the future. But for here, now and for whatever future anyone can foresee, America has turned out to be our Promised Land.

Many American Jewish leaders greeted Neusner's piece with shock, even outrage. Because Neusner's claim was so much at variance with what American (and other) Jews had always assumed, his article was greeted as virtually heretical by some leaders of the Jewish community. What upset many was not only his unbridled optimism about American Jewish life, but his scathing critique of what he saw as Israel's disappointing record:

Zionism promised that the Jewish state would be a spiritual
center for the Jewish people. But today, . . . [a]part from some
fine fiction, Israeli art and creative life have made only a slight
impact on American Jews. . . . The not very-well-kept secret
is that except in a few areas of natural strength, such as
archaeology of the Land of Israel or Hebrew language studies, Israeli scholarship is pretty dull. After Martin Buber, not
a single Israeli thinker has made a mark outside the intellectual village of Jerusalem. After Gershom Scholem, not a single Israeli scholar in the study of Judaism has won any
audience at all outside of the State of Israel. Everyone can
boast about locale. But who, today, is listening?

Neusner went on to critique Israel for a lack of religious pluralism and a host of other maladies that, he argued, detracted from
its traditional place at the center of Jewish life, and that—to his
mind—bequeathed that role to the American Jewish community.

Many observers objected to Neusner's hyperbolic tone, claiming that he had spoken about a very subtle issue in black-and-
white terms. Others pointed to evidence that American Jews *were*
assimilating. Some noted examples of genuine anti-Semitism in
America and still others named Israeli scholars who do have
impact around the world. Some respondents suggested that
Neusner had failed to take account of the role Israel played in
instilling pride in Diaspora Jews, thus enabling them to continue
their work of building the Jewish communities in which they
lived. Still others pointed to a profound renaissance of traditional
Jewish learning that, they claim, far outshadows anything that is
happening in the Diaspora.

But whether Neusner was correct or incorrect, or more likely,
the degrees to which he was both right *and* overstated, is not
what is crucial for our discussion. For our purposes, what matters
is that such a visible Jewish personality pronounced publicly—
and in a national, non-Jewish publication at that—that *shelilat ha-*

golah, the denigration of the Diaspora, was fundamentally wrongheaded.

Despite the centuries, the profoundly different backgrounds and the wildly different religious worldviews that separate them, all those authorities make the same point: there *is* authentic, legitimate and passionate Jewish life to be lived outside the State of Israel. That should not, of course, deny that the bulk of the halakhic tradition still sees living in Israel as the ideal. Nor should it in any way minimize our awareness that Israel is a reality with profound and dramatic implications for Jewish life. The creation of the State of Israel is undoubtedly the most important historical event for Jews in the last two thousand years, of more significance, ultimately, than even the Shoah. Diaspora Judaism is more enriched by Israel than anyone can articulate, and Jewish life in Israel is spiritually and nationally fulfilling in certain ways that Diaspora Jewish life could never emulate. Perhaps most tellingly, statistics suggest that because Israel's Jewish population is growing so rapidly and that of the Diaspora is diminishing, Israel will soon be the world's largest Jewish community.

All that having been said, however, the denigration of the Diaspora is a harmful, shortsighted approach to Jewish life. For the foreseeable future, there will continue to be very large Diaspora Jewish communities, and those communities need a vision, a sense of purpose. No longer can we expend energy arguing about whether we are legitimate. There is ample evidence in the tradition that Diaspora life, while perhaps not what the tradition might have originally envisioned, *is* authentic Jewish life. For us, therefore, the important task is to develop a conception of what our contribution to the world might be.

WHAT THE DIASPORA MIGHT COME TO MEAN

Critical ideas in Jewish life have always been developed by actual Jews living real lives. Jewish philosophy never developed in a vacuum, and Jewish attitudes to the Promised Land were no exception.

For a long time, it was safe to dream of a return to the Promised Land. It was safe to plead with God to restore Jewish independence in Israel and to "gather our exiles from the four corners of the earth," because it did not seem likely to happen. As long as Jews had little opportunity to transport themselves to a Jewish homeland, the dream of restoring Zion was valuable and safe. The dream restored hope. It reminded an impoverished and disenfranchised people of a rich national history, and suggested that their days of grandeur could once again come to be.

But when dreams come true, life often becomes very complicated. When the State of Israel was created in 1948, Jews throughout the world cheered and celebrated. Some danced in the streets. They raised money, waved Israeli flags, worked for Zionist causes all across the world. But for the most part, they did not leave their homes. Glued to their radios in November 1947 as if their lives hung in the balance during the United Nations vote, few of those Jews realized what was about to happen—two thousand years of dreaming would suddenly become reality, and Jews would ironically discover that most of them preferred the dream to reality.

Now, half a century later, contemporary Jews still live with the incongruity of having both a tradition formulated when they had no land and a contemporary reality in which that land is accessible. For many Jews, important though Israel is, it will not be home, at least in a physical sense. If honesty matters, therefore, American Jews shall have to be forthright about the decisions we have made. Many of us have decided to stay. We have made that decision for personal, professional or sometimes inchoate reasons. But that is what we have decided, and we need a mission. We need a sense that life in the Diaspora is not second-rate or illegitimate. American Jews need to commit themselves to discovering what it is that Jews can contribute wherever they have chosen to live. That task is not nearly as difficult as it might seem.

CONTRIBUTIONS TO JEWISH LIFE
THAT ONLY THE DIASPORA CAN MAKE

The legitimacy, perhaps even the necessity, of Diaspora life stems from the fact that an integral part of the Jewish mission is about Jews' modeling and broadcasting their message to the non-Jewish world. Jews cannot do their work in a vacuum. The tradition's assertion that the descendants of Abraham, Isaac and Jacob need to be a blessing to the world requires that Jews be in contact with the world outside their own community. Where better to do that than in the Diaspora?

Where better than in the Diaspora can Jews make their claim about the possibility of survival, even in the face of political weakness? If part of the Jewish mission is to be gently critical of society's values and mores, isn't it almost necessary by definition that at least major portions of the Jewish people live in non-Jewish society? To be sure, all this presupposes that Jews will take these missions seriously. But if we do, Israel cannot be our only platform. We simply wouldn't be heard.

As important as it might be to use the Diaspora as a platform for the proclamation of the values we discussed in Chapters Four, Five and Six, Diaspora Jewry plays yet another significant role in contemporary Jewish affairs. Because American Jews are so prone to romanticizing Israel, we have long overestimated the Jewishness of the Jewish state. We have too often bought into the fallacy that while Diaspora Jewry is disappearing as a result of assimilation, the State of Israel will virtually guarantee Jewish identity to the Jews who live there.

Today, however, Jewish leaders know better. They know that although the future of Diaspora Jewry hangs very much in the balance, things are not much more assured in Israel. To be sure, Israeli Jews all speak Hebrew, have some conversance with the holidays, and get at least an elementary Jewish education in the public school system. But Israel is also a country with a deep divide between the "religious" and the "secular," in which the "grays" of American Jewish life are almost nonexistent. It is a country in which Westernization is rapidly spreading across society, and in which, painfully and ironically, Israelis are also beginning to ask themselves, Why be Jewish?

Some radical Israeli intellectuals have even argued that the history of Israel should be told as part of the history of the Middle East, denying that Judaism as a religion should play a major role in Israeli cultural life. Most famous of these intellectuals was Yonatan Ratosh (1908–1981). Ratosh, founder of a group called the "Canaanites" (as opposed to Jews), was a poet who believed that Israeli Jews had more connection to Israeli Arabs and to Maronites in Lebanon than to Diaspora Jews, because the Israeli Jews, Arabs and Maronites shared a bond of land. While Ratosh began by *predicting* that most Diaspora Jews would not come to Israel, he gradually grew to *hope* that they would not come. Ultimately, after the Six Day War in 1967, Ratosh saw the opportunity for a broad regional peace. He suggested that Palestinian Arabs should no longer consider themselves part of the Arab nation, and urged Israeli "Hebrews" not to see themselves as part of world Jewry. A strange position coming from the Jewish state.

And Jewish tradition and commitment is in trouble even in less radical portions of Israeli culture. In the Israeli secular public schools, Jewish studies are disappearing from the curriculum. This is not an accident, but rather, is a response to some secular Israelis' personal experience with a close relationship between the secular government and the religious parties. In the minds of too many Israelis, Jewish religion equals Orthodoxy, and Orthodoxy inevitably leads to religious coercion. That is not a fair reading of Orthodoxy, obviously, but in some circles there is now a fear of Jewishness in the Jewish state. For others, Jewish tradition in a rapidly Westernizing society seems simply irrelevant. In Israeli academic circles, "post-Zionism" is now a buzzword, indicating that many of the original assumptions about what the Jewish state would be are now highly controversial. But whatever the reason, one conclusion is all but inevitable: Israel is only one generation behind the United States in facing its own Jewish identity crisis.

Ironically, the assumption that Israeli Jewish identity is secure in at least the religiously right-wing portions of Israeli society is also unfounded. Paradoxically, when one moves to the extreme-right positions in the Israeli religious spectrum, support for Israel as a state becomes tenuous, and at the outer reaches, with groups like the *Neturei Karta* (who believe that only the Messiah can reestablish the Jewish state), it even turns into hostility. Again, this is a radical extreme in Israeli society, but its presence is felt.

Simply put, living in the Land of Israel is an important Jewish value, but it is unfortunately no guarantee of healthy Jewish (or even Israeli) identity. In Israel, just as in America, there is much work that needs to be done.

And here is where contemporary Diaspora Jews are uniquely poised to help. It is in the Diaspora that pluralistic models of Jewish life have taken root, offering alternatives to Jews with varying spiritual needs. Those alternatives, though developing, are all but nonexistent in Israel. It is in the Diaspora that liturgical creativity thrives, in which new models of Jewish leadership have been created, and in which a wide variety of educational endeavors have already sprung up, each struggling to create new avenues for promoting Jewish identity when it is challenged as never before. It is in the Diaspora that summer camps, for children as well as adults, have opened new vistas in Jewish education. It is primarily in the Diaspora, and not in Israel, that Jews are fashioning new forms of Jewish life that they believe are suited to the needs of modernity.

Has the Diaspora solved the Jewish identity problem? Are the liberal Jewish denominations successfully addressing the problems they were created to solve? Not yet. But Diaspora communities have at least acknowledged the challenge, which unfortunately is still more than can be said for most elements of the Israeli community.

Obviously, neither community has a monopoly on solutions to the problem of Jewish identity. But as Israelis struggle to define reasons for maintaining Jewishness in the Jewish state, Diaspora Jews have a contribution to make. Jews outside the Land of Israel face similar challenges, and have experimented with ideas that might help Israeli society. If we focused on recognizing American Judaism's potential contributions, instead of delegitimizing Diaspora Jews, we might enable American Jews and Israelis to transcend their long-standing tradition of mutual condescension.

Does the world need the Jews? Yes, it does. And Israel needs Diaspora Jews. American Jews have a vital role to play. It is time to start. First, we need to acknowledge that role. Then, we need to find the courage to search honestly for the answers that both American and Israeli Jews need so desperately.

Yes, Israel is the Jewish home in ways that no other place can be. But the Bible's text is clear: when God spoke to Abraham and Jacob, promising them that they and their descendants would be blessings to the world, God spoke as they left their homes, not as they sat comfortably within them. God's promises to Abraham (Genesis 12:2 and 22:15–18) come as Abraham leaves his father's home, and as he is away from home on a journey to Mount Moriah to sacrifice his son. And God's promise to Jacob (Genesis 28:12–14) comes when Jacob is in the midst of a journey, sleeping away from home, fully cognizant of his complete vulnerability. The Torah does not seem to believe that one must be "home" to be this blessing; if anything, being away from home creates both unique vulnerabilities and unique opportunities.

MOSES' WORDS to the Jewish people, uttered thousands of years ago, ring true now more than ever:

> 6For you are a people consecrated to the LORD your God: of all the peoples on earth the LORD your God chose you to be His treasured people. 7It is not because you are the most

numerous of peoples that the LORD set His heart on you and chose you—indeed, you are the smallest of peoples; ⁸but it was because the LORD favored you and kept the oath He made to your fathers. . . .

(DEUTERONOMY 7:6–8)

Moses seems to have understood what some contemporary Jews do not: God (to use the Torah's language) did not pick the Jews because they would be the majority where they did their work. That is not necessary. The question that ultimately matters for Jews is not so much where they will do their work, but whether they will do it at all. What matters is not place, but identity. To the extent that Jews no longer believe we have a mission, we have lost our ability to explain to other Jews why they ought to choose Judaism. To reverse the trend, Jews—wherever they may be—need to regain that sense of mission. Israel offers some unique opportunities, while America offers others. Arguments about where Jews should live are convenient because they shield Jews from the real question about how they will live Jewishly and what they believe they are here to do. It is time to drop this defense; there is work that needs to be done.

CHAPTER EIGHT

"Choosing to Be Chosen"— Turning Vision into Reality

*I*n September 1996, *Life* magazine published a photo-essay about Jews in America. Appearing just shortly before Rosh Ha-Shannah, the story told how on the Jewish New Year, Jews

> will begin chanting beautiful ancient blessings as candles flicker in the gathering darkness of their homes. They will share loaves of sweet, amber bread and apples dipped in honey. In the morning, they will enter tabernacles where white-robed cantors sing the praises of the Lord and loud blasts are trumpeted on ram's horns. Then they will embrace one another and offer a traditional greeting: "May you be inscribed for a good year in the Book of Life." . . . And then [after the holiday], their ancient identities will once again recede as they reenter the American mainstream.

For generations of Jews weaned on the dream that we could have both deep Jewish resonance and complete participation in American life, this picture would have been a virtual vision of perfection. But a new generation, wondering if a few holidays and a handful of rituals will really sustain Jewish identity, realizes that there are profound dangers when our "ancient identities . . . recede." Which raises painful questions: Can we make it here? Or is it now too late?

But painful though these questions may be, they are not new. In many senses, Jews today are the spiritual heirs of the biblical matriarch Rebekah, who when pregnant with twins and profoundly uncomfortable asked *lammah zeh anokhi*—"Why do I exist?" (Genesis 25:22). God's response, "Two nations are in your womb, two separate peoples shall issue from your body" (Genesis 25:23), is an assurance and a parallel to the contemporary Jewish condition.

Jewish life today is rife with discomfort. Like Rebekah, Jews today are caught in the struggle between two nations. Ours, of course, is a struggle not between two fetuses, but between two images of who we might be. It is not a struggle between Jacob and Esau, but a conflict that is fundamentally internal. It is strife not between brothers, but between two parts of a national soul. It is the dilemma we feel upon realizing that we cannot be completely at home in America and at one with its values and at the same time committed to lives of Jewish substance and moment.

Does the tradition itself say anything about all this? Because these dilemmas are so ancient, it should not surprise us that it does. Indeed, surviving assimilation is such a constant and critical issue for Jews that the Jewish calendar even devotes a holiday to addressing that theme. Surprising though it may seem, that holiday is Purim.

PURIM AND ITS TIMELESS QUESTIONS

Because Jews in America too often live their Jewish lives vicariously through their children, too much of Jewish life is child-oriented, without attention to the themes it raises for adults. The problem with Judaism lived exclusively for our children is not that it takes children seriously, but that it discounts adults. It assumes that holidays like Purim are cute and fun, but that they have little to say to adults about serious and existential issues. Nothing could be further from the truth.

On Purim, Jews read the Megillah, a Hebrew word for

"scroll" that often refers to the Book of Esther. Esther tells the story of the evil Haman, who plotted to kill the Jews but who was ultimately thwarted by Esther (one of the king's "wives") and her relative Mordecai. By the end of the story, it is Haman and his sons who are hanged, while the Jews prevail and help themselves to the spoils of victory.

On the surface, the Megillah is an amusing tale of palace intrigue and national survival. But upon closer examination, particularly in light of the customs that Jews observe on Purim, it becomes clear that something much more profound is at stake.

The heros of the story, Mordecai and Esther, are in many ways not unlike the American Jews with whom this book is concerned. How do we know this? In part, from their names. Modern biblical scholars assert that although Mordecai and Esther are now classic Jewish names, that was not always the case. Indeed, at the time of the story, Mordecai and Esther were names of Babylonian gods. Mordecai was based on the name of the Babylonian god Marduk, while Esther is derived from the name of the goddess Ishtar.

That is no small point. To name one's Jewish children after the god or goddess of the prevalent culture is an astounding statement of assimilation. It would be like naming a Jewish child today Chris, or Christine. Though possible, that almost never happens. In the committed Jewish community, it simply never happens. But it happened to Mordecai and Esther, which reveals something about their parents' agenda. They, like many American Jews today, wanted to blend into the society around them; they did not want to be noticed.

Yet that is not all we know about Mordecai's and Esther's desire to assimilate in the culture around them. Indeed, the Megillah explicitly states that when she was brought to be examined in order that she might be brought to the king's harem, "Esther did not reveal her kindred or her people, for Mordecai instructed her that she not say" (Esther 2:20). Mordecai was conscious of the fact that revealing her Jewishness might eliminate her from the competition. He instructed her not to say anything about it, and she obeyed. What we have in Esther, therefore, is not simply a story about people poised to become Jewish heros. Esther and Mordecai start out as assimilated Jews, eager to keep their Jewishness private and their climb to power rapid.

Their tension is a profound one, a pull that has tugged Jews in competing directions for thousands of years. The tradition understood that, and began to assemble a variety of customs around the holiday of Purim that reflect an awareness of that struggle. Take the custom of costumes, for example. Despite our common contemporary misconceptions, Purim is not simply a Jewish Halloween. It is not a holiday about ghosts or goblins, nor is it simply devoted to the pure pleasure of dressing up. It is about identity and about the struggle of not knowing exactly who to be. Wearing costumes and masks is a way of giving expression to Mordecai's and Esther's dilemmas. "Who am I?" "Who do I want to be?" "Do you recognize me?" "Do I want you to?"

Add to the story of the Megillah and the tradition of costumes the custom of drunkenness on Purim and you find a holiday that also affords respite and escape from the persistent tensions of wondering who to be. The tradition actually says that Jews should drink until they are so inebriated that they cannot tell the difference between Mordecai and Haman (*Shulhan Arukh, Orah Hayyim* 695:2)! Whether Jews today ought to drink that much is an entirely separate question; what matters for our purpose is what the Book of Esther and the holiday of Purim are about. They are about identity, conflict, internal turmoil. They are about the masks that all of us are at times tempted to wear, and about the stress that attends to always hiding. They are about us.

One final point about the Book of Esther and the holiday of Purim: Esther is essentially a book about ethnic Jews. The Megillah is rather notorious in biblical literature for its omission

of any mention of God. God plays no role in the lives of Mordecai and Esther, at least as far as the text of Esther is concerned.
Indeed, when Mordecai implores Esther to intercede with the
king to avoid the destruction of the Jews,

> [13]Mordecai had this message delivered to Esther: "Do not
> imagine that you, of all the Jews, will escape with your life by
> being in the king's palace. [14]On the contrary, if you keep
> silent in this crisis, relief and deliverance will come to the
> Jews from another quarter, while you and your father's
> house will perish. And who knows, perhaps you have
> attained to royal position for just such a crisis."
>
> (ESTHER 4:13–14)

In any other book of the Bible, one would expect mention of
God at this juncture. Mordecai's message to Esther virtually begs
for mention of God, but he seems to refuse to accede. All he can
say is that "relief and deliverance will come to the Jews from
another quarter." But what that quarter is, he cannot say.

How similar to the predicament of modern Jews. Struggling
between competing definitions of who we are, painfully conscious of the threat to *our* existence, we desperately hope that
relief and deliverance will come from some other quarter. But
from where?

In our era, though, matters are different than they were for
Mordecai and Esther. For us, the threat from which we need
relief and deliverance is different and we do know where it will
come from. For Jews today, the threat is no longer Haman and his
gallows, but our own inability to bring energy, enthusiasm and
passion to Jewish life. And the solution is different, as well. American Jews can count on relief and deliverance neither from God
nor from palace intrigue. Deliverance from this predicament will
have to come from us.

REIMAGINING AMERICAN JUDAISM

That is the conclusion to which the Purim holiday tries to lead us. Today, survival is up to American Jews themselves. Purim is about rededicating ourselves to making that survival a reality.

That, of course, will not be easy. We face a myriad of challenges, one of which has been the focus of this book—recovery of our sense of "chosenness," a sense of purpose, a reason for being. It is recovery for the Jews what many Americans have found in their sense of "manifest destiny." We need a sense of mission, for we have become, to paraphrase Abraham Joshua Heschel, "messengers who've forgotten our message."

This book has argued that we have our work cut out for us if we want to resume the role of messenger. For the Judaism that lives in America today cannot recover or transmit those messages. Contemporary American Judaism, in most of its forms, is too detached from the textual and ritual traditions that give Jewish life not only its richness, but its sense of how to be a blessing for the rest of the world. To recover a sense of mission and importance, American Jews have to become comfortable once again with chosenness. To do that, we need to reengineer the way we raise and teach children and adults; indeed, we need to reassess many of the assumptions that have characterized American Jewish life for decades, if not for generations. How shall we accomplish that?

The End of the Sound Bite Era

When contemporary Jews are exposed to a sophisticated presentation of tradition, one of their most common reactions is "Why did I always think that this tradition was simply an amalgam of quaint little stories?"

Many of us ask similar questions about other parts of the tradition that we rediscover as adults. Why were we never given opportunities to wonder what chosenness might mean? Why did we never encounter the meaning of "holy" as "separate" in Jewish life? Why is my own tradition so foreign to me?

There are many reasons for the ways Jewish tradition was transmitted, but one of the most important is that Jews in America typically stop studying Jewish life long before we are ready to think as adults. Imagine that we had stopped studying literature at the age most Jews stop studying Judaism. Would we still love to read? Would we still find ourselves roaming through bookstores, wishing that we had more time for all the books that beckon to us? Probably not. If the last time we had been taught to read and to appreciate literature was at the age of thirteen or sixteen, we would have no interest in books. They would seem daunting, inaccessible, ultimately irrelevant.

American Jews thus need to redesign their education system from the ground up. Schools, camps and other programs can be developed for children, but adults need to be addressed as well. If we are serious about Jewish education, we cannot allow it to stop at the age of thirteen, or even sixteen. That's exactly when we just begin to have the skills to confront complex ideas.

Perhaps we need to begin to think of Jewish education as "minority education," as a way we transmit a culture that is always at risk of being swallowed up by the society and culture around it. But at present, we have no idea how to do that. It's ironic, indeed, that the Dalai Lama came to Jews to ask us to teach *him* how to survive in exile. Do we have it so well figured out?

Having grown up with an education system that taught them very little, American Jewish adults must now become autodidacts. Having been failed by schools that were designed to make Jewish life unobjectionable and undemanding, many of us know far too little about serious and sophisticated Jewish life. We will have to educate ourselves. We have to find the teachers who can make this tradition come alive. We need to read some of the myriad of books on Jewish life that now line the shelves of major bookstores across the country; we need to provide for ourselves the education that no one ever gave us.

Jews are also beginning to recognize that whatever we teach ourselves about our tradition, it has to go far beyond the surface. It is time for depth. The sound bite era of Jewish education is exhausted and ineffective. Its time is over. Thoughtful Jews, well educated in other domains of their lives, will find no sustenance or excitement in a simplistic tradition that has quick and immature answers to profound questions. Though we know that there is much sophistication, angst and ambivalence in the Jewish tradition, most Jews never get a sense of that ambivalence from the "Reader's Digest" version of Judaism that we all too often provide. To get a sense of the wonder, the sophistication and the richness of our tradition, we will need to examine it firsthand. American Jews live in a culture that produces CDs with titles like *Mozart's Greatest Hits*. It's an absurdity, this version of culture and sophistication. But Jews in America have bought into this consumerist version of Jewish education hook, line and sinker. That has to change.

Not a Tradition of Bystanders

Revamping the educational system of American Jewish life is not all that finding "relief and deliverance" will take. Given what we have seen in the preceding chapters, it has now become clear that Judaism makes its case about chosenness and purpose largely through the way it exhorts Jews to live. As I argued for at least one of many possible conceptions of chosenness in Chapters Four through Six, we saw that the substance of Jewish life simply cannot be communicated without commitment to Jewish learning and observance. Painful, perhaps, but true. Nothing in Jewish tradition says that Jews are chosen simply by virtue of being; rather, chosenness in the tradition is conditional. Jews are chosen if—and only if—they live so that they stand for something.

The Jewish community in America, however, has not wanted to make that claim. Our leaders feared that by placing too many demands on Jews, it would force us to flee. They imagined that in an era in which Jews could easily decide not to remain Jewish, the logical step was to raise as few "obstacles" to Jewish identification as possible.

It is important, though, not to lay the guilt for our current predicament at the feet of previous generations' leaders. Those leaders did a wonderful job of preserving Jewish life in America. At every step of the way, they were trying to address the specific needs of their community as they saw them, and to plot what they thought was the most appropriate and responsive course. All we know now is that what may have worked a generation ago no longer works today. The issue is not who is at fault; the question is how to begin the repair. The issue is not the leaders of the past; the issue is us—the Jews of the present.

Jews today want more Judaism, not less. It should not be surprising that those elements of the Jewish community that seem to be attracting the most interest and that are apparently inspiring the most passionate commitments to Jewish life are precisely those communities that encourage more creativity, more commitment and more involvement. Not less. After all, in what other areas of life do we dare imagine that things can matter if they do not make demands on us? We know better. Relationships that matter require effort. Raising children well does not mean lowering standards. People who know and love music know the difference between music and Muzak. The former inspires, the latter fills time.

If we are to be honest, American Jews will need to acknowledge that Jewish tradition speaks if and only if it is lived; there is no way to appreciate it from the sidelines. Hanukkah speaks most loudly and clearly when Jews do more than buy gifts and light candles; singing its songs, studying its texts, attending to the correct placement of the menorah—these are the small but crucial details that begin to add up to a message that matters. Jewish tradition's rituals and *mitzvot*—its "commanded" behaviors—are the way we begin to internalize the central Jewish claim that it is not the individual, but community, that lies at the heart of meaningful living.

The Link Between Living and Learning— The Death of "Autonomy-Centered" Judaism?

That realization poses major challenges for a Jewish community that now recognizes the necessity of serious Jewish learning but that also wants to reserve the right to determine exactly how it will practice Judaism. The liberal movements in American Judaism have always insisted that they were just as interested as anyone else in Jewish knowledge. They simply asserted that they wished to leave decisions about behavior up to their constituents. Serious education, they insisted, could take place regardless of one's level of behavior. But matters have not been quite that simple. There is a direct—and astounding—correlation between levels of commitment in behavior and levels of commitment to Jewish learning.

The pattern is clear and undeniable—those Jews who are more committed to traditional behaviors tend to know and to study more. Similarly, the less traditional a community's behavior, the lower the educational standards in its Jewish educational institutions. Why? Because, as we have seen, behavior is not a neatly separable component of Jewish life; it is impossible to separate Jewish ideas and Jewish values from Jewish traditions. The tradition's observances are the way it gives expression to those ideas and values; without one, the other makes little sense. After a certain point, there is a cognitive dissonance in studying these traditions intensively without committing to living them. Few of us can be disconnected anthropologists about our own world. At a certain point, as we study a tradition that continually beckons to us and asks us to commit to its way of life, we either need to move in that direction, or we want to stop hearing the calling voice.

We know now that the illusion of extraordinarily well-educated Jewish communities, some of which would take Jewish tradition and behavior seriously and some of which would not, is just that—a pipe dream. The evidence is in: by and large, secular Judaism has failed to create an educated laity, while the most traditional elements in our community have raised generation after generation of deeply learned Jews.

None of this, however, should be construed as suggesting that it is only the most traditional elements of our community that can survive, or that the more liberal and progressive strands of Judaism must ultimately disappear. Nothing could be further from the truth. The issue here is not *which* version of Jewish observance and commitment Jews subscribe to, but rather, that we acknowledge that survival as Jews in this open and pluralist society will require investment in *some* version of intensive Jewish living. This book has made little mention of the major Jewish movements or denominations, not because of accidental omission, but because those divisions are often much more destructive than they are useful. Increasingly, we are finding passionate, committed Jews in all these walks of life. We are also discovering that those contemporary Jews who become passionate about study and about serious encounter with Jewish ideas and values also tend to become increasingly committed to living the tradition that expresses them. This happens in all the movements, in all walks of Jewish life. Is there ultimately going to be a close correlation between Jewish sophistication and Jewish commitment? Deep in our hearts, we know the answer, and it is clear. The answer is yes.

CHOSENNESS AND THE POSSIBILITY
OF REUNIFICATION

A return to a serious encounter with chosenness will require tremendous effort and courage from a community long accustomed to a passive way of Jewish life. But in addition to all the possible rewards and gains that would flow from a reconstituted vision of American Jewish life, another is equally important. In encountering chosenness anew, American Jews may find that we can repair our fractured and wounded community. How so?

Time and again, God reminds Abraham, Isaac and Jacob that being a Jew means bearing a message for the world at large. Too much of Jewish liturgy is universal for anyone to claim that a totally inward Jewish existence, one focused on Jews and Judaism alone, is what the tradition stands for. Precisely the opposite is the case. Jews need to begin to assert that there is absolutely no correlation between Jewish insularity and Jewish authenticity. It is one of the great tragedies of American Jewish life that those most often seen as the most authentic are those who are least involved with the outside world. There is a sad irony about a Jewish world in which "social action" and "religious seriousness" too often seem mutually exclusive. Does Jewish religious seriousness have to minimize our involvement with the outside world, with non-Jews and their culture, their wisdom and their needs? Jewish tradition speaks clearly on this: if that is what committed Judaism is to become, there is little reason for Judaism to survive.

As we reimagine American Jewish life and identity, we may find new partners and allies. Those Jews who have considered themselves committed to social action as their Jewish expression might well find a renewed interest in the more overtly religious elements that had, thus far, seemed irrelevant or even anathema. They will recognize that if they want their own message about repairing the world to be distinctly Jewish, they will need to tap into the world of Jewish text, ritual, *mitzvah* and tradition that gives their work Jewish resonance. Or they can continue unchanged, doing important universal work barely clothed in Jewish garb, knowing in the bottom of their hearts that such a mission will not speak to anyone about the importance of Judaism.

Conversely, the community of "religious" Jews may suddenly find themselves open to partnerships with those who had previously had nothing to share with them. Religious differences among Jews will never disappear; perhaps, given a tradition that relishes debate and ambivalence, that is even good. But we can learn to bind ourselves together through our differences. It is now becoming more rare for Jews to be united because of enemies from the outside. The story of Purim and the obvious way in which a threat from the outside awakens Esther's Jewish self raises an important question—can Jews awaken a sense of Jewish importance without that threat from the outside? Perhaps this search for a compelling American Jewish identity will allow us to become partners and fellow seekers once again.

AT THE VERY beginning of this book, we suggested that there are different sorts of Jews, with different interests and different needs. Among them, we said, are Jews for whom spirituality is crucial. Those Jews live in the hope that Jewish life will enable them to touch the transcendent, to feel God's presence at more than fleeting moments, to believe that their lives have value, that they are filled with meaning.

Others, we said, are more dubious about spirituality. They live with a different focus, and want to know not what Judaism can do for their internal, spiritual existence, but what it does for the world. They want a Jewish life that is focused not on what they call religious issues, but on repair, on healing, on bringing light to a world too often marked by darkness.

As conflicting as these approaches may seem, Jewish tradition says that they are ultimately not that different. What we've seen is that Judaism sees its rituals and traditions as tools not only for the spirit, but for reminding Jews that unless we repair the world, we have no reason for being. And it suggests that the only way to make "social action"—that much bandied about phrase—distinctly Jewish is to imbue it with resonances from the deepest and most spiritual parts of our tradition. There is, Jewish tradition says, no neat divider between matters of the soul and matters of the world. Judaism fully and richly lived is about both. It gives

Jews a chance to lead, to teach, to feel and to heal. It also gives us a chance to matter.

This book has argued that one critical step on the road to mattering is reengaging the notion of chosenness, of taking seriously the responsibility of being a blessing to the outside world. This suggestion is offered in the hope that it will help more Jews find their way home. It is born not out of conviction that the image of chosenness offered here is the only legitimate one, but rather, that confronting the question of what chosenness might mean has the capacity to enable Judaism to become once again a passionate, vibrant and compelling tradition.

But what this book *has* insisted on is the importance of uniqueness, of difference from the rest of the world around us. What that difference is may change with time, but part of being a responsible Jew in each generation is to think about what the content of our uniqueness might be at any given point in time. For chosenness is not a static idea. What chosenness is in one generation is not what it will be in another. What the world needs now is not what it needed a thousand years ago. And therefore, what Jews have to offer now cannot be what we offered in the past. Because of that, how each Jew construes what chosenness ought to mean will depend on how she or he evaluates the world and its condition. Different Jews' conceptions of what Judaism needs to say will depend upon what each of us thinks the world needs to hear. But that Jews need to say something—something powerful, unique and distinctively and authentically Jewish—is beyond debate. Your answers need not be those of this book. But each of us needs an answer to the question with which we began: What would the world be missing if it woke up one morning and there were simply no Jews left?

MORE THAN two hundred years ago, in 1791, a young German-Jewish immigrant to the United States named Rebecca Samuels wrote a letter to her parents, who were still in Europe. She described her new life in America, assuring them that "one can make a good living here, and all live in peace. . . . As for the Gentiles, we have nothing to complain about . . . Jew and Gentile are as one." Just several lines later, however, Samuels's wholly upbeat tone soon gave way to a more ominous prediction. "Dear Parents," she continued, "I know quite well you will not want me to bring up my children like Gentiles. [Yet] here they cannot become anything else."

This book is committed to the proposition that Rebecca Samuels was wrong. If she meant that Jewish life in America would be fraught with tensions, she was obviously right. But if what she really meant was that her children would in fact inevitably grow up to be Christians, then she was wrong. Why? Because we are not yet willing to surrender. There are still many American Jews who do not want to give up the quest for vibrant Jewish life in America. We still want to matter, and to matter as Jews. We still want our children to have meaningful Jewish lives, though we may not be certain what that entails. Most American Jews still harbor a hope that their grandchildren will also be Jews. For us, the critical questions are about how to do that, how to be part of a larger culture and to preserve fulfilling Jewish life at the same time.

That means asking hard questions our community has not faced honestly enough. In part, we have to ask ourselves, what would survival look like? When interfaith couples say that they are raising their children as Jews, what do they mean? Are they talking about a label, or are they talking about some specific content in their children's lives?

What makes a Jew? A certain number of years of Hebrew school? A Jewish mother, regardless of education? A visceral sense that when someone says "Jew" they are talking about us?

We are no longer certain what it means to have or to be a Jewish grandparent. When the next generation of American Jewish children hear the phrase "Jewish grandparents," what images will come to mind? For many Jews today, images of Jewish grandparents are rich with memories of fragrances in the kitchen, accents, distinctly different worldviews from those of society at large. What issues will define us to our grandchildren as Jewish?

Those are the questions we have to begin answering. We need to create a vision of American Judaism that gives meaning and substance to the phrase "Jewish survival." We need a conception of what that survival is, how we might measure it, and why it might be important. That, we now know, will require a dramatic shift in our thinking as American Jews.

Will American Jews buy into this project? Will they make the investment that a rich and fully lived version of Jewish life will require? Without question, some will not. They do not care enough about Jewish life to change very much, and painful though this admission is, there is probably little that we can do to attract them. But there are also many others.

Despite outward cynicism, ours is a generation of Jews who desperately want to make a difference. We want to know that our lives and our loves, our triumphs and our trials, our dreams and our fears are not for naught. More than anything, we want to live lives that we can look back on with a sense that we have made a real contribution to a world that needs us; we want to know that we stood for causes that deserved our attention and that the values that propelled us forward were more than passing phases and fads. Jewish tradition offers us just that opportunity.

We are heirs to a tradition that beckons to us, asking us to join a two-thousand-year-old tradition of demanding the most from ourselves and our society. It begs us not to despair, but to face today's challenges with the passionate belief that we can still matter. Genesis puts it plainly: "Be a blessing." It's really that simple. Jewish life urges us to commit to a way of living predicated on the belief that despite all our previous accomplishments, our brightest days and greatest contributions belong not to the past, but to the future that still lies ahead.

Notes on Sources

Does the World Need the Jews? quotes extensively from translations of original Jewish texts. Though I have adapted many of these sources to the context and style of this book, I have been aided by several superb translations.

Translations of biblical passages are taken primarily from the *Tanakh: The Holy Scriptures According to the Traditional Hebrew Text* (Philadelphia: Jewish Publication Society of America, 1985) and from the CD-ROM version of that JPS Bible published by Logos Research Systems and JPS. For translation of mishnaic passages, I relied primarily on Jacob Neusner's innovative translation, *The Mishnah* (New Haven: Yale University Press, 1988), often with some modification. Translations from the Tosefta are essentially mine, though especially in the case of sources on witnessing and capital punishment, I made extensive use of Jacob Neusner's translation, *The Tosefta —Neziqin: The Order of Damages* (New York: Ktav Publishing, 1981), again with some modification. For translations of talmudic passages, I relied on *The Soncino Talmud* (London; Soncino Press, 1977) and the CD-ROM version of that translation published by Soncino in cooperation with Davka Software. For translations of the *Pesikta Rabbati,* I am indebted to the work of William G. Braude in his *Pesikta Rabbati* (New Haven: Yale University Press, 1968), which I have used virtually without modification.

For translations of liturgical passages from the prayer book, I have used primarily *The Complete Artscroll Siddur* (New York Mesorah Publications, 1985), which is virtually unparalleled for its highly literal translation. The *Artscroll Siddur* was helpful particularly with translations of *Al Ha-Nissim, Ma'oz Zur,* the *Havdalah* service (to which I made numerous changes), *Ahavah Rabbah* and the weekday *Amidah*. The translation of *Aleinu* is basically that of *Siddur Sim Shalom* (New York: Rabbinical

Assembly and United Synagogue of America, 1985). The translation of the *Hatikvah* is taken from the *Encyclopedia Judaica.*

A small portion of the material in this book relies on ideas in articles or monographs I have published over the past several years. The discussion of decisions about having children is influenced by work that I did for *"Give Me Progeny . . .": Jewish Ethics and the Economics of Surrogate Motherhood,* published by the University of Judaism in the UJ Paper series (Vol. 8, No. 1, November 1988). I relied occasionally on ideas I had originally published in a monograph written for the American Jewish Committee, entitled *Behaving and Believing, Behaving and Belonging* (1995). Finally, I also borrowed an occasional phrase from my earlier book, *God Was Not in the Fire: The Search for a Spiritual Judaism* (New York: Scribner, 1995). A small section of Chapter Five (on law in the Christian tradition) is heavily based on *God Was Not in the Fire.*

While writing this book, I published very early drafts of Chapters Three and Four in the *Jewish Spectator.* They appeared, respectively, as "Rethinking America's Hospitality: New Challenges to American Jewish Identity" (Fall 1995) and "Re-reading Chanukah: Judaism's Festival of Survival" (Winter 1995).

For transliteration of Hebrew and Aramaic words and names, I have generally followed the transliteration system of the *Encyclopedia Judaica.* Commonly used words such as *chutzpah* and *mitzvah* employ a more well known transliteration system, using "ch" instead of "ḥ" and "tz" instead of "z."

In general, I have sought to use gender-free language when discussing God. Even at the cost of an occasionally awkward sentence structure, I have consistently avoided terms such as "He" or "His" when referring to God. I made exceptions in the case of translations, where it seemed to me preferable to portray the literal meaning of the original source as faithfully as possible. Integrity in our Jewish quests, I believe, demands that we confront the texts as they do speak, not necessarily as we might like them to.

Glossary of Hebrew Names and Terms

The following is a list of Hebrew or Aramaic words and Jewish terms that appear throughout the book. The definitions that follow are not technical definitions. Rather, they are popular ones, designed only to assist the reader in understanding this book.

Abrabanel: Don Isaac Abrabanel (1437–1508), a renowned biblical commentator and the finance minister for King Ferdinand and Queen Isabella of Spain. When the Jews were expelled from Spain in 1492, he accompanied them into exile. Also known as Isaac ben Judah Abrabanel.

Abraham: the first of the Jewish patriarchs and, by tradition, the first monotheist and the founder of the Jewish faith.

Abram: Abraham's birth name, which was later changed to Abraham as a symbol of his relationship with God.

Ahavah Rabbah: literally "Abundant Love." The blessing that directly precedes the *Shema,* it thanks God for the gift of Torah and for having chosen the Jewish people.

Aleinu: this prayer closes the liturgical service by pronouncing God's oneness and wholeness, and emphasizing the special relationship that Israel has with God.

Al Ha-Nissim: this prayer, which is added into the liturgical service on Purim and Hanukkah, thanks God for the miracles that were performed on these holidays. It is placed in the middle of the *Amidah* and in the Grace After Meals.

Al Het: an acrostic prayer recited repeatedly on Yom Kippur (the Day of Atonement), which lists a number of sins committed over the course of the year, for which we ask forgiveness.

aliyah: based on the Hebrew word that means "to go up," this term is used to refer to immigration to Israel.

Amalek: an ancient people mentioned in the Torah as a group that attacked the Israelites on their journey from Egypt to the Promised Land. The Torah commands that the Jews blot out the memory of Amalek.

Amidah: the central prayer of the Jewish liturgy. The weekday version (as opposed to versions for Sabbath and holidays) is also known as the *Shemoneh Esrei,* or the "Eighteen Benedictions." In much of rabbinic literature, the *Amidah* is also called *Ha-Tefillah* or *"the* prayer."

Amos: the first of the literary or later prophets, he lived and prophesied around 750 B.C.E. He is most well known for his proclamations about justice.

Ararat: the name of a geographic area in Armenia. According to the Torah, Noah's ark came to rest on the top of Mount Ararat.

Babylonian Talmud: compiled between 400 and 600 C.E., the Babylonian Talmud is an extensive commentary on the Mishnah. The Babylonian Talmud, composed of both legal and ethical writings, is considered the most important document of rabbinic Judaism.

Bar Kokhba: a warrior thought by many (including Rabbi Akiva) to be the Messiah, Bar Kokhba led a revolt against the Roman occupation in Palestine from 132 to 135 C.E. The revolt was a bitter failure for the Jews, who suffered devastating population losses in the battle.

Bava Batra: literally the "last gate," this tractate of Talmud, found in the Order of Damages, focuses mainly on laws concerning real estate and personal property.

Birkat Ha-Mazon: the Grace After Meals, recited by Jews after a meal in which they have eaten bread. This lengthy blessing thanks God for providing food for humankind and mentions the centrality of Israel.

bris: a shortened form of the Hebrew phrase *Brit Milah,* which means "Circumcision of the Covenant." It refers to the circumcision ceremony usually performed on the eighth day of a boy's life, formally welcoming him into the Covenant.

challah: a special braided egg bread, eaten as part of Sabbath and Festival meals.

Children of Israel: a term used in the Bible to describe the Jewish people.

chutzpah: a popular Yiddish word used to describe extreme self-confidence, to the point of audaciousness.

Deuteronomy: *Devarim* in Hebrew, this is the last of the Five Books of Moses. Most of the book is devoted to Moses' farewell address to the Israelites before his death, as they prepare to enter the land of Israel.

emet: a Hebrew word that means "truth."

Book of Esther: a book of the Bible. This biblical text is read each Purim, as it tells the story of the attempted destruction of the Jews of Persia. It concludes with the mandate that Purim be celebrated by Jews of all future generations.

Ethics of the Fathers: a tractate in the Mishnah that records moral aphorisms of the rabbis. While most of the Mishnah is legal in nature, the *Ethics of the Fathers* (or *Pirkei Avot,* as it is known in Hebrew) is more concerned with religious values and folk wisdom.

Feinstein, Rabbi Moshe (1895–1986): one of the greatest halakhic (legal) authorities of the twentieth century, Rabbi Feinstein was recognized by many as the titular head of Orthodox Judaism in America.

galut: a Hebrew word that means "exile," commonly used to refer to Jewish communities in the Diaspora. Though there are other Hebrew words, such as *tefuzot,* that also mean Diaspora, *galut* is the most commonly used term in modern colloquial Hebrew.

Gemara: an Aramaic word that means "learning" or "teaching," it commonly refers to that portion of the Talmud that is the rabbis' discussion of the Mishnah. The Talmud is comprised of Mishnah and Gemara.

Gittin: a tractate of the Mishnah and Talmud, found in the Order of Women. It deals primarily with matters related to divorce and the issuing of a *get,* the Jewish legal document of divorce.

goy kadosh: literally "a holy nation." The Torah uses this phrase to refer to the Jewish people in Exodus 19.

Haftarah: a reading from the prophetic books of the Bible that is recited in the synagogue on Sabbath and Festivals after the Torah has been read. Usually, though not always, the selection from the prophets bears some thematic connection to the Torah portion read directly before it.

Haggadah: the text that Jews read on Passover during the Seder. The *Haggadah* fulfills the religious obligation to tell the story of the exodus from Egypt in each generation. The plural is *Haggadot.*

halakhah: a Hebrew term that means "Jewish law," the word actually comes from the root which means "to go." Thus, *halakhah* essentially means "the way we are to go." The plural is *halakhot.*

Haman: a villain of the Purim story, recounted in the biblical Book of Esther. According to tradition, he plotted to have the Jewish community of Persia murdered.

ḥanukkiah: a nine-pronged candelabrum that is the symbol of the holiday of Hanukkah. One candle is lit each night in memory of the miracle of the eight nights that the oil burned in the Temple after it was rededicated by the Maccabees. Additionally, there is one candle, the *shamash,* used to light the other eight.

Hanukkah: an eight-day winter holiday celebrating the rededication of the Temple in Jerusalem after it was recaptured from the Greeks by the Hasmoneans. Today it is celebrated with a variety of rituals, the most well known of which is the lighting of the Hanukkah candles.

Hanukkah *gelt:* literally, "Hanukkah money." In traditional Jewish communities, Jewish children would receive a small number of coins on Hanukkah as a present.

Hasidic: belonging to or stemming from the Jewish community that had its roots in the pietistic movement started by Israel Baal Shem Tov (1699–1761).

Hatikvah: the Israeli national anthem, written in 1878 by Naphtali Herz Imber. *Hatikvah* was first the anthem of the Zionist movement and after the state was founded, it became Israel's national anthem as well. *Hatikvah* means "The Hope."

Havdalah: a Hebrew word meaning "separation" or "distinction," this is also the name of the ceremony used to mark the conclusion of Sabbaths and Festivals.

Herzl, Theodor: Herzl, who lived from 1860 to 1904, was one of the notable Zionist leaders ultimately responsible for the creation of the State of Israel. Herzl determined that as long as Jews lived in non-Jewish surroundings, anti-Semitism would persist. He believed that Jews could only be safe in a land of their own, thereby laying the foundations for modern political Zionism and the creation of the Jewish state.

Hilkhot Mat'not Aniyim: literally, "the laws of giving to the poor," this term often refers to the section of Maimonides's *Mishneh Torah* that deals with the obligation to give *tzedakah,* commonly translated as "charity."

Hilkhot Shabbat: literally, "the laws of Shabbat." Often, this term refers to the section of Maimonides's great legal treatise (the *Mishneh Torah*) that deals with the laws of Sabbath observance.

Hosea: a prophet who lived and preached in the northern kingdom of Israel around 700 B.C.E. He is most known for his passion for the covenant with God, and his analogy that God's relationship with Israel is much like a husband's with his unfaithful wife.

intifada: the Arab uprising in the West Bank and Gaza Strip that began in 1987 and lasted for several years.

Isaac de Leon: author of the *Megillat Esther* (published in 1591), a commentary on Maimonides's legal work, the *Mishneh Torah.*

Isaiah: among the most well known of the later prophets of the Bible, Isaiah lived in the eighth century B.C.E. Most of his prophecies contain condemnation of Israel for disobeying God's commands and foreshadowing of their punishment should they not change their behavior.

Jacob: the grandson of Abraham and therefore the third of the three forefathers of Judaism. Jacob received the name "Israel" after he wrestled with the angel of God. Jacob's twelve sons became the twelve tribes of Israel.

Jereboam: in the Book of Kings, Jereboam was chosen by the people of Israel to lead a revolt against Reheboam, King Solomon's son, who was a cruel and arrogant king. After the battle, the kingdom was divided into Judah and Israel, and Jereboam became the first king of Israel, the northern kingdom.

Joel: one of the twelve "minor" biblical prophets, Joel lived around 400 B.C.E. The focus of the Book of Joel is a call to Israel to repent for its sins.

Judah: following Solomon's kingship over Israel, the kingdom was divided. The northern kingdom, made up of ten of the twelve tribes, was called "Israel," and the southern, comprised mostly of the tribes of Judah and Benjamin, was called "Judah."

Kaddish: an Aramaic prayer recited in different forms throughout the service. The most familiar form is that recited by mourners. The *Kaddish* is a prayer that praises and sanctifies God's name.

kadosh: literally, "holy." This Hebrew word also has other connotations, such as "separate" or "distinct."

kashrut: a Hebrew term that refers to the body of Jewish dietary laws.

kedushah: a Hebrew word that means "holiness." *Kedushah* is also the name of a section of the *Amidah,* in which the congregation refers to the angels of heaven and their praise of God.

Keilim: a tractate of the Mishnah in the Order of Purities. It deals with laws of ritual purity.

ketubbah: the traditional Jewish marriage document, which guarantees women, among other things, a financial settlement in case of divorce. In the ancient Near East, this was a radical change from the typical treatment of women.

Ketubbot: a Talmudic tractate in the Order of Women. It discusses primarily the *ketubbah,* the traditional document of Jewish marriage.

Kiddush: a Hebrew word meaning "sanctification." It generally refers to a prayer recited on Friday evening and Saturday morning that sanctifies the Sabbath day. It is usually recited over a goblet of wine.

Kiddushin: a talmudic tractate in the Order of Women that discusses primarily laws of marriage.

kippah: the Hebrew term for the traditional skullcap worn to cover one's head as a sign of humility before God.

Knesset: the Israeli parliament, whose 120 members are chosen when voters select parties, not individual politicians. Each party then determines the individual leader that will be placed in that party's elected seats.

Kuzari: an imaginative description of an argument made on behalf of Judaism before the king of Khazaria. Written by Judah Ha-Levi in the twelfth century.

Leviticus: in Hebrew, *Va-yikra.* This is the third of the Five Books of Moses, which is comprised mainly of priestly regulations of sacrifices and other elements of Temple worship.

Lubavitcher Rebbe: The rebbe is the charismatic spiritual leader of the Lubavitch community, an active and highly visible segment of the Hasidic community. The most recent Lubavitcher Rebbe was Rabbi Menachem Mendel Schneersohn, whose adherents believed him to be the Messiah.

Maccabees: a family of religious zealots who rebelled against Greek rule over Jerusalem and then all of Judea in 167 B.C.E. The holiday of Hanukkah celebrates the Maccabees' recapturing of the Temple and its rededication.

Maimonides: Judaism's most important philosopher, he lived from 1135 to 1204. Author of the famous *Thirteen Principles of Faith*, Maimonides also wrote a major philosophic treatise *(The Guide for the Perplexed)* and a legal code (the *Mishneh Torah*), among many other works.

Malachi: one of the Bible's "minor" prophets, Malachi prophesied in approximately 500 B.C.E.

Ma'oz Ẓur: a well-known Hanukkah song, "Rock of Ages," apparently composed in the mid-thirteenth century.

matzoh: the unleavened bread Jews eat during the holiday of Passover.

maya be-alma: literally, in Aramaic, "mere water." The talmudic term for a fetus up until forty days after conception.

Menaḥot: a talmudic tractate in the Order of Holiness, dealing primarily with laws of the meal offering in the Temple.

mezuzah: a small ritual object that is affixed to doorposts and that contains sacred texts inside. The command to affix these texts to the doorpost is found in the Torah and recited as part of the *Shema.*

Midrash: a Hebrew term that means "exploration" or "investigation." It generally refers to rabbinic narratives or homilies that explore scriptural sources for additional insight and meaning.

mikveh: Hebrew term for a ritual bath. Typically, the *mikveh* is used by women before marriage and after their menstrual periods (before resuming sexual relations with their partners), and by men in some communities before Sabbaths and Festivals.

minyan: a Hebrew word that literally means "counting"; it is generally used to refer to the prayer quorum of ten Jewish adults.

Mishnah: The earliest major document of Rabbinic Judaism, it was compiled by Rabbi Judah the Patriarch in approximately 220 C.E.

Mishneh Torah: one of Judaism's most important legal compilations organized by Moses Maimonides in 1180.

mitzvah: a Hebrew term that means "commandment." The plural is *mitzvot.*

Mount Moriah: the mountain upon which the Torah says Abraham was asked to sacrifice his son Isaac.

Mount Nebo: the mountain upon which the Torah says Moses died.

Mount Sinai: the mountain known as the place upon which the Jewish people received the Torah several months after they left Egypt, as they began their journey across the desert to the Promised Land.

mourner's *Kaddish:* the prayer recited by those who lost close relatives. The mourner's *Kaddish* does not mention death, but rather praises God.

Nahmanides: also known as Ramban, one of the most important biblical commentators and talmudic scholars of the medieval period. He lived from 1194 to 1270.

Neturei Karta: a group of ultra-Orthodox Jews who deny the legitimacy of any Jewish state established before the coming of the Messiah and who therefore do not recognize the State of Israel.

Noah: the biblical character, portrayed as a righteous man who "walked with God" and who was chosen to build an ark and to save humanity and the animal world from God's flood.

Numbers: the fourth book of the Five Books of Moses. It is called *Ba-Midbar* in Hebrew.

Omer: literally, the first sheaf cut during the barley harvest. The ritual of the "Counting of the *Omer*" takes place during the forty-nine days between the start of Passover and the holiday of Shavu'ot.

Passover: the eight-day festival during which Jews refrain from eating all leavened foods and products. The holiday takes place in the spring and celebrates the exodus of the ancient Israelites from Egypt.

Pesikta Rabbati: a medieval Midrash on the Festivals of the year.

pirsuma de-nissa: Aramaic for "the proclamation of the miracle." This is the reason given by the Talmud for placing the Hanukkah candles outside the front door of one's house, or today, in the window.

Purim: the festival that takes place on the fourteenth or fifteenth day of the Hebrew month of Adar, which commemorates the victory and survival of the Jews of Persia during the time of Esther. It typically falls in February or March.

Rabban Gamaliel: the name of several Palestinian rabbis. Rabban Gamaliel II, who lived toward the end of the first century C.E., was known for his keen intellect and political power.

Rabbenu Tam (1096–1171): Rashi's grandson, and one of the most important legal authorities of the Middle Ages.

Rabbi Eliezer: a rabbinic sage of the late first century C.E.

Rabbi Judah Ha-Levi (1075–1141): an important Hebrew poet and philosopher; author of the *Kuzari*.

Rabbi Judah the Patriarch: the codifier of the Mishnah. Rabbi Judah collected and gave order to many of the previously oral teachings of the rabbis, and called his work the Mishnah. The Mishnah was codified in approximately 220 C.E.

Rabbi Yose bar Rav Judah: a second-century C.E. rabbinic teacher and the elder colleague of Judah the Prince.

Rabbi Zera: a late-third-century, early-fourth-century C.E. scholar who was active mainly in Israel.

rabbinic literature: a term used to refer to Judaism's oral tradition, a compilation that began to form approximately 250 years before the common era and continued until the sixth century C.E.

Rashi: an acronym for Rabbi Solomon ben Isaac of Troyes (1040–1105), perhaps the greatest Jewish commentator on the Bible and Talmud.

Rav Judah: a mid-second-century rabbinic teacher whose full name was Rav Judah bar Ilai. Commonly called simply Rav Judah, he came from the Galilean town of Usha.

Red Sea: also known as the "Sea of Reeds" from the Hebrew word *yam suf.* The biblical tradition identifies the Red Sea as the sea that engulfed Pharaoh's army.

Rosh Ha-Shannah: the Jewish holiday that commemorates the beginning of a new Jewish year. It typically falls in September or very early October.

Sanhedrin: the assembly of teachers and scholars that served as both a supreme court and as a legislature in Palestine during the Second Temple period until approximately 70 C.E.

schwartze: a Yiddish term for "black" but used derogatorily in reference to African-Americans.

Seder: a ritual meal on the first two nights of Passover commemorating the exodus from Egypt. The central feature of this meal is the recitation of the *Haggadah.* Only one Seder is performed in Israel, on the first night.

Seleucids: the people originally from the city of Seleucia, from whom the Maccabees recaptured the Temple in 164 B.C.E.

Seven Noahide Commandments: seven basic rules the rabbis deduced from the Bible that they said applied to all human beings, Jewish and gentile alike. Some scholars suggest that these are similar to Judaism's conception of natural law.

Shabbat: the Hebrew word for Sabbath. The seventh day of the week; a "day of rest," which begins at sundown on Friday and ends Saturday night.

Shabbetai Zevi (1626–1676): a Jewish scholar and charismatic leader whom many considered to be the Messiah. When he ultimately converted to Islam, his followers were devastated and a deep depression swept across parts of the Jewish community.

Shaḥarit: the morning service in the Jewish liturgy, on both weekdays and Shabbat and Festivals.

Shavu'ot: the "Festival of Weeks," a holiday celebrating the giving of the Torah to the Jewish people by God atop Mount Sinai. It falls seven weeks and one day after the beginning of Passover, usually sometime in May or June.

sheigitz: a Yiddish word for "non-Jew," but used in a derogatory manner.

shelilat ha-golah: a Hebrew phrase that means "denigration of the Diaspora." It refers to a position taken by some elements of Israeli society who claim that Jewish life outside Israel is intrinsically dysfunctional.

Shema: a Hebrew word that means "Hear!," the *Shema* is also the name of a part of the Jewish liturgy that declares faith in God and God's oneness. It is a central piece of the liturgy, portions of which are included in the phylacteries worn by some Jews and in the *mezuzah* attached to their doorposts.

Shemini Azeret: roughly translated as "the Eighth Day of Assembly," this is the Hebrew name for the festival that follows immediately after the last day of Sukkot, the Festival of Tabernacles. It usually falls in September or early October.

shiksah: a Yiddish word for a non-Jewish woman, which has a terribly derogatory connotation.

Shoah: a Hebrew word meaning "calamity," or "devastation," it is the Hebrew term used to refer to the Nazi Holocaust.

Shul: a Yiddish word for "synagogue."

Shulhan Arukh: a Hebrew phrase that literally means "a set table," it is also the name of Judaism's classic code of Jewish law, edited by Rabbi Joseph Karo and published in 1565.

siddur: a Hebrew word meaning "order," it is also the Hebrew term for the Jewish prayer book, containing the daily and Sabbath liturgy.

Sifrei: a very early rabbinic commentary on the Book of Deuteronomy.

Sukkot: a holiday known as the "Festival of Booths." It takes place in the fall and commemorates the experience of the Jewish people in the desert when they lived in temporary, unstable dwellings.

tallit: a Jewish prayer shawl, worn by men (and today, by some women as well) during morning prayers.

Talmud: a Hebrew word meaning "teaching," it is generally used to refer to the Babylonian Talmud, rabbinic Judaism's greatest compendium of legal and ethical teachings. Jews in what is today called Israel also produced a Talmud, known either as the "Jerusalem Talmud" or the "Palestinian Talmud." When the word "Talmud" is used alone, however, the reference is almost always to the Babylonian Talmud, the more frequently studied of the two.

Temple: the central Jewish location of worship and sacrifice in ancient Jerusalem. There were two Temples, the first destroyed by the Babylonians in 586 B.C.E., the second by the Romans in 70 C.E.

Torah: a Hebrew word that means "teaching," it commonly refers to the Five Books of Moses, the first five books of the Hebrew Bible.

Tosefta: an Aramaic word that literally means "addition," it is generally used to refer to a collection of the teachings of the Sages in the last few centuries before the common era and the first two centuries of the common era. The Tosefta is arranged just like the Mishnah, and contains teachings that Rabbi Judah the Patriarch did not include in the Mishnah.

Trei Asar: a Aramaic phrase that means "twelve," it generally refers to the twelve "minor" prophets in the Hebrew Bible.

Tur: also known as the *Arba'ah Turim,* it is the fourteenth-century compilation of Jewish laws and customs by Rabbi Jacob ben Asher.

tzedakah: a Hebrew word commonly translated as "charity," but that more precisely means something like "righteousness."

Uzziah: the king of Judah (the more southern of the two Jewish kingdoms); he reigned for fifty-two years, from 785 to 734 B.C.E.

Viddui: a "Confession" that is part of the Jewish liturgy. It is recited on Yom Kippur and at select other occasions such as on one's deathbed, and in some communities before marriage as well.

yarmulke: the Yiddish term for the traditional skullcap worn to cover one's head as a sign of humility before God.

yeshivah: a Hebrew word for academies of traditional Jewish learning. The plural is *yeshivot.*

Yevamot: literally "levirate marriages" or marriages of a childless widow to her husband's younger brother. This custom was designed to perpetuate the name of the deceased brother. *Yevamot* is also the name of the first tractate in the Order of Women in the Mishnah and Talmud.

yiddischer kopf: a Yiddish phrase that literally means "Jewish head," but which is used to suggest that the person who has it is bright.

Yom Kippur: a Hebrew phrase that means the "Day of Atonement," it refers to the Jewish holiday that falls the week after Rosh Ha-Shannah and is commonly considered the holiest day of the year. On this day Jews repent their sins and seek the strength to live better lives during the upcoming year.

Yoreh De'ah: one of the four sections of the *Shulhan Arukh,* it discusses the dietary laws, interest on loans, purity and mourning.

zedek: a Hebrew word meaning "righteousness."

Zur Yisrael: a Hebrew phrase that means the "Rock of Israel." In classical Jewish texts, this phrase almost always refers to God. In the Israeli Declaration of Independence, it was interpreted by religious Zionists to mean God, and by secularists to represent the Jewish spirit or passion for survival.

Notes

The following notes provide sources for quotations
found throughout the book.

Introduction: Andersen Versus Disney

22 Seymour Martin Lipset and Earl Raab, *Jews and the New American Scene* (Cambridge: Harvard University Press, 1995), pp. 26–27.

25 Most of the material on these Holocaust deniers is found in Deborah Lipstadt, *Denying the Holocaust: The Growing Assault on Truth and Memory* (New York: Plume/Penguin, 1993), pp. 183–201.

27 The column by Sharod Baker appeared in the Columbia *Spectator*, October 12, 1995, p. 3.

27 Peter Freeman was quoted in the *Forward*, October 20, 1995, p. 4.

29 Michael Goldberg, *Why Should Jews Survive?: Looking Past the Holocaust Toward a Jewish Future* (New York: Oxford University Press, 1995), pp. 161, 168.

Chapter 1: The Promise and the Reassurance

33 Philip Roth's comments were made at a roundtable discussion in Jerusalem on June 18, 1963. They were reprinted in the *Congress Bi-Monthly*, September 13, 1963, pp. 19–41. This particular remark is found on page 21.

37 The passage from Allan Bloom about studying with friendship in partnership with "wise old books" is taken from *Giants and Dwarfs: Essays, 1960–1990* (New York: Touchstone, 1991), pp. 10–11.

48 The Pittsburgh Platform is widely reprinted. This quotation is taken from Elliot N. Dorff, *Conservative Judaism: Our Ancestors to Our Descendants* (New York: United Synagogue of America, 1985), pp. 236–37.

49 Rabbi Samuel Goldenson's remarks are cited in the *Central Conference of American Rabbis Yearbook 1939* (New York: Jewish Publication Society of America, 1940), p. 346.

50 Comments about the Skirball Cultural Center were reported in the *Forward*, April 19, 1996, in an article entitled "Editing Out Abraham in Los Angeles: New Skirball Center Uses Universalism to Attract the Unaffiliated."

Chapter 2: To Be the Chosen People

55–56 The quotation from the letter critiquing Will Herberg is taken from a letter to the editor of *Judaism: A Quarterly Journal* by Abraham F. Citron (July 1952), p. 275.

62 While the convert's "transformation" is complete, there is one curious detail of Jewish law that should be noted. While most Jews are prohibited from marrying a *mamzer* (a child born of an adulterous relationship), a convert is not subject to that prohibition (*Shulḥan Arukh, Even Ha-Ezer* 4:22). Why that is the case is not entirely clear. I am grateful to Rabbi Yosef Kanefsky for pointing out this complexity.

63 Richard J. Herrnstein and Charles Murray, *The Bell Curve: Intelligence and Class Structure in American Life* (New York: The Free Press, 1994), p. 275.

63 The quotation from Mark Twain about the intelligence of Jews was cited in Stuart Schoffman, "The Jewish Elixir," *The Jerusalem Report*, December 2, 1993.

63–64 Twain's letter describing Jews as the "cunningest brains in the world" is cited in Janet Smith, *Mark Twain on the Damned Human Race* (New York: Hill and Wang, 1962), pp. 174–75.

64 The most complete study on the subject of Jews' intelligence is a very recent one. It is Sander L. Gilman, *Smart Jews: The Construction of the Image of Jewish Superior Intelligence* (Lincoln: University of Nebraska Press, 1996). Gilman points to the issues with Fitzgerald and Redford, among others, in Chapter Six: "The End of Another Century: The Image in American Mass Culture," pp. 173–206.

81 The two poems are reprinted in *The Silver Treasury of Light Verse,* ed., Oscar Williams (New York: Mentor, 1957), p. 169.

Chapter 3: Blending In or Standing Out

89 Details of the murder of Schwerner, Goodman and Chaney and the larger conspiracy of which it was a part may be found in the *American Jewish Yearbook 1965* (New York and Philadelphia: American Jewish Committee and Jewish Publication Society of America, 1965), p. 185, in an article by Lucy Dawidowicz.

90 The circumstances surrounding the reading of the poem on WBAI and its aftermath are described by Edward T. Rogowsky in the *American Jewish Yearbook 1969* (New York and Philadelphia: American Jewish Committee and Jewish Publication Society of America, 1969), pp. 83–85.

90 *Fear of a Black Planet* was released in 1990 by Def Jam Records. We requested, but were denied, permission to quote the lyrics at length.

91 Michael Jackson's *HIStory* album was released on June 20, 1995, by Epic Records, a division of Sony Music.

92 The quotations, anecdotes and data regarding Louis Farrakhan and the Nation of Islam and the black community's response have been widely documented. This discussion has been deeply informed by a collection of these sources in Lipset and Raab, *Jews and the New American Scene,* p. 101ff.

94 Sally Mugabe's remarks were quoted in the *Jerusalem Post,* July 16, 1985.

95 The quotation from Mary Daly about Lot's daughters is from Mary Daly, *Beyond God the Father* (Boston: Beacon Press, 1973), p. 117.

96 The characterization of German feminist religious writings is taken from Katharina von Kellenbach, *Anti-Judaism in Feminist Religious Writings* (Atlanta: Scholars Press, 1994), p. 101.

96 Letty Cottin Pogrebin's article "Anti-Semitism in the Women's Movement" appeared in the June 1982 issue of *Ms.,* Vol. 10, pp. 45–46.

96 Susanna Heschel's article "Anti-Judaism in Christian Feminist Theology" appeared in *Tikkun,* Vol. 5, No. 3 (May/June 1990), p. 25ff.

96 Gloria Anzaldúa, ed., *Making Face, Making Soul, Haciendo Caras* (San Francisco: Aunt Lute Foundation, 1990), p. xx. All the quotations from Anzaldúa are found on this page.

101 Carol Gilligan, *In a Different Voice* (Cambridge: Harvard University Press, 1982); and John Gray, *Men Are from Mars, Women Are from Venus* (New York: HarperCollins, 1993).

104 Emil L. Fackenheim, *God's Presence in History: Jewish Affirmations and Philosophical Reflections* (New York: Harper Torchbooks, 1972). His section related to our discussion of the "614th Commandment" and what he calls the "commanding voice of Auschwitz" can be found on pages 84–95.

Chapter 4: "Not by Might and Not by Power"

109 Twain's reflections on the "immortality" of the Jew were first published in *Harper's Magazine,* September 1899. They are reprinted in Smith, *Mark Twain on the Damned Human Race,* pp. 176–77.

111 The quotation by Blaise Pascal is taken from *Pensées,* trans., W. F. Trotter (New York: Modern Library, 1941), pp. 618–19.

134 Adrienne Rich, *Your Native Land, Your Life: Poems* (New York: Norton, 1986), p. 17. The poem itself is untitled. It is numbered "XV," and is part of a series of poems entitled "North American Time."

134–135 "Light One Candle" is by Peter Yarrow, 1983. It appears on the Peter, Paul and Mary album *No Easy Road to Freedom,* 1987.

136 This quotation by the Dalai Lama and the subsequent citations are taken from Rodger Kamenetz, *The Jew in the Lotus: A Poet's Rediscovery of Jewish Identity in Buddhist India* (New York: HarperCollins, 1994), pp. 2 and 106–7.

Chapter 6: Standing Uncomfortably Outside the Mainstream

172 The quotation by Woodrow Wilson is cited in Arthur M. Schlesinger, Jr., *The Disuniting of America: Reflections on a Multicultural Society* (New York: Norton, 1992), p. 35.

172 The description of the Ford Motor Company English School graduation is taken from Stephen Meyer III, *The Five Dollar Day: Labor Management and Social Control in the Ford Motor Company, 1908–1921* (Albany: State University of New York Press, 1981), pp. 160–61.

174 This and the preceding quotation from the JNF are from reporting in the *Forward,* May 17, 1996, p. 2.

175 I am grateful to Thomas Fields-Meyer for a critically important conversation in the summer of 1993 that prompted me to think about the complicated phrase "Judeo-Christian ethic." Tom forced me to rethink old notions and ill-conceived ideas, and I appreciate his gentle but forceful prodding.

185–86 Schlesinger, *The Disuniting of America*, p. 74.

190 Allan Bloom, *The Closing of the American Mind: How Higher Education Has Failed Democracy and Impoverished the Souls of Today's Students* (New York: Simon and Schuster, 1986), p. 337.

192 The quotation by Leonard Jeffries is cited in Lipset and Raab, *Jews and the New American Scene*, p. 101.

193 Arthur Butz, *The Hoax of the Twentieth Century* (Torrance, CA: Noontide, 1976). For a superb discussion of this episode, see Lipstadt, *Denying the Holocaust*, especially Chapter Seven.

196–97 405 US 438 (1972). For a very useful discussion of *Eisenstadt v. Baird*, see Phyllis Coleman, "Surrogate Motherhood: Analysis of the Problems and Suggestions for Solutions," in the *Tennessee Law Review*, Vol. 50, 1981, p. 76.

199 Robert N. Bellah et al., *Habits of the Heart* (New York: Harper and Row, 1985), p. 142.

Chapter 7: "Exile" or "Diaspora"?

221 There *is* a word in Hebrew which means Diaspora. It is *tefuzot*. However, the more generic *galut*, which means both "Diaspora" as well as "exile," is by far much more commonly used in everyday parlance.

227 Jacob Neusner, "Is America the Promised Land for Jews?" in the *Washington Post*, March 8, 1987.

232 Much has been written about Yonatan Ratosh and the "Canaanites." A good introduction, upon which I also relied, is Yoram Bronowski's article "Canaanism: Politics or Poetry?" in *Midstream: A Monthly Jewish Review*, Vol. 32, No. 5 (May 1986), pp. 48–51.

Chapter 8: "Choosing to Be Chosen"

236 The name of the article in the September 1996 issue of *Life* is "Portraits of a People." It includes photography by Frédéric Bren-

ner, and text by Charles Hirshberg. The quoted passage is on pages 60–61.

242 The phrase "minority education" was first suggested to me by David Resnick, in his "Jewish Multicultural Education: A Minority View," in *Religious Education*, Vol. 91, No. 2 (Spring 1996), pp. 209–21.

250 The story about Rebecca Samuels is cited in Lipset and Raab, *Jews and the New American Scene*, p. 45.

Suggestions for Further Reading

As interest in Jewish life and culture has intensified over the past decades, dozens of wonderful and insightful books have appeared on a variety of topics related to Judaism. There are many other superb volumes not listed here, but for readers interested in pursuing further some of the issues raised in this book, these volumes should provide an appropriate place to begin. A more general reading list about Jewish topics such as spirituality, prayer, God and ethics is found at the conclusion of *God Was Not in the Fire: The Search for a Spiritual Judaism*.

Introduction: Andersen Versus Disney

Andersen, Hans Christian. *The Complete Andersen: All of the 168 Stories by Hans Christian Andersen.* Trans., Jean Hersholt. New York: Heritage Press, 1942. This is the standard collection of Andersen's tales and includes "The Little Mermaid."

Goldberg, Michael. *Why Should Jews Survive? Looking Past the Holocaust Toward a Jewish Future.* New York: Oxford University Press, 1995. Goldberg's book asks a similar question to the one raised in this book, but takes a very different approach. Though published by an academic press, it is accessible to the lay reader and is filled with thoughtful insights throughout.

Gordis, Daniel. *God Was Not in the Fire: The Search for a Spiritual Judaism.* New York: Scribner, 1995. A discussion of the ways in which Jewish life gives expression to our spiritual and most personal yearnings. *God Was Not in the Fire* examines Judaism's impact on our inner lives and spiritual selves.

Kamenetz, Rodger. *The Jew in the Lotus: A Poet's Rediscovery of Jewish Identity in Buddhist India.* New York: HarperCollins, 1994. An extraordinarily popular book, this volume traces how encountering Buddhist India in the company of several Jewish leaders helped an American Jew rekindle his attachments to Jewish life. Because his search has universal qualities, the book is of interest to a wide audience.

Lipset, Seymour Martin, and Earl Raab. *Jews and the New American Scene.* Cambridge: Harvard University Press, 1995. A fascinating and erudite study of the position of Jews in modern America and of the implications of our now comfortable status for Jewish identity in the future.

Roof, Wade Clark. *A Generation of Seekers: The Spiritual Journeys of the Baby Boom Generation.* San Francisco: Harper San Francisco, 1993. This is not a book about Jews, but its discussion of the spiritual yearnings of contemporary Americans is relevant to the condition of Jews today. This is a scholarly volume, but it is still highly readable. Its case studies are fascinating and not easily forgotten.

Chapter 1: The Promise and the Reassurance

Fox, Everett. *The Five Books of Moses: A New Translation with Introductions, Commentary and Notes.* New York: Schocken, 1995. Fox's approach is novel and refreshing: he tries to translate the Torah in a way that captures the sound and feel of the original. Much of Chapter One of this book examines the Torah's own story of the Jews. Fox's translation and his thoughtful commentary are a wonderful way to encounter this story afresh, whether for the first time or the hundredth.

Johnson, Paul. *A History of the Jews.* New York: Harper and Row, 1987. Though there are many one-volume histories of the Jews, this is among the most accessible. It is rather recent, and its non-Jewish author has a palpable awe for the accomplishments of Jews throughout history. For readers interested in a broad sense of who the Jews have been and what they have accomplished throughout their history, this is the place to begin.

Lipstadt, Deborah. *Denying the Holocaust: The Growing Assault on Truth and Memory.* New York: Plume/Penguin, 1993. Lipstadt's work is the best on the subject of Holocaust denial. More information on the Bradley Smith episode, discussed briefly in our chapter, can be found in Lipstadt's work, pages 183–201.

Meyer, Michael A. *Jewish Identity in the Modern World*. Seattle: University of Washington Press, 1990. For readers interested in other discussions of Jewish identity, this highly readable collection of lectures is a wonderful place to begin. Meyer's book focuses on the enlightenment, anti-Semitism and Zionism.

Plaut, Gunther, ed. *The Torah*. New York: Union of American Hebrew Congregations, 1981. For readers interested in encountering the Bible's description of the early origins of the Jews firsthand, this is a wonderful and thoughtful commentary. The text is presented in Hebrew, with a good English translation and many worthwhile commentaries. All five books are found in one volume.

Chapter 2: To Be the Chosen People

Eisen, Arnold M. *The Chosen People in America: A Study in Jewish Religious Ideology*. Bloomington: Indiana University Press, 1983. Eisen's book is by far the most thoughtful discussion of how the concept of the "chosen people" has been used and adapted in the history of American Judaism. An academic work, but eminently readable with fascinating insights throughout. Very worthwhile.

Gilman, Sander L. *Smart Jews: the Construction of the Image of Jewish Superior Intelligence*. Lincoln: University of Nebraska Press, 1996. Gilman is a scholar at the University of Chicago. In this fascinating study, he shows how stereotypes such as the "smart Jew" permeate society, and how they have a dark underside, such as suggesting that the Jew may have superior intelligence but lesser virtue. A worthwhile and detailed addition to our brief discussion of this issue.

Gordis, Daniel. *God Was Not in the Fire*. New York: Scribner, 1995. See Chapter Three for further discussion of the Binding of Isaac, mentioned only briefly in this chapter.

Kamenetz, Rodger. *The Jew in the Lotus: A Poet's Rediscovery of Jewish Identity in Buddhist India*. New York: HarperCollins, 1994. A "travelogue" of the author's journey to the Dalai Lama and the encounter between Jewish and Buddhist leaders, this book is noteworthy in part because it recounts how this encounter helped its Jewish author rediscover the idea that Jews have important contributions to make to the world around them.

Novak, David. *The Election of Israel: The Idea of the Chosen People*. Cambridge: Cambridge University Press, 1995. Many contemporary Jews are troubled by the concept of the "chosen people," which our chapter redefines slightly. Novak's extraordinarily scholarly book is one of the best for those interested in a history of how the idea of the chosen people has evolved over time.

Chapter 3: Blending In or Standing Out

Biale, Rachel. *Women and Jewish Law: An Exploration of Women's Issues in Halakhic Sources.* New York: Schocken, 1984. For readers interested in a discussion of Judaism and feminism, this is an important volume. Biale is highly critical of some of Judaism's traditional stances. Even those who disagree with her will find her discussion thoughtful and her collections of original sources extremely useful.

Dershowitz, Alan M. *Chutzpah.* Boston: Little, Brown, 1991. This popular volume does more than give insight into one of America's best-known Jews. Dershowitz's discussion of his family's fear of being seen as a *shanda fur de goyim* (an embarrassment in front of the gentiles) sheds light on what was once a paramount issue for American Jews. An important volume for the issues it raises about Jewish identity in America.

Fackenheim, Emil L. *God's Presence in History: Jewish Affirmations and Philosophical Reflections* New York: Harper Torchbooks, 1972. Fackenheim is one of the most important Jewish philosophers of the twentieth century. His section related to our discussion of the "614th Commandment" and what he calls the "commanding voice of Auschwitz" can be found on pages 84–95.

Glazer, Nathan. *American Judaism.* Second edition, revised; with a new introduction. Chicago: University of Chicago Press, 1989. This is the classic study of Jews in America. The new introduction in particular is a wonderful discussion of how Judaism is struggling to get beyond an earlier self-definition that saw Jews as an embodiment of the values of American liberalism.

Greenberg, Blu. *On Women and Judaism: A View from Tradition.* Philadelphia: Jewish Publication Society of America, 1983. A wonderful book on feminism and Judaism written from the perspective of the Orthodox community. Readers may be surprised to see how committed to feminism a noted Orthodox figure like Blu Greenberg can be.

Greenberg, Simon. *The Ethical in the Jewish and American Heritage.* New York: Jewish Theological Seminary / Ktav Publishing, 1977. This thoughtful volume is one of the classic statements of the ways in which Jewish and American values coincide. Though my book takes exception to some of the assumptions behind such comparisons, Greenberg's book is thoughtful and erudite.

Heschel, Susanna. *On Being a Jewish Feminist.* New York: Schocken, 1983. The daughter of the famed philosopher Abraham Joshua Heschel, Susanna Heschel is an accomplished scholar in her own right. This collection of essays, a wonderful introduction to many of the basic issues that Jewish feminists confront, is now a classic.

Prager, Dennis, and Joseph Telushkin. *Why the Jews: The Reason for Anti-Semitism.* New York: Simon and Schuster, 1983. Our discussion of Jews' treatment at the hands of non-Jews throughout our history inevitably raises questions about the whole issue of anti-Semitism. Prager and Telushkin's book asks a question few can avoid. Their answer may not appeal to all, but this is a thought-provoking and illuminating work.

Schneerson, Menachem Mendel. Adapted by Simon Jacobson. *Toward a Meaningful Life: The Wisdom of the Rebbe.* New York: William Morrow, 1995. The Rebbe, who lived from April 1902 through January 1994, was the leader of the highly visible Lubavitch sect of Judaism. This book is unique, since its editor was the personal scribe and secretary for the Rebbe, and excerpted the Rebbe's many writings for a broader audience.

Von Kellenbach, Katharina. *Anti-Judaism in Feminist Religious Writings.* Atlanta: Scholars Press, 1994. Though this volume is a technical read in places, it is a critical contribution to the discussion of feminist attitudes to Judaism. It illustrates how Judaism has been depicted in major American and West German feminist theologies, calling on feminist theologians to create a teaching of respect to combat the pervasive tradition of Christian anti-Judaism.

West, Cornel, and Michael Lerner. *Jews and Blacks: The Hard Hunt for Common Ground.* New York: Putnam, 1995. In the face of the often growing hostility between Jews and blacks, this volume is a breath of fresh air. West and Lerner are important representatives of the black and Jewish communities, respectively, and though some of their proposed solutions have been criticized as unrealistic, their discussion of the problem is thoughtful and respectful.

Wolpe, David. *Why Be Jewish?* New York: Holt, 1995. In an exceedingly brief and readable essay, Wolpe manages to make a poetic and thoughtful case for Jewish belonging. Wolpe's characteristic poetic style is no less evident here than in his other wonderful books.

Chapter 4: "Not by Might and Not by Power"

Biale, David. *Power and Powerlessness in Jewish History.* New York: Schocken, 1986. The question of how powerless the Jews have really been throughout their history is the subject of this extraordinarily interesting book. Biale argues that though the Jews did not always have power in the classic sense, they had more than we commonly believe and they created different sorts of power. A fascinating companion to our discussion of Jewish "powerlessness."

Englander, Daniel, ed. *The Jewish Enigma.* New York: George Braziller, 1992. A fascinating and eminently readable discussion of why the Jews have survived and the factors that have contributed to our survival.

Goldberg, Michael. *Why Should Jews Survive? Looking Past the Holocaust Toward a Jewish Future.* New York: Oxford University Press, 1995. Goldberg's excellent volume argues that the Holocaust plays an unhealthy role in Jews' thinking about why our survival matters. He proposes a radically new idea behind Jewish survival: we must survive—and we will—because that is what God intends. Though such an argument may not strike all modern readers as plausible, this is an extremely thoughtful and readable book that virtually compels its readers to think in new and unexpected ways.

Goodman, Phillip. *The Hanukkah Anthology.* Philadelphia: Jewish Publication Society of America, 1992. Our chapter presents a reading of Hanukkah somewhat different from what most contemporary Jews have heard. For those interested in more background, rituals and celebrations associated with Hanukkah, Goodman's book is a classic. Goodman has written a series of "anthologies" on the various Jewish holidays. All are a good introduction to the basic ideas and customs of the festivals they discuss.

Greenberg, Irving. *The Jewish Way: Living the Holidays.* New York: Simon and Schuster, 1988. While there are quite a number of "how to" books about the Jewish holidays, none comes close to this one in explaining in thoughtful and sophisticated language the meaning behind them and the spiritual sophistication of the Jewish calendar year. Greenberg is deeply learned and profoundly insightful; this book has become a classic. Readers interested in yet another reading of Hanukkah would do well to examine this wonderful volume.

Wolfson, Ronald. *The Art of Jewish Living—Hanukkah*. New York: Federation of the Jewish Men's Clubs, 1990. Wolfson has become one of the most popular teachers of Judaica in the country. His book is of the "how to" genre of Jewish holiday books. It is a superb volume, which will enrich the celebration of any family that takes its suggestions and advice to heart. Wolfson has written similar volumes on Passover and Shabbat, each of which is a wonderful introduction to those celebrations.

Chapter 5: Distinctiveness, Spirituality and Moderation

Bleich, David. *Judaism and Healing: Halakhic Perspectives*. New York: Ktav Publishing, 1981. Our discussion of abortion will undoubtedly raise questions about Jewish medical ethics in general. Bleich is the preeminent writer on the subject. Readers interested in Jewish medical ethics should also consult books by Fred Rosner, MD. Both Bleich and Rosner write from an Orthodox perspective, but even readers interested in a different orientation will profit from the careful attention to classical sources in these volumes.

Feldman, David. *Marital Relations, Birth Control and Abortion in Jewish Law*. New York: Schocken, 1974. Without question the classic work on the subject, this book is unsurpassed for its detail and analysis. Though it is not always an easy read, it is sufficiently accessible for the ambitious lay reader. Chapter One, which runs only eighteen pages, has a superb review of the structure of Jewish law.

Gordis, Robert. *Judaic Ethics for a Lawless World*. New York: Jewish Theological Seminary of America, 1986. An interesting argument that a major thrust of Jewish life is the goal of providing ethical standards for an otherwise lawless world. This book is accessible to the lay reader, and provides important background to Judaism's attitudes on many different ethical dilemmas. Interesting as a corollary to our suggestion that Judaism provides moderation to an otherwise "unmoderated" world, though the actual argument is very different.

Herring, Basil F. *Jewish Ethics and Halakhah for Our Time: Sources and Commentary.* New York: Ktav Publishing and Yeshiva University Press, 1984. An excellent introduction to Jewish ethics, Herring's book addresses several issues in medical ethics, and is outstanding in its illustration of how contemporary Jewish ethical thinking makes use of classic legal sources.

Neusner, Jacob, ed. *The Mishnah.* New Haven: Yale University Press, 1988. For those interested in learning more about the Mishnah, this is the most accessible translation available. Neusner is by far the most prolific scholar in Mishnaic studies, and this translation also contains a superb introduction that points to many of the issues we've been examining.

Prager, Dennis, and Joseph Telushkin. *Nine Questions People Ask About Judaism.* New York: Simon and Schuster, 1981. There is no one more committed to the premise that Jews have a message to the world than Dennis Prager. Central to Prager and Telushkin's argument is Judaism's introduction to the world of ethical monotheism. While that claim is not identical to our argument, it is certainly related to our suggestion that Jews are expected to serve as the conscience of society in a prophetic and even "subversive" fashion.

Roth, Joel. *The Halakhic Process.* New York: Jewish Theological Seminary of America, 1986. Though highly technical and difficult, Roth's book is an excellent summary of how Jewish law works and how law in Judaism evolves. It has been criticized for its commitment to a philosophy known as legal positivism, but is still an exceedingly valuable contribution to the field. Ambitious readers interested in learning more about Jewish law will find no better place to start.

Waskow, Arthur. *Seasons of Our Joy: A Celebration of Modern Jewish Renewal.* New York: Bantam, 1982. Self-described as "a new-age guide to the Jewish holidays," this volume will give readers a sense of the many different ways the Jewish holidays can be interpreted. Readers might find it interesting to compare Waskow's treatment of the *Omer* with the very different reading offered in our chapter.

Chapter 6: Standing Uncomfortably Outside the Mainstream

Borowitz, Eugene. *The Masks Jews Wear.* New York: Simon and Schuster, 1973. One of the preeminent thinkers of the Reform movement,

Borowitz's work is always provocative and illuminating. This book, an examination of how America has influenced the identity of modern Jews, is still fascinating almost a quarter of a century after it was written.

Meeks, Wayne A. *The Moral World of the First Christians*. Philadelphia: Westminster Press, 1986. An academic work by a non-Jewish scholar, this is perhaps the best and most readable introduction to Christianity's Jewish roots from a Christian perspective. This is a fascinating volume for readers interested in the shared roots of Judaism and Christianity.

Neusner, Jacob. *A Rabbi Talks with Jesus: An Intermillennial, Interfaith Exchange*. New York: Doubleday, 1993. A very creative and imaginative work, this book tries to imagine what a rabbi would have felt listening to Jesus. In so doing, Neusner explains why he believes most Jews did not find early Christianity satisfying or appealing. A wonderful, readable book for those seeking a better sense of where Judaism and Christianity differ.

———. *Tzedakah*. Chappaqua, N.Y.: Rossel Books, 1982. A very readable introduction to Jewish attitudes to charity, including a useful appendix of primary sources.

Novak, David. *Jewish Social Ethics*. New York: Oxford University Press, 1992. This series of collected papers, all by Novak, takes a rigorous philosophical approach to the question, what are Jewish social ethics? Though some of the content is on the difficult side, Novak's book will make a strong impression on readers by showing just how much Judaism does have to say about these issues.

Silver, Abba Hillel. *Where Judaism Differed*. New York: Macmillan, 1956. Though somewhat apologetic by today's standards, this book was a classic in its day. Many modern Jews will find its argument about how Judaism is different from other traditions somewhat unsatisfying, but as a timepiece, it is fascinating. It is still an interesting essay on the substance of Jewish life, well worth reading.

Chapter 7: "Exile" or "Diaspora"?

Halkin, Abraham S., ed. *Zion in Jewish Literature*. Lanhan, Md.: University Press of America, 1985. A wonderful anthology of sources on the place of Israel in Jewish writing, beginning with the Bible and proceeding chapter by chapter through rabbinic literature, medieval writing and modern works. There is much more here than just the sources; some of the century's greatest Jewish minds have woven those sources into delightful essays. A wonderful introduction to this dimension of Jewish thought, easily accessible.

Halkin, Hillel. *Letters to an American Jewish Friend: A Zionist's Polemic.* Philadelphia: Jewish Publication Society of America, 1977. Halkin is certainly correct when he calls his book a "polemic," but it is also a classic polemic. A series of letters from a hypothetical American-turned-Israeli to a friend still in America, it reflects the classic arguments about why Jewish life in Israel is the only real, authentic option for Jews. The last twenty years have complicated the issue, and Halkin's book does not address many of the responses that American Jews might make today. But its passion is compelling; this is a wonderful place to begin for readers interested in thinking more about the place of Israel in Jewish life.

Hartman, David. *Conflicting Visions: Spiritual Possibilities of Modern Israel.* New York: Schocken, 1990. It took the tragic assassination of Yitzhak Rabin to bring many of the tensions in Israeli life to the attention of many American Jews. But Hartman, one of Israel's most interesting philosophers, wrote this work long before Rabin was murdered. Hartman, a committed Zionist, is also a moderate, and in this book he explores Israel's condition and some of its spiritual implications.

Hertzberg, Arthur. *The Zionist Idea: A Historical Analysis and Reader.* Garden City, N.Y.: Doubleday, 1959. This is by far the best one-volume collection of writings from various Zionist thinkers. The material is not always easy, but the vast majority is accessible to the lay reader. Those interested in this subject will be eminently assisted by the introductory essay on Zionism (approximately one hundred pages long), still considered the best of its kind.

Ravitzky, Aviezer. *Messianism, Zionism and Jewish Religious Radicalism.* Trans., Michael Swirsky and Jonathan Chipman. Chicago: University of Chicago Press, 1996. Professor Ravitzky examines the ways in which Orthodox and ultra-Orthodox Jews have responded to Zionism and Israel in light of the traditional idea that Jewish exile would end only with the coming of the Messiah, and offers a fascinating glimpse into the differences between groups that often seem to us indistinguishable.

Chapter 8: "Choosing to Be Chosen"

Artson, Bradley Shavit. *It's a Mitzvah: Step-by-Step to Jewish Living* New York: Behrman House and the Rabbinical Assembly, 1995. After finishing *Does the World Need the Jews?*, readers may want to know how to begin to make Jewish tradition and commitments a greater part of their life. Artson's book is the latest contribution to this genre. It is a superb, highly accessible book, with creative ideas and suggestions of where to turn for further learning.

Gordis, Robert. *A Faith for Moderns.* New York: Bloch Publishing, 1971. This volume is one of the best-known rational defenses of religion and tradition in general, Judaism in particular. The final two chapters, "The Meaning of Jewish Existence" and "The Ultimate Goal," are particularly germane to the issues we have raised.

Heilman, Samuel C. *Portrait of American Jews: The Last Half of the 20th Century.* Seattle: University of Washington Press, 1996. Focuses on the East Coast, but Heilman is among the best of the sociologists of the American Jewish community. This book is a portrait of assimilation patterns in the American Jewish community, and offers a troubling prognosis for the future of Jewish life in this country.

Neusner, Jacob. *Death and Birth of Judaism: The Impact of Christianity, Secularism and the Holocaust on Jewish Faith.* New York: Basic Books, 1987. Primarily a scholar of the rabbinic period, Neusner is also a thoughtful commentator on the American Jewish scene. This is one of his most important contributions on the subject. Somewhat controversial in parts, it is extremely thoughtful and provocative.

———. *Israel in America: A Too Comfortable Exile?* Boston: Beacon Press, 1985. Neusner's prescriptions for how to live as a Jew and as an American are thoughtful and challenging. This brief set of essays makes for very interesting reading, and is easily accessible to the newcomer.

Seltzer, Robert M., and Norman J. Cohen, eds. *The Americanization of the Jews.* New York: New York University Press, 1995. This collection of essays addresses such topics as Jews and the American liberal tradition, and the adaptation of Jewish religious life to American society. It's not a book intended for popular audiences, but it is nicely written and raises many interesting ideas.

Strassfeld, Michael, and Sharon Strassfeld. *The Jewish Catalogue*, Vols. I–III. Philadelphia: Jewish Publication Society of America, 1973, 1976 and 1980. Products of the 1960s revival in Jewish spirituality, these paperback volumes have become classics. They contain excellent introductions to countless Jewish rituals, combining humor, wisdom and much practical advice. Though stylistically slightly dated, they remain excellent both as a reference and for getting started in Jewish ritual life.

Index of Primary Sources

Subject Index

ABOUT THE AUTHOR

DANIEL GORDIS is a Vice President of the University of
Judaism in Los Angeles and Dean of its Ziegler School of
Rabbinic Studies. Rabbi Gordis is also the author of *God
Was Not in the Fire: The Search for a Spiritual Judaism*. He lives
with his wife and three children in Los Angeles.